Praise for

THE ART OF
SPIRITUAL DREAMING

"Harold Klemp, . . . leading authority on the spiritual nature of dreams."

—*Body Mind Spirit* magazine

"Some dreams create, some dreams heal, some dreams initiate; this remarkable book encompasses them all."

—Stanley Krippner, Ph.D.,
coauthor, *The Mythic Path*

"Harold Klemp breaks important new ground in the spiritual significance of dreams."

—Rosemary Ellen Guiley, author,
Dreamwork for the Soul and
The Encyclopedia of Dreams

"Harold Klemp's new book is a definitive work. It offers the best tips on interpreting spiritual dreams I've ever read. This book is a knockout!"

—Arielle Ford, author, *More Hot Chocolate
for the Mystical Soul*

"It is my conviction as well as my personal experience that much personal healing can take place in our dreams. Harold Klemp's book, *The Art of Spiritual Dreaming* leads the way to our exploring the full potential of dreams."

—Gerald G. Jampolsky, M.D., author,
Love is Letting Go of Fear and
Forgiveness, the Greatest Healer of All

THE Art of SPIRITUAL DREAMING

Also by Harold Klemp

Ask the Master, Books 1 and 2
Child in the Wilderness
A Cosmic Sea of Words: The ECKANKAR Lexicon
The Living Word, Books 1 and 2
A Modern Prophet Answers Your Key Questions about Life
Soul Travelers of the Far Country
The Spiritual Exercises of ECK
The Temple of ECK
The Wind of Change

The Mahanta Transcripts Series

Journey of Soul, Book 1
How to Find God, Book 2
The Secret Teachings, Book 3
The Golden Heart, Book 4
Cloak of Consciousness, Book 5
Unlocking the Puzzle Box, Book 6
The Eternal Dreamer, Book 7
The Dream Master, Book 8
We Come as Eagles, Book 9
The Drumbeat of Time, Book 10
What Is Spiritual Freedom? Book 11
How the Inner Master Works, Book 12
The Slow Burning Love of God, Book 13
The Secret of Love, Book 14
Our Spiritual Wake-Up Calls, Book 15

Stories to Help You See God in Your Life

The Book of ECK Parables, Volume 1
The Book of ECK Parables, Volume 2
The Book of ECK Parables, Volume 3
Stories to Help You See God in Your Life,
ECK Parables, Book 4

MAHANTA

This book has been authored by and published under the supervision of the Mahanta, the Living ECK Master, Sri Harold Klemp. It is the Word of ECK.

The *Art of*
SPIRITUAL
DREAMING

HAROLD KLEMP

ECKANKAR
Minneapolis

The Art of Spiritual Dreaming

Copyright © 1999 ECKANKAR

The terms ECKANKAR, ECK, EK, MAHANTA, SOUL TRAVEL, and VAIRAGI, among others, are trademarks of ECKANKAR, P.O. Box 27300, Minneapolis, MN 55427 U.S.A.

Printed in U.S.A.

Compiled by James Davis,
Adrian McBride, and Mary Carroll Moore

Edited by Joan Klemp and Anthony Moore

Text illustrations by Valerie Taglieri and Ron Wennekes

Back cover photo by Robert Huntley

Library of Congress Cataloging-in-Publication Data

Klemp, Harold.
    The art of spiritual dreaming / Harold Klemp.
       p.   cm.
    Includes index.
    ISBN 1-57043-149-3 (alk. paper)
    1. Dreams—Religious aspects—Eckankar (Organization) 2. Eckankar (Organization)—Doctrines. I. Title.
BP605.E3K53   1999
299'.93—dc21   99-25358
                                      CIP

Contents

Foreword xi

1. **Dreams and Our Spiritual Journey** 1

Dreams Happen in a Real World • Your Hidden Life • Earth Academy • Dream Treasure • Handy Spiritual Tool • Your Source of Everyday Guidance • Forgotten Road to Heaven • You Have a Dream Guide • Dream Travel Protection • The Way of Contemplation • Mental Obstacles • Insights through Dreams • What Is a Spiritual Dream? • Universal Nature of Dreams • Waking-Life Lessons • A Fallen Robin • Greater Destiny • Waking Dreams • Exploring Your Inner Worlds • The Purpose of Life • *Spiritual Exercise:* The Blue Curtain of God

2. **The Dream Master** 23

Wake-Up Call • Working with a Dream Teacher • The Mahanta • My Early Experiences • Personalized Teachings • The Mahanta Never Interferes • *Spiritual Exercise:* Inviting the Dream Master • How the Mahanta Communicates • The Inner Teachings • *Spiritual Exercise:* To Remember Your Dreams • How to Remember Experiences • Dream Guidance • How the Mahanta Works with Dreams • Grasping the Significance of Dreams • Dreams Are Memories • *Spiritual Exercise:* To Soul Travel • Overcoming Fear • Going with the Flow • First Dream Experiences • Movement into Higher Consciousness • Coming Back the Knower • *Spiritual Exercise:* A Soul Travel Dream Technique • Drawing Back the Curtain • Degrees of Realization • *Tip:* It Takes Practice • The Reality of the Inner Worlds • *Spiritual Exercise:* For Direct Knowingness • Spiritual Geography

3. **Beginning Your Dream Study** 49

Overlooking the Commonplace • *Tip:* Study the Details • Developing Your Dream Memory • *Spiritual Exercise:* The Golden Cup • The Expanse of the Inner Worlds • *Tip:* Nap Time—An Easy Start to Dream Study • Map of the Dream Worlds • Clearing Up Dream Messages • Dream Censor • Forgetting the Dream • *Tip:* Writing to Slip Past the Censor • The Rest of the Story • *Spiritual Exercise:* The Rest of the Story • Nightmares and

Spiritual Obstacles • Downside of Expectations • *Tip:* Drawing the Curtain of Memory • Personal Habits as Obstacles • *Tip:* Three Steps for Better Dreaming • Fasting Can Remove Blocks • *Tip:* On Fasting • *Tip:* Recalling Your Inner Experiences • Recording Your Dreams • *Tip:* Keeping a Dream Journal

4. **Uncovering Your Past Lives through Dreams**........................... 69

Ultimate Purpose of Dream Study • Dream Insight for Our Lives Today • *Tip:* On Past-Life Study • Visit to the Old American West • Tools for Unfoldment • Self-Responsibility versus Faith • Guillotine Dream • *Tip:* Thoughts Have Life • Are You Aware of Your Dream Karma? • *Tip:* Avoiding Unconscious Karma • A Labor of Sisyphus • By Hard Experience • Soul's Total Experience • Present Tools • The Role of Karma • Insight from a Past Life • Drumbeat of Time • Lessons from the Past • Growing in Understanding of Yourself • The Inner Worlds and Past Lives • Inquisition Dream • A Fuller Understanding of Past Lives • Victim Consciousness • Self-Responsibility

5. **Dream Glimpses of the Future** 93

Dreams Can Speak in Symbols • Key to Understanding Dreams • *Spiritual Exercise:* For Higher Dream Awareness • Dream Big, Work Hard • Interpreting a Dream • How to Get Help • End-of-the-World Dreams • Strengthen Your Weak Points • Nightmares • Golden-tongued Wisdom • Prophecy for the Moment • Your Own Path to God • Taking a Chance on Life • Waking Dreams • Another Waking Dream • A Matter of Trust • Try Again • Appearance of God's Love • Interconnected Wheels • A Dream of Death • Recurring Dreams • Prophetic Dreams • Above the Time Track

6. **Eight Types of Dreams,** Part 1 121

Eight Types of Dreams • Daydreams • Dreams of Initiation • Remembering Initiation Dreams • Dreams of Intrusion • Screen of Protection • *Tip:* Cut Back on Contact • Losing Confidence in Yourself • *Tip:* Take Precautionary Measures • Dreams Teach You Strength • Creating Your Own Protection • *Tip:* Protection Techniques • Methods of the Black Magician • *Tip:* How to Survive a Psychic Attack • *Spiritual Exercise:* The Mountain of Light • Use Your Own Resources • Develop Your Creativity • Beam Me Up, Scotty! • Dreams of Release from Fear • Unexpected Rescue

7. **Eight Types of Dreams,** Part 2 .... **141**

Natural Way to Remember Dreams • Waking Dreams • Fateful
Bus Trip • Locked Out • Copper Coins • Contact Lenses •
Wall Hangings • Golden-tongued Wisdom • Glass Etchings
• Fortune Cookie • Dreams of Understanding • A Beached
Whale • Golden Seeds • Repaying a Debt • Dreams with the
Mahanta • Recognizing the Mahanta • Sound Experience •
River Run to God • The Richness of Dream Experiences

8. **Understanding Your Dreams** **163**

Beginning to Interpret • Three Levels of Dreams • Dream
Symbology • Creating Your Own Dream Dictionary • *Tip:* The
Dream Dictionary • Dream Guidance • Translator Function
• Effect of Interference • A Dream about Habits • How to
Change a Dream Yourself • *Spiritual Exercise:* Into the
Light • Dreams of Flying • *Tip:* Dream Characters • Is It
Real, or Is It a Symbol? • The Meaning of a Dream Marriage
• Interpreting Spiritual Dreams • *Tip:* Invite the Mahanta
Along • Fear of Death in Dreams • *Tip:* The Value of the
Spiritual Exercises of ECK • Sharing Dreams • Soul's
Freedom • Dream Advice • Overcome Procrastination • *Tip:*
How to Interpret Your Dreams

9. **Dream Healing and Help in Everyday
   Life** **189**

Letting Go of Fear • Dreams about Your Health • Dreams and
Diet • Healing Dreams • Healing the Past through Dreams
• *Spiritual Exercise:* How to Heal Yourself • If You Don't
Like It, Change It • *Spiritual Exercise:* Game of Chess •
Overcoming Panic • *Spiritual Exercise:* How to Go Slower
• *Tip:* Using Dreams to Understand the Outer Life • Dream
Guidance: Plan Better • Help in Business • Dream Help with
Finances • Learning How to Help Others • *Tip:* Don't Act
Blindly on a Dream • Overcoming Fear of Death through
Dreams • Meeting Loved Ones in Dreams • Helping Others
in Dreams • The Power of Dreams

10. **Experiences with ECK Masters** **213**

Meeting the Master Again • Dream Master Visit • *Spiritual
Exercise:* The Dhyana Technique • Help from ECK Masters
• Help to Move beyond Fear • Spiritual Perspective • Spiritual Experiences as a Child • The Motorcycle Man • Light
and Sound • Looking for Happiness • First Connection •
Accepting the Love • A Dream with Rebazar Tarzs • *Spiritual Exercise:* Beach Walk with Rebazar Tarzs • A Dream
with Gopal Das • *Spiritual Exercise:* Meeting Gopal
Das • When the Seeker Is Ready • Golden Wisdom Temples

• How to Visit Temples in Your Dreams • *Spiritual Exercise:* Temple Technique • Seeing Loved Ones in Dreams • Finding the Master in Dreams • A Dream Class with Fubbi Quantz • Secret Teachings

11. Active Dreaming 243

Dream Letter • Dream Softens Fear of Death • Inner Communication Line • Going beyond Passivity • *Spiritual Exercise:* The Big Stone Statue • *Tip:* See Yourself Alive in Spirit • Soul Travel in Dreams • Opening the Heart Center • *Spiritual Exercise:* How to Open Your Heart • Levels of Heaven • *Spiritual Exercise:* The Formula Technique • *Tip:* Recording the Experiences • Working Consciously with Sound and Light • *Spiritual Exercise:* Dreaming Consciously • *Tip:* How Do I Get Back? • Sound Experiences • Night Sounds • Celestial Light • Series Dreams • Opening the Inner Vision • Wah Z • Dream Music • *Spiritual Exercise:* Golden Musical Notes • Dreams of Teaching • *Spiritual Exercise:* Getting Answers in Dreams

12. Dream Travel to Soul Travel 267

Self-Realization • *Spiritual Exercise:* Journey on an Ocean of Light • Soul Travel and Spiritual Unfoldment • Dreams to Soul Travel • *Spiritual Exercise:* Using the Imaginative Body • What Is Soul Travel? • Natural Movement out of the Body • Steps to Higher Consciousness • Begin with a Dream • Remembering Your Inner Experiences • Here's a Soul Travel Experience • Soul Travel Today • The Vision Experience • The Dream Experience • Giving and Receiving • The Soul Travel Experience • The ECKshar Experience • Hearing and Seeing God • Promise of the ECK Masters • Soul's Dream of God

Glossary 287
Index 289

Foreword

What are spiritual dreams?

There is an ancient and universal tradition about the true nature of dreams which has lost favor in modern times. This view holds that dreams are of divine origin, that they are a portal to spiritual worlds, and that they bear messages from heaven and prophetic insights.

The Gilgamesh saga of ancient Mesopotamia shows us that dreamers used various techniques to increase the chances that a deity would appear in their dreams. A god might send a dream message to a single priest or a group of dreamers. The Egyptians were said to believe that dreams were caused by the soul taking out-of-body journeys during sleep. In the Old Testament, God says, "Hear my words: If there is a prophet among you, I the Lord make myself known to him in a vision, I speak with him in a dream."

In Jacob's famous dream at Bethel, he saw a ladder reaching up to heaven, with angels ascending and descending upon it. At the top was the Lord. When Jacob awoke from the dream he exclaimed, "How awesome is this place! This is none other than the house of God, and this is the gate of heaven."

The Chinese also believed that the soul could separate from the body during sleep and journey into the spiritual worlds, where it could communicate with the departed, then return to the body with memories of the visit. High Chinese officials were expected to seek divine guidance through their dreams so they would obtain the insights needed for wise political judgment.

In ancient India the soul was also thought to leave the body during sleep and visit other places. Indian texts also state that children dream of impressions from past lives and that old people could dream of the world to come. The Greeks, such as Homer, believed dreams had a divine origin and that the messages were often direct and readily understood. Like nearly all ancient cultures, the Greeks believed that the soul was able to leave the body at night, take trips into other worlds, and visit with the gods. The list goes on, but these examples show the widespread belief held by our ancestors in the spiritual nature of dreams.

It is one of the greatest losses of modern psychology in its pursuit of scientific foundations that this ancient view was discarded. For spiritual dreams are as prevalent today as they were in ancient times.

Thousands of people are reporting out-of-body journeys in the dream state—journeys to distant locations on earth or to higher spiritual dimensions. They are reporting prophetic dreams, past-life dreams, telepathic dreams, healing dreams, and dreams of illumination and divine love, guidance, and protection. The dreamers having these kinds of adventures are too numerous to ignore.

Harold Klemp, the spiritual leader of Eckankar, Religion of the Light and Sound of God, is one of the foremost advocates of spiritual dreaming in the world today. He draws upon his own insights and experiences, as well as those of many other spiritual dreamers whose personal adventures fill these pages.

The dream teachings of Eckankar define the nature of Soul. You are Soul, a particle of God sent into the worlds (including earth) to gain spiritual experience.

The goal in ECK is spiritual freedom in this lifetime, after which you become a Co-worker with God, both here and in the next world. Karma and reincarnation are primary beliefs.

Key to the ECK dream teachings is the Mahanta, the Living ECK Master. He has the special ability to act as both the Inner and Outer Master for ECK students. He is the prophet of Eckankar, given respect but not worship. He teaches the sacred name of God, HU, which lifts you spiritually into the Light and Sound of God, the ECK (Holy Spirit). Purified by the practice of the Spiritual Exercises of ECK, you are then able to accept the full love of God in this lifetime.

Sri Harold Klemp is the Mahanta, the Living ECK Master today. He has written many books, discourses, and articles about the spiritual life. Many of his public talks are available on audio- and videocassette. His teachings uplift people and help them recognize and understand their own experiences in the Light and Sound of God.

This book is a compilation of Harold Klemp's public writings on dreams. It goes beyond the usual dream book: it places spiritual dreaming in its rightful place at the center of the whole subject of dreams.

The assumption is made right from the start that spiritual dreams are real, that they are a vital part of life, and that they are an essential and key element in one's spiritual growth.

Do you want to understand the nature and reality of your dreams? And experience the wondrous potential for love and happiness they can bring into your life? Then try the tips and spiritual exercises given in these pages. They will introduce you to the dream teachings of Eckankar—a road to your inner worlds and the art of spiritual dreaming.

Our dreams are the forgotten road to heaven.

1

Dreams and Our Spiritual Journey

*D*reams—the stuff of wonder, fear, the unknown—are always certain to pique our curiosity.

Dreams were the reason for the good fortune of Joseph of the Old Testament. He overcame all odds—treachery by his brothers, slavery, and imprisonment—to rise in stature and power until he was second only to the mighty pharaoh of Egypt.

Dreams hold an aura of mystery. They give power to anyone who can—or claims to—interpret them. Elias Howe, inventor of the sewing machine, tried for years to develop his invention, but without success. Until, in a dream, he got orders to finish it or pay with his life. Strong motivation, indeed.

Among the many examples of the influence of dreams, there is the one of Samuel Clemens, the American humorist known as Mark Twain. He foresaw the death of his brother Henry, who also worked on the riverboats of the Mississippi River during the 1850s. One night, Twain awoke from a nightmare in which he saw the metal coffin of his brother. On it lay a bouquet of white flowers, a red rose in the middle. A few weeks later, his brother

Dreams hold an aura of mystery. They give power to anyone who can—or claims to—interpret them.

suffered severe injuries from a boiler explosion on the river. He died shortly after.

Upon his arrival a few days later, Twain found the setting exactly as it had appeared in his dream. Some people had taken pity upon his brother and had collected money to buy an expensive metal coffin, instead of the wooden boxes usually used in river accidents. As Twain paid his last respects, a woman entered the room and placed on the coffin a bouquet of white flowers with a single red rose in the middle.

Dreams touch every level of our life.

DREAMS HAPPEN IN A REAL WORLD

Dreams touch every level of our life. They may let us glimpse the future, or give suggestions for healing, or share insights into our relationships. Above all, they can and will steer us more directly toward God.

What is this fantasy about dreams?

First, understand that the dream world is anything but a fantasy. A "confused" dream simply shows the inability of our mind to accept truth head-on, so it bends the facts and artfully weaves them into a story line that is less likely to cause us distress. Yes, dreams are real.

A mother listening to her young daughter tell of an inner experience from the night before dismissed it offhand as only a dream. The girl quickly corrected her. "Not just a dream, Mom," she said. "It was real."

So, first, understand that the land of dreams is an actual place. Second, any experience you gain in the dream world is as useful to you spiritually as any of those you may have here in the human body.

To grasp the universal nature of dreams, take a step back and imagine that you are standing at the top of all worlds. The identity that can do that, to command a view even of creation itself, is the real you—eternal Soul. Soul is a child of God, and, by nature, Godlike. And so It can share in the divine attributes of wisdom, joy, freedom, and divine love.

So why doesn't It? Why don't you?

Your dreams are like a telescope that can give a better view of something that is normally out of reach: your spiritual side. That includes how you act, feel, reflect, think, react, and even love. Most people fear putting the telescope of dreams to their eye, afraid of what they might see.

Your Hidden Life

Dreams are a direct line to the sea of our hidden life, much like a fishing line dropped from a small boat into a bottomless sea.

A person who learns to dream well can usually take everyday life in stride, because dreams give him or her a perception that others cannot help but notice. An understanding of dreams can steady us for the surprises of the day, and so aid us in learning to manage stress with more foresight and grace.

Dreams often tell what's coming.

A friend from the air force and I keep in touch with an exchange of letters every few months. Usually, he comes for a visit in the dream world on the inner planes while writing me a letter. Next morning, I'll tell my wife about our visit on the inner planes.

"Ray must be writing a letter again," I say.

Dreams are a direct line to the sea of our hidden life, much like a fishing line dropped from a small boat into a bottomless sea.

And it usually comes a few days later.

Dreams are like that fishing line dropped from a boat into the sea. They are much more than a communication link, which the line suggests: Our memory of dreams is a glimpse of the full spiritual life that each of us leads beyond the physical. Our daily physical life has as little scope or variety as might exist in a rowboat. A full spiritual life, on the other hand, includes all events around the boat (human self), including those within the sea, on the land, and in the sky of existence.

Dreams are a large part of each person's hidden life, and it's this sea of experience that we want to look at.

Our memory of dreams is a glimpse of the full spiritual life that each of us leads beyond the physical.

EARTH ACADEMY

A woman we will call Sue went through a divorce and other problems that brought on a weariness of living. In the past, at the height of distress, she often had a series of troubling, recurring dreams about the last days of school, usually just before final exams. She could not stomach the thought of having to deal with a single day more of classes. It was easier to skip them. The next morning, Sue would awaken with a deep loathing for the problems of living.

Then the realization struck her: She just wanted to go home to God. Weary of the lessons of life, she was tired of having to face still another boring lesson, a repeat of a spiritual law she had refused to learn in the past.

These she called her quitter's dreams.

Through the dream teachings of ECK, Sue has come to understand that life on earth is like an academy, a camp of discipline where people learn the laws of Divine Spirit (ECK). In her case, the ECK is cleaning out old wounds and pouring Its healing Light and Sound into the dark, infected areas of karma in her life. The emotional pain she so often feels is from her resistance to the changes of Divine Spirit. As the pain of life drives itself deeper into her, she nevertheless feels the love behind it opening her heart wider to God.

When she remembers to look at herself in a spiritual light, she sees the deep capacity for love this pain has brought her. The realization fills her with wonder. Now she can rise in the morning and greet the new day with eagerness and grace.

DREAM TREASURE

Another sort of dream may tell a dreamer where to look for an actual treasure. Yet the real experience may be a test of spiritual grace.

A young woman and her husband moved from a small, crowded apartment into a house her father owned. Shortly before moving day, she had two separate dreams that told of money hidden somewhere in their new home. Busy with the move, she set the dreams aside.

When it was time to connect the gas for heating and cooking, she called the utility company, which sent a serviceman. He checked all the appliances that used gas and found a paper bag hidden behind an old oven.

"Do you want this paper bag?" he asked the young woman. "It could catch fire back here."

Remembering her two dreams, she quickly replied, "Yes, give it to me, please." Casually, she

When she remembers to look at herself in a spiritual light, she sees the deep capacity for love this pain has brought her.

placed it on the kitchen table, in full view, though in her heart she suspected it was full of money. After the serviceman had left, she opened the bag and indeed found a large wad of cash.

Yet this house was the property of her father. Instead of saying "Finders keepers," she put the cash in a safe place for her father, who was out of town for the weekend. Upon his return, she gave him the full amount, for it had never occurred to her to keep any for herself. He, in turn, let her keep it all—in appreciation for her love, grace, and honesty.

This young woman did profit from her dream. When the serviceman had handed her the bag, she took it calmly and placed it on the kitchen table in plain sight—as if it were of no value. This calmed suspicion and any chance that he might tell others about her good fortune, only later to have someone try to break in and steal it. Told in her dreams about the contents of the paper bag, she could act wisely and safeguard it for her father, the real owner.

A dreamer lives in many worlds at once.

HANDY SPIRITUAL TOOL

A dreamer lives in many worlds at once. And yes, dreams do enrich life.

Dreams are a spiritual tool of the Holy Spirit to help you find your way to God. Take advantage of this help. There is so much more to life than you'll ever find in something so small as a rowboat, or as narrow as the human state of consciousness.

A study of dreams the ECK way can help you enter a more productive, calm, and graceful life.

YOUR SOURCE OF EVERYDAY GUIDANCE

Dreams can tell us everything we need to know to get along in this life. Yet how many people really believe that? If people actually did, the study of dreams would be much more prominent in our society than it is today.

Most of my life I also paid little regard to dreams. My early dreams were of two kinds: the bad and the good. The first were nightmares, and the less they came, the better. Even the good dreams had little to recommend them, since everything in them was topsy-turvy. I usually blessed the deep and dreamless sleep, because in that unknowing state there was a kind of refuge which did not threaten my waking life.

In fact, my recollection of dreams started to flower shortly after I began my study of Eckankar in 1967. My desire to Soul Travel had aroused my curiosity about the invisible worlds, and soon I bought a notebook to record any adventure that might occur there.

Dreams taught me to face myself, let me see the future, took me to the heavens of God, and even apprised me of impending illness and where to obtain the cure. During my years in ECK, my respect for the inner teachings of dreams has grown considerably.

Dreams taught me to face myself, let me see the future, took me to the heavens of God, and even apprised me of impending illness and where to obtain the cure.

FORGOTTEN ROAD TO HEAVEN

Our dreams are the forgotten road to heaven.

This was once a nearly absolute truth. That is, until the teachings of ECK surfaced in 1965 to encourage people to look for the lost doorway between heaven and earth: their dreams.

Dreams are the starting point for many who wish to begin the spiritual journey to God and do it in the easiest possible way. There is simply no better way to start than with our dreams. Good works may carry us far along this holy journey, and prayer is indeed a boon, but generally we can learn more about the true nature of God through the secret knowledge of dreams.

YOU HAVE A DREAM GUIDE

Daydreams, night dreams, contemplation, Soul Travel— all are steps in the pursuit of heaven.

Daydreams, night dreams, contemplation, Soul Travel—all are steps in the pursuit of heaven. In Eckankar, the student is under the protection of a spiritual guide known as the Mahanta. This is the Spiritual Traveler, the Dream Master.

As the Mahanta, he is the Inner Master, the one who comes on the inner planes to impart knowledge, truth, and wisdom. But he also has an outer side. Here he is known as the Living ECK Master. Thus, the spiritual leader of Eckankar can work both inwardly and outwardly with all who come to learn of God and life.

DREAM TRAVEL PROTECTION

Once he requests it, a person who travels in his dream worlds is assured of the Mahanta's protection. This is helpful because in those lower heavens that lie between earth and the true worlds of God, there are shady people who like nothing better than to cheat or harm innocent people.

In Africa, for instance, the power of black magic is very strong. An African man reported a dream in which a group of men and women took him to a high place. Unknown to him, these people were warlocks and witches. When they reached the top of this place, which was a towering seawall, a woman in the group told him to jump into the sea. But he knew that all who jumped from that height never came back.

"Jump!" she urged. As if hypnotized, he began to move toward the edge of the wall. At that moment, the Mahanta appeared. The group vanished. The Master smiled and patted the dreamer on his shoulder; then the dreamer awoke.

What few would recognize is that the Mahanta prevented the dreamer's death. It often happens that a dreamer, who does not have the protection of the Mahanta, simply dies in his sleep. The doctor writes off the cause as heart failure or some other physical condition. Often as not, however, the dreamer had wandered beyond the safe limits of his inner world and met a psychic criminal, who was responsible for his death. An experience that did not have to be, had he known of the Mahanta, the Living ECK Master.

THE WAY OF CONTEMPLATION

The student of ECK finds that his dreams become ever more spiritual as he continues his search for God.

Dreams are one road to heaven. Another way to enter is through contemplation: a few minutes each day of spiritual relaxation in which the individual sits with his eyes shut and sings the holy name of God. This word is *HU.* The Inner Master comes, in time, to take him into the worlds of heaven, the Far Country.

More often, though, we start our study of heaven through dreams. They are a most natural way. The student of ECK finds that his dreams become ever more spiritual as he continues his search for God.

Mental Obstacles

The mind is the chief obstacle in the search for God. It tries to have the dreamer forget dreams in which the Mahanta imparts divine wisdom. So the Dream Master must bypass this wall created by the mind.

One way the Mahanta, the Living ECK Master accomplishes this is seen in a dream study by a member of Eckankar. When the Mahanta wanted to remind her to avoid gossip and honor the Law of Silence, she had a dream in which something unpleasant was in her mouth. When the Master's lesson was on the "play" of life, her dream experiences dealt with school, group meetings, clubs, dorms, households, even pageants. When it was necessary for her to recall travel through higher levels of consciousness, her dreams were of stairs, steps, elevators, mazes of rooms, and even of herself on a child's swing.

Dreams are a road to heaven. They are not the only road; they do not go straight to the highest heaven, but they do offer a sound beginning for anyone who sincerely wants to find God.

Insights through Dreams

In ECK, we are familiar with dreams of past lives. Other dreams give us insight into our health, family concerns, love interests, business plans, and guidance in how to live our lives with minute-to-minute care, if we are interested in developing our study of dreams to such a degree.

But the most important dream category is the spiritual dream. It tells us something about our present life, with all its struggles.

We learn about hidden motives, which most people wish to leave undisturbed in the dark corners of their minds.

WHAT IS A SPIRITUAL DREAM?

Here is a spiritual dream, so that when you have one you have a measure to compare it with.

A dreamer awoke in her dream to find herself alongside the ocean. A high mound of sand ran parallel to the water, like a breakwater. She noticed she was on the side nearest the ocean. Looking closely at the mound of sand, she found little booklets buried in it and picked one up. An ECK Master came and read the message in the booklet for her.

"You've won a white used car," he said.

Used? She pulled another booklet from the mound, hoping for a message that said she had won a new white car. Instead, the ECK Master read: "You've won $113,000 in groceries." A second before she awoke, she found herself on the other side of the mound, away from the ocean.

A dreamer awoke in her dream to find herself alongside the ocean.

The spiritual meaning came to her loud and clear: She had taken a step backward in her spiritual life. It came as a shock to her to see how attached she had become to worldly things. Only a month earlier she had written a two-word letter to the Living ECK Master: "I'm ready." She meant, for a higher state of consciousness.

This dream was a humbling experience. She now realized that the Mahanta had given her the used car in the dream because it was right for her at the time. It was the Master's gift, no matter how "used" it may have seemed to her. She was thus able to take a new look at herself, honestly. From that dream she was then able to move up spiritually as was her desire.

Many more stories are told throughout this book about dreamers who have been enriched by their dreams. The study of dreams is an art, a highly interesting spiritual endeavor. It gives deep satisfaction to all who wish to learn more about themselves through their own experience.

Above all, dreams are of priceless spiritual worth to us, because they open our personal road to heaven.

UNIVERSAL NATURE OF DREAMS

The universal nature of dreams transcends all cultures. Symbols may vary from place to place, but these are minute details. To deal with dreams only from the level of symbols is to treat them in a light, superficial way.

The universal nature of dreams reflects the universal being, Soul.

By *the universal nature of dreams,* I mean that dreams are working continuously in our lives. They are working not only when we are asleep but also when we are awake. The universal nature of dreams reflects the universal being, Soul.

One evening I was out working in the yard. I had just finished mowing the grass and was setting up the hoses to water my geraniums, a gay mixture of white, pink, and red. They're set along the driveway to greet me when I come home. Some of my neighbors have commented on how nice they look.

One neighbor, being pulled down the sidewalk by his huge dog, stopped to tell me how pretty the geraniums were. "Plants need love just like animals," I said. "Just like your dog."

I think I caught him off guard. He must have

just gotten home from work. Tired and hungry, he still had to take the dog out for its duty walk before he could relax and enjoy dinner. It was probably the last thing he felt like doing right then.

But after I made that comment, he looked at his dog as if to say, Excuse me for being so rude. I understand why you must have your walk.

WAKING-LIFE LESSONS

This man was an example of the universal dreamer. In the course of his everyday life, through his own ears, he got a lesson on how to treat his pet better.

I didn't say it to preach to him. Actually, it didn't even occur to me until after I spoke that he might have been a little upset about having to take the dog for a walk. But it was part of his waking dream to meet with a neighbor who would awaken him to be more conscious of what he was doing in his daily chores.

It was part of his waking dream to meet with a neighbor who would awaken him to be more conscious of what he was doing in his daily chores.

A FALLEN ROBIN

My neighbor and his dog continued on their walk. As I turned back to the geraniums, I kept hearing a peeping sound, like a little bird in distress, followed by the song of a full-grown robin. Why all the commotion?

I followed the sound to a small tree where I found a nest. In it were two young robins. The parent robins were off gathering worms to feed into those young, gaping beaks. At this point my eyes saw a third robin. It had fallen out of the nest and was lying at the base of the tree. The nest had become almost too small for three robins. This young one must have carelessly walked to the edge of the nest and slipped off.

The parents probably had mixed feelings about their little one on the ground at the base of the tree. They showed great distress, yet their instincts drove them to feed only the babies in the nest.

So, I'm standing by the geraniums, wondering whether to interfere in this little family's karma.

Finally I decided. I went to the garage and looked around for something to pick the robin up with. Fortunately, the nest in that small tree was just a little higher than my head. And though there were some hitches to placing the little robin back in its home, I'll spare you the details.

GREATER DESTINY

In a way, this illustration also is part of the universal nature of dreams.

The little birds in the nest are like people before they find the two aspects of the Holy Spirit, the Light and Sound of God.

The little birds in the nest are like people before they find the two aspects of the Holy Spirit, the Light and Sound of God. They're in a little nest and feel safe and secure. Somebody always takes care of them. Life rolls on just perfectly. Ignorance is bliss. But gradually life becomes less and less perfect as these little creatures grow bigger and the nest starts to get crowded.

They're in a little nest and feel safe and secure.

There are stirrings within one little bird that say its destiny is greater than this small nest, which seems to grow smaller by the day. After all, how long can you eat somebody else's worms? Why not spread your wings and see if there's something else to eat out there.

This little bird is like Soul before It finds truth. The natural order of life is growth and spiritual unfoldment. Like it or not, believe it or not, accept it or not, life says you are going to grow spiritually, until someday you outgrow your present state of consciousness.

Spiritually, this has also happened to you.

You too were once a young robin fallen from the nest before your time. An experience showed you there is more to life than you knew up to that moment—something much greater than the nest of the human consciousness. The Inner Master temporarily helped you back into your old state of consciousness until you had the strength spiritually to venture forth into these new worlds too.

And at the moment you could fly freely, to find the nourishment you craved spiritually, you entered a brand new world.

At the moment you could fly freely, to find the nourishment you craved spiritually, you entered a brand new world.

WAKING DREAMS

Many of you have passed beyond the beginners steps of inner experiences to the more advanced ones of outer experiences: waking dreams or the Golden-tongued Wisdom, two ways the Holy Spirit speaks to us in our waking life.

A waking dream is usually an experience from the Mahanta, the Inner Master, that points out a spiritual lesson with an example in your outer life. The Golden-tongued Wisdom is the voice of the Inner Master that jumps out at you to impart some spiritual insight. It might come through words spoken by another person in a golden moment.

Once you are able to see the connection between your inner and outer lives, you will never again be happy in your old nest.

Of course, there are people who try to go back.

But that's like a young bird trying to fit back into a broken eggshell.

EXPLORING YOUR INNER WORLDS

There is a universal force that operates in the background of our lives to establish harmony.

So how do you begin the adventure of exploring your spiritual worlds? There is a universal force that operates in the background of our lives to establish harmony.

It is the ECK, otherwise known as the Audible Sound Current, the Holy Spirit, the Voice of God, and as the Light and Sound of God.

How do you find these two aspects of the Voice of God? Usually, it starts with your dreams. The pathway to the Light and Sound includes: (1) *belief* in ECK, the seedbed of unfoldment; (2) *experience,* the cultivator; and (3) *awareness,* the rich harvest.

Dreams, as a tool of awareness, can tell a dreamer how in or out of tune he is with the Light and Sound—and thus, with himself. For example, let's look at a businessman named Jerry. His productivity at work had slipped because of poor work habits. So he was unhappy, ready to blame his family and associates for things gone wrong.

One night he had a dream in which he was a student again. His instructor had given him and his classmates an open-book test for homework. They were to turn it in for grading at the next class period.

At home, Jerry answered most of the questions before losing the test among a stack of other papers on his desk. He later found it. But just before class the next morning, he discovered an awful mistake. Somehow he had put his answers on someone else's test paper. By then it was too late to complete his own test, so he decided to stay home and risk an absence from class.

After class, a classmate told him that the instructor had graded their tests but had then sprung a second test on the class. Suddenly, Jerry was two tests behind. Troubled, he awoke.

What did his dream mean?

The instructor was the Dream Master, the Mahanta. Like a teacher, he sets a program of spiritual study for everyone in Eckankar. This study involves every part of a person's life and may partly reflect in his dreams.

The dream showed Jerry filling out someone else's test paper in error. At his office in the day-to-day world, Jerry often let others convince him to help them do their work, but at the expense of his own. Clearly a mistake. His classmates in the dream represented a spiritual standard that he could reach with a minimum of effort. So to regain harmony with the spiritual standard of ECK, he must set new priorities at work.

His dream told of an important principle: Life goes forward; keep up or fall behind.

That was shown by the teacher grading the tests of Jerry's classmates, while handing out another test during the same class. Because of Jerry's absence, he was quickly two tests behind. It pointed to a widening gap between him and Divine Spirit.

In a capsule, this dream had a warning: "You're out of tune with life. Get back in step!" Once he set new priorities, his discontent vanished.

THE PURPOSE OF LIFE

Dreams, visions, and other experiences mean little by themselves. Yet in the scope of our whole

His dream told of an important principle: Life goes forward; keep up or fall behind.

spiritual life, they are good signs of how much we are in accord with life. In fact, the whole point of life is to teach us how to reach agreement with the Voice of God, the Light and Sound. Many people thus find the road to their inner worlds through the teachings of ECK.

Often, however, it takes a personal tragedy to drive us in search of the meaning of life.

A mother, very close to her son, found Eckankar after his death in a motorcycle accident. Devastated by her loss, she was unable to find comfort at church. She regularly cried through the entire service. If only there was a way to feel closer to God, then maybe He would help her understand why the accident had occurred. More important, where was her son now? Was he all right? She constantly prayed for help.

Five months later, while at her lowest ebb, she had an experience that changed her life. At first, she thought it was merely a dream, but it was actually Soul Travel.

The mother awoke in vivid consciousness in the other worlds. A bespectacled woman with grey streaks in her dark hair met her, and they talked for a few minutes. "Do you know my son?" she finally asked the woman, giving his name.

"Of course I know him," said the woman. "He lives right over there in that white house." The scene was a normal setting of cottages, such as near a lake resort.

She and her son had a long conversation. He assured her his health was better than it had been on earth. Then looking closely at her, he said, "I know what you're doing to yourself. Please stop. You're only hurting yourself." Before they parted,

Often it takes a personal tragedy to drive us in search of the meaning of life.

she asked to hold him in her arms, since she didn't get a chance to do so before his death. Laughing, he said, "OK, Mom."

Soul Travel had put her right there with her loved one. She could actually feel him in her arms. Then she awoke.

His scent still lingered with her, and a peaceful, happy feeling lasted for weeks before it began to fade. She was now determined to learn where he was. Somewhere on earth, she knew, somebody had the answer. That's when her sister introduced her to Eckankar. The first book she read was *The Spiritual Notebook* by Paul Twitchell, the modern-day founder of Eckankar. It convinced her that here was the answer to her prayers. Here was an explanation that made sense.

Grief for her son still overtakes her on occasion. She wants the Mahanta, the Living ECK Master to help her regain the peace felt while with her son during Soul Travel. So she does the Spiritual Exercises of ECK daily. And she directs her efforts to seeing the Light and hearing the Sound—keys to the secret worlds of God.

Stories like this may inspire one to search for truth and love too, but finding them depends upon doing the right thing. For those in ECK, it is doing the spiritual exercises. They are in the ECK books and discourses, and take twenty to thirty minutes a day. Simply a love song to God or a conversation with Divine Spirit, they can help you find a new appreciation for life. Many people develop their own spiritual exercises, once they catch the knack of it from the ECK teachings.

Soul Travel had put her right there with her loved one. She could actually feel him in her arms.

Spiritual Exercise: The Blue Curtain of God

Here's an easy spiritual exercise called "The Blue Curtain of God." The first part awakens the seeing power of Soul.

Find a time to sit or lie down for ten to twenty minutes when you will not be disturbed. Shut your eyes, but imagine you are gently looking at a dark blue curtain on the wall before you. The first few days, expect to see only the rich blue curtain. Sooner or later, some color of the Light of God will shine from it.

The second part of the spiritual exercise attunes your spiritual hearing.

While looking at a blue curtain, begin to softly sing the word *HU* (say, "hue"), an old name for God honored by saints for thousands of years. After a few minutes, sing HU to yourself, making no audible sound. Continue to sing for a few more minutes until you wish to stop. Then sit quietly, still looking at the rich blue curtain before you.

Throughout this short exercise, carry in your heart a feeling of love for God.

After finishing your devotion, go about the day as usual. Then at bedtime, think briefly of the blue curtain again and the word *HU*. Quietly, to yourself, say, "Show me Thy Will, O God. Teach me to love Thee."

Over the next few days, try to remember your dreams. No matter how inconsequential they may seem, write down any images to jog your memory for contemplation later. The Mahanta or the Holy Spirit will use dreams to give you special guidance and understanding.

Spend time in your universe of dreams. You will find the grace of more insight, harmony, and joy in your spiritual life.

Solomon supposedly said, 'There is no new thing under the sun.' He was right. But what I am trying to show people is that there is something new beyond the sun.

2

The Dream Master

J work in the capacity of the Inner and Outer Master. As the Outer Master I give people the outer teachings. I can tell them about the books of Eckankar and how the books can help them start to see the secret teachings.

As the Inner Master I come to them in the dream state. I talk to them and meet with them. Gradually they become aware of the secret, inner teachings, through the dream state. Then I can begin showing them there's more to life than they could ever have imagined.

Solomon supposedly said, "There is no new thing under the sun." He was right. But what I'm trying to show people is that there is something new beyond the sun.

I can begin showing them there's more to life than they could ever have imagined.

WAKE-UP CALL

An individual planned to go to an Eckankar seminar. She and her husband had been out very late the night before they were to leave, and she was concerned that they would oversleep. When she finally got into bed at two-thirty in the morning, she asked the Dream Master, "Please help me get up by seven o'clock so that I can get to the train station in time."

She had been asleep for a few hours when suddenly she was jolted awake by the doorbell ringing. She tried to ignore it and go back to sleep. But it rang over and over, making a horrible racket.

"Who's there?" she called out. Nobody answered, but the ringing continued.

Very agitated by now, she jumped up, ran to the door, and jerked it open. She was quite surprised to find that no one was there. On her way back to the bedroom, she glanced at the clock and saw that it was one minute after seven. She realized she had gotten her wake-up call right on schedule.

WORKING WITH A DREAM TEACHER

Some people not in Eckankar have similar experiences, and misunderstand them. They say, "An evil force is trying to enter my life!" They do not recognize that it is a good force working in their behalf.

This is important to know: The Dream Master will come when you ask.

The wake-up call came to the ECKist because she had asked. This is important to know: The Dream Master will come when you ask. You first have to learn to ask, and then you have to learn to recognize when he speaks. Our whole concern in ECK is how to become more conscious individuals; to become more conscious of who and what we are.

Usually I work with you in the dream state. The true test of a Master ought to be that he can not only work with you outwardly and physically, but also inwardly. There are few individuals who have this power. Even in ECK there are some students who aren't conscious of this inward help. The best I can say is: Be patient. I am happy for those who have experiences with either myself or the other

ECK Masters. Spirit is not divided; these ECK Masters are merely the manifestation of Divine Spirit on a certain plane of the inward heavens.

THE MAHANTA

The Mahanta is a state of consciousness. It is a spiritual state of consciousness very much like the Buddha consciousness or the Christ consciousness. The Living ECK Master is the other half of the title *the Mahanta, the Living ECK Master.* This means the outer spiritual teacher, myself.

The Mahanta is a state of consciousness.

The teachings of Eckankar speak very directly and very distinctly of the two parts of the Master: the Inner Master and the Outer Master. The Inner Master is the Mahanta, and the Outer Master is the Living ECK Master.

The Inner Master is not a physical being. It is someone you see in the inner planes during contemplation or in the dream state. He may look like me, he may look like another ECK Master, or he may even look the same as Christ. All it is, really, is the merging of the Light and Sound of God into a matrix, into a form which appears as a person. This, then, becomes the inner guide which steers a person through the pitfalls of karma, the troubles we make for ourselves through ignorance of the spiritual laws.

The Master often works in the dream state because it is easier to get through. Fears can inhibit and prevent one from exercising the freedom and power and wisdom which are the birthright of Soul. In the dream state, the Inner Master can begin working with you to familiarize and make you comfortable with what comes on the other side.

MY EARLY EXPERIENCES

During my first year in Eckankar, I had a couple of experiences with the Light and Sound of God, the ECK; but the memory quickly faded, and I forgot about it. I began to worry, because it didn't seem that I was having any experiences.

One night as I was drifting off to sleep, I asked Sri Paul Twitchell, who was the Living ECK Master of the time, to help me. As I inwardly expressed this desire, I saw him sitting in an easy chair, watching me. I was pacing the floor in front of him, walking back and forth with my hands behind my back in the classic thinker position. I asked, "Paul, when am I ever going to have experiences on the inner planes— with you or with the Light and Sound of ECK?"

Of course, I didn't realize that it was happening. This was in the dream state, and I believed that I was wide awake. He looked at me for a long while, and then he turned his head to look at a picture of a lady. She had been on the earth plane about 199 years, and the picture showed scenes of her entire life. It showed scenes of her childhood, her adulthood, and her many experiences. Paul turned to me again and pointed to the picture. "I don't know how to break this to you," he said. "You are a young man, but even when you get to be this woman's age, it doesn't look good."

I knew it was all over. "Yeah," I said, "the spiritual path is too hard. It doesn't look as if I'm ever going to make any progress on this path to God at all."

Paul just sat there with his arms folded, looking at me. Finally, I walked away very much upset.

Immediately, I woke up in my bed. I was really upset and out loud I asked the question, "When am

I asked, "Paul, when am I ever going to have experiences on the inner planes—with you or with the Light and Sound of ECK?"

I going to have an inner experience with the Sound and Light?"

The dream had come about so naturally that it took me nearly half a day to figure it out. The ECK Masters work in subtle ways.

PERSONALIZED TEACHINGS

Some people have difficulty remembering their dreams, but others are very aware of working with the Dream Master. This is a very real being, someone not generally known in the more contemporary teachings on dreams. People outside of ECK who hear of the Dream Master try to fit him into some kind of symbology: "Oh, yes, he represents your inner urgings and strivings to reach satisfaction and happiness, and therefore, blah, blah, blah."

They don't understand, of course, that the Mahanta, the Living ECK Master is the Dream Master and that he can work with you on a one-to-one basis. He can help you understand the attitudes that affect your health and bring insight into problems you may be having with others.

THE MAHANTA NEVER INTERFERES

The ECK Masters never interfere in another person's state of consciousness without his permission. I hold your personal life sacred and won't intrude in any way, even in the dream state, without your permission. There are always the do-gooders who want to dry out the drunk, when maybe the drunk doesn't want to be dried out. Or they want to save the soul of the man who has committed a crime and is on his way to the gallows.

The ECK Masters never interfere in another person's state of consciousness without his permission.

We really don't have that right. Soul must have the freedom of Its own state of consciousness.

Spiritual Exercise: Inviting the Dream Master

The Dream Master, who is really the Mahanta, the Living ECK Master, will not work with the dreamer unless invited in some way.

Before going to sleep, inwardly give permission to the Dream Master to be with you.

Before going to sleep, inwardly give permission to the Dream Master to be with you. Imagine unburdening yourself, giving your problems to him, and letting your mind relax its concerns and worries. Ask the Dream Master to help clear up the karmic conditions of whatever is standing in the way of your spiritual growth.

Then go to sleep, aware that you are resting in the care of the Dream Master who will look out for your best interests.

HOW THE MAHANTA COMMUNICATES

In the air force I had a friend who was quite a mentalizer. We had some pretty interesting conversations during breaks at work. He liked to quote facts, but occasionally he would forget the name of something. Finally he would give up trying to remember, and we'd go back to work.

About three weeks later, he would look over at me and say the word he hadn't been able to think of before. "Thanks," I'd say and go right back to work.

It was as if the three weeks since our conversation on the subject had collapsed, and we picked up right where we had left off. He had the ability to set up a line of inner communication between us, so that I wasn't caught off guard when he said the forgotten word out of nowhere. I always knew just what he was referring to.

This is often what happens with the Mahanta and you. Out here in the role of spiritual leader of Eckankar, I am only able to hint at the spiritual truth that exists here and in the other worlds. Part of the fault is mine, because I simply don't have the words. An equal part of the fault lies with the listener, for not having the ability to understand what is being said.

THE INNER TEACHINGS

There is a link that can bridge that gap, and this is known as the inner communication of the Mahanta with the student. When the Master speaks with the student through the inner communication, sometimes a mere phrase triggers all kinds of memories from the dream state. It can happen when you are sitting in the audience at an Eckankar seminar or in your home listening to a tape of the talk. That certain phrase suddenly seems to convey a book of truth to you.

These are the inner teachings, the secret teachings. The insight that comes from the Golden-tongued Wisdom—those golden moments when the Holy Spirit speaks directly to us—whether spoken by me or someone else, is the working of the ECK. It is trying to lift you into a higher state of consciousness.

One of the gems of truth, a golden jewel of God, has been placed in your path. When the moment occurs, look closely at the experience and weigh it

The insight that comes from the Golden-tongued Wisdom—those golden moments when the Holy Spirit speaks directly to us—whether spoken by me or someone else, is the working of the ECK.

carefully. Try to get all the value out of it that the Master has put into it.

Spiritual Exercise: To Remember Your Dreams

This exercise is for people who don't dream but want to. Just before you go to sleep, sit quietly on your bed. Close your eyes. Chant the word *HU* very softly, or if someone is in the room with you, chant it silently to yourself. HU is a special word, the ancient name for God. You could call it the manifested Word or the Sound; it has a power of its own.

As you take the time to sit there and chant HU, the name of God, you are making a commitment with Divine Spirit. Chant HU in a long, drawn-out way for three or four or five minutes, and let yourself settle down. Then wait for a few more minutes before starting the next step.

For those who have been unable to remember their dreams, simply chant the word *dream* spelled out. Chant it out loud, letter by letter: D-R-E-A-M. Do this for about five minutes. Next, chant the same thing quietly for a few minutes, and then just go to sleep. As you are falling asleep, say, "I would like to remember a significant spiritual dream." With this method, you are asking for truth to come through the dream state.

For those who have been unable to remember their dreams, simply chant the word dream *spelled out.*

How to Remember Experiences

To some, the ECK dream teachings seem almost too humble, yet this is how the ECK works. A dream experience can be as simple as a wake-up call.

I used to hear a knocking sound, as if someone had rapped sharply on the door to my room. It would happen about forty-five minutes to an hour before my alarm clock was set to wake me for work. The sound was so clear that, as I gradually came back to the physical body, I actually thought someone had knocked on my door. But when I got up and opened the door to look, no one was there.

It usually happened that the knock interrupted one of my inner experiences. Since there was still time before I had to get ready for work, I could take the opportunity to write down the dream while the memory was fresh.

The knocking sound frightened me at first; I didn't know who was doing it or what was happening. Eventually I realized that it was the Dream Master and that he was saying, "I have given you an experience on the other planes that has meaning for you. I want you to remember it. Wake up and write it down." The wake-up call gave me the time and opportunity to record whatever had come through.

Soon I stopped questioning the knocking and whatever other means the Dream Master used to awaken me. When it came, I just got up, opened my dream journal, and wrote down what had occurred in the dream state.

DREAM GUIDANCE

Many followers of ECK are given guidance through the dream state. A situation may be mocked up by the Dream Master to simulate something that is causing the ECKist concern in his daily life. Through this dream, the ECKist is shown what he should or should not be doing if he wants to

Many followers of ECK are given guidance through the dream state.

resolve the situation.

A husband and wife bought a horse, which they named Sid. Their plan was to train the horse, and when it reached a certain age, they would resell it. Of course, it never occurred to them to wonder how Sid felt about all this.

About a year later, the husband had an unusual dream in which he found himself entering a crowded bar. Seeing one unoccupied table, he went over and sat down. A man came over and introduced himself. "Hi," he said. "I'm Sid, your horse."

The dreamer thought this was the funniest thing he had ever seen. "My horse in a dream, looking like a man," he said. "This is really wild."

The only thing that bothered him about the dream was that this man had a tooth missing, whereas his horse did not.

The dreamer and his horse got to talking. Sid said, "You know, I love you and your wife. I'd like to stay with you. I've never had owners before who could Soul Travel and meet with me in the dream state so we could talk things over."

This is pretty far out, the dreamer thought.

"Sid," he asked, "I notice you've been limping on one of your hind legs. Is there something wrong?"

"I'm having a problem with that foot," said Sid. "It's just a minor thing, but if you can get a farrier to trim my hoof, I could walk better." And they continued talking.

When the man awoke and told his wife about the dream, they shared a good laugh over it. She thought the part about the missing tooth was really hilarious.

Later that morning as they walked to the stable, they saw a crowd around Sid's stall. The ECKists

> *The dreamer thought this was the funniest thing he had ever seen. "My horse in a dream, looking like a man," he said. "This is really wild."*

rushed over, afraid that something dreadful had happened to their horse.

The owners saw a little bit of blood on the door of the stall, but Sid seemed to be all right. The husband put a halter on the horse and led him outside. "If you plan to ride him, just don't put a bit in his mouth," one of the grooms advised him. "Your horse somehow got his mouth caught on the door lock, and his tooth broke off."

Husband and wife looked at each other. "The missing tooth in your dream," she said. Without another word, they leaned over to check the horse's hind foot. Just as Sid had said in the dream, his hoof needed trimming.

Just as Sid had said in the dream, his hoof needed trimming.

The Dream Master sometimes manipulates the dream state so that Soul may communicate with Soul, whatever Its form. Since the man might have totally discounted a dream about a talking horse, the Master changed the image to one the dreamer could accept. This is just one of the ways the Dream Master works.

How the Mahanta Works with Dreams

One woman, newly on the path of ECK, had a dream that demonstrates how the Inner Master often works with us and how the ECK comes into one's life. It happened through the dream state so it would come to her gently. Instead of having an experience of the Sound and Light pouring in directly, which might have shocked her consciousness, the Inner Master saw that it was necessary to take it a little bit slow for the sake of her well-being and stability.

The dream was this: She was watching TV on the inner planes when a news flash announced an earthquake. Running outside, she saw that all the big buildings, including a university up the street, had started to crumble and shatter. She noticed that although the university had fallen into a heap, it didn't bother her. A little farther down the street was a skyscraper bank building, and because of the earthquake it started to tilt. It remained standing but ended up leaning against the capitol building. Then she saw a huge block building, peculiarly shaped with rounded edges, shake loose from its foundation and come sliding down a hill right past her.

She asked someone what the dream meant and was given this interpretation: "Well, looks like there are going to be changes in your life and in your finances." And that was OK as far as it went.

GRASPING THE SIGNIFICANCE OF DREAMS

Spirit had come into her consciousness when she began the Spiritual Exercises of ECK, and she saw this on the inner plane as the earthquake.

What happened was that Spirit had come into her consciousness when she began the Spiritual Exercises of ECK, and she saw this on the inner plane as the earthquake. It shook her foundations. When Spirit comes in, It has to kind of shake us awake.

The earthquake was the ECK coming into her consciousness, and the university represented the mental structure, the mental thought process which is generally very strong in some of us as we step onto the path. It stands in the way of Spirit working freely in our life. This mental process is the one that works by logic and reason. It says, If I go to that party tonight, I know this or that will happen; so I'm not going. Pretty soon we can become withdrawn and inward, and we start missing out on life.

When she saw this university building fall in the earthquake, it meant that the ECK was coming in and working to break down that rigid, unbending Mental body to make it the servant of Soul, instead of trying to make Soul be the servant of mind. She said she hadn't felt badly about it.

Then the bank building shifted over. A lot of times we think our security depends on how much is in our bank account or wallet. When this building started to lean, the security in money wasn't quite as strong and upright as before. It had lost a bit of its character, and the reliance on money wasn't as strong.

But Spirit had come in. There's more reliance on Spirit when you come to know that as you work in your daily life, the ECK will let you take the first step, then It will take the second, and so on.

The big blocks from that building with the rounded edges that slid by her were some of the huge blocks of karma that can pass off in the dream state. This helps to get rid of karma from our past so that we can be free, so that we can be open to let Divine Spirit begin working through us. It brings an upliftment of consciousness and begins paving our way and making it better.

Let Divine Spirit begin working through us. It brings an upliftment of consciousness and begins paving our way and making it better.

DREAMS ARE MEMORIES

Dreams are not merely symbolic messages from the subconscious, though many people accept them only in that way. Dreams may have symbolic messages, but only at the most superficial level. All the books listing thousands of dream symbols make much ado about nothing. Symbols are but the surface of the experience.

The dream world is actually an imperfectly remembered Soul Travel experience. When the memory is not very vivid, we call it a dream.

This is why I have linked Soul Travel and dream travel so closely together. Basically they are the same thing. They are not dreams, and they are not really Soul Travel. They are your experiences of life in greater worlds. And this is actually the best definition of Soul Travel: your experiences of life in the spiritual dimensions, in the greater worlds of God.

Unless you have the experience yourself, you can't really understand what it is all about. But these inner experiences are as important in gaining wisdom, knowledge, and understanding as any experience here on earth.

> *The dream world is actually an imperfectly remembered Soul Travel experience.*

 ## Spiritual Exercise: To Soul Travel

Some of you want Soul Travel, which is usually an advanced state beyond the dream state. Again, sit on your bed or on the floor, shut your eyes, and look into your Spiritual Eye. This is located at a point just above and between the eyebrows. Don't expect to see anything there; just chant HU, the holy name of God.

Then spell out *Soul Travel*, chanting each separate letter: S-O-U-L T-R-A-V-E-L. Do this about three times out loud and then three times quietly.

OVERCOMING FEAR

The Living ECK Master wants to teach people: (1) just to dream; (2) once they dream, to separate their mental distortions from an authentic inner experience; and (3) how to travel in and out of the body in full consciousness.

This is a tall order. First, he must overcome people's fear.

In the beginning stages in ECK, the coming and going of Soul is generally taught through the dream state. The spiritual leader of Eckankar, which at the present time is myself, may come to you in the dream state and casually invite you to go for a short walk. A more exotic experience can scare a person at first. If he gets scared, he's right back in the body, locked in tight for another couple of weeks.

Soul is not a brave entity when the human consciousness is strong. It cowers within the body, occasionally peeking out at the world. Every time something strange comes past, It crouches back in the body.

But it's stuffy in there, so out Soul comes again— not very far—to take another look around, keeping hold of the body. And at the first sign of trouble or danger, Soul zips right back in. If this happens enough times, the person sits down and writes me a very earnest letter: "I'm not having any luck with Soul Travel. Can you please help me?"

Soul is not a brave entity when the human consciousness is strong.

I work in many different ways to help a person overcome this fear. I give down-to-earth talks about ECK and Soul Travel and suggest natural, commonplace spiritual exercises for him to try. On the inner planes he is taken out into the other worlds in such a gentle, natural way that he often doesn't realize he was out until he wakes up in the body and remembers the experience. At that point he might swagger a bit, but the next night, there's Soul hanging on to the body again. Fear doesn't go away very fast. It usually takes more than one Soul Travel experience to rid a person of the fear of death, so he can go forward and live his life fully.

GOING WITH THE FLOW

There are many different ways to look at life. When a problem comes up, we can fight it or just let nature run its course. But we often feel compelled to beat the clock: We get impatient with the natural cycle of an event and want to hurry things along.

Farmers don't get much time off, especially on a dairy farm, with the morning milking, evening milking, and endless chores in between. But one Sunday afternoon, a dairy farmer decided to take a few hours off and get some rest. He stretched out on the couch and closed his eyes, planning to take a short nap. Suddenly he heard a strange noise coming from the basement. He listened intently for a moment, but it wasn't repeated. Figuring it must be his imagination, he relaxed and drifted off to sleep.

The noise sounded again and jolted him awake. This time he jumped up and ran down into the basement to investigate. There was no one there. Wondering what it could have been, he went back upstairs and lay down on the couch.

His eyes had barely shut when he heard the strange noise again, even louder than before. Once again he ran down to the basement. He looked very carefully in all the corners. If an intruder had gotten into the house, he wanted to take care of it right then and there.

The noise seemed to be coming from the furnace. Since it was summer, the old, wood-burning furnace had not been used for some time. He opened the door and looked inside.

To his amazement, gazing out at him from the dark interior of the furnace was a soot-covered wood duck.

The farmer and the wood duck stared at each other for a moment. The duck didn't make a move to come out, and the farmer certainly wasn't about to go in after it. But he had to do something.

The farmer considered the possibilities. Finally, being the kind of person who likes to let things run their natural cycles, he decided on a course of action.

Leaving the furnace door open, he swung open the two doors that led out of the basement. Why not let the duck find its own way out to the patch of blue sky showing through the cellar doors? That done, the farmer went back upstairs to the couch and finally got some rest.

A few hours later he went back down to the basement. Just as he suspected, the furnace was empty; the sooty wood duck was gone. The farmer shut all the doors, satisfied that the problem had been solved in a natural way. Even though he was not an ECKist, he was actually working with an ECK principle.

Even though he was not an ECKist, he was actually working with an ECK principle.

Later he figured out what had happened. The wood duck had probably been flying along when it saw the chimney of the farmhouse and decided it would be a good place to build a nest. Wood ducks do this in old, hollow trees and other closed-in places. Somehow it flew down the chimney, managed a sharp turn where the pipe turned, made its way down about ten feet of thick pipe, and ended up in the furnace. At this point it must have panicked, wondering how it was going to get out of there.

That's when it started making the noise that the farmer heard.

As I listened to this story, I couldn't help wondering what I would have done if I had been asleep upstairs, heard a noise in the basement, and found a duck in the furnace. A few years ago I probably would not have let nature take its course. Instead, I would have gotten a broom handle and started poking it around in the furnace until the duck came flying out at full speed. I could imagine it reeling blindly into the washing machine and the woodpile, which would have made it angry enough to charge at the first moving thing it saw—which would have been me.

When a person pushes a natural cycle, he is asking for trouble.

In our spiritual life we, too, lie asleep, until the Master wakes us up with some noise during the dream state that will get us off the couch.

FIRST DREAM EXPERIENCES

In our spiritual life we, too, lie asleep, until the Master wakes us up with some noise during the dream state that will get us off the couch.

When people first come into Eckankar, they sometimes have slightly upsetting dreams or inner experiences. They awaken in a near world of the Astral Plane, which is almost identical to the physical world. They think they are waking up right here, but Soul is moving into the other worlds.

They are really coming awake in the dream state. The phenomenon we call Soul Travel is beginning.

MOVEMENT INTO HIGHER CONSCIOUSNESS

Soul Travel simply means the movement of Soul into higher states of consciousness.

It may take the form I just described. When we, as Soul, are awakened by a noise, we jump up startled. Not yet sure that Soul is eternal and lives forever, we view any noise that comes while we lie asleep and unprotected as a threat to our physical self. Then, as we look around, all of a sudden we think, *Hey, I feel different. I feel good!* And slowly the realization comes that we are on a higher plane than the physical state of consciousness.

With this higher state of consciousness comes a degree of perception, happiness, and a mental clarity beyond description. It is a state in which the individual feels natural, where he says, "This is what I am: I am Soul, I am eternal, and I would like to stay here forever."

But as quickly as he says, "here forever," meaning apart from the physical body asleep on the couch, Soul returns there. It happens as soon as the attention goes back to the physical body.

With this higher state of consciousness comes a degree of perception, happiness, and a mental clarity beyond description.

Coming Back the Knower

Now having proof that there is life beyond the physical body, the person constantly strives to return to this higher state. It's an exciting, interesting experience, and the way to bring it about is through the spiritual exercises.

When he is ready for it, the person is given this experience in the other worlds of God, in the heavens which are spoken of in the many different religions. And once he has the actual experience, he comes back the knower. I would like to think of the initiates of ECK as the knowers, not the believers. There is a world of difference between knowing and believing.

Spiritual Exercise: A Soul Travel Dream Technique

If you are interested in Soul Travel, you can try out a technique tonight in your dreams.

If you are interested in Soul Travel, you can try out a technique tonight in your dreams.

Close your eyes, and place your attention very gently on the Spiritual Eye, the spot slightly above and between the eyebrows. Then chant HU, and fill yourself with love. This feeling of love is needed to give you the confidence to go forward into an unknown, unexplored area. One way to fill yourself with love is by calling up the warm memory of a past occasion that filled you with pure love.

Then look inwardly for the individual who is your ideal at this time—whether it is Christ or one of the ECK Masters.

In a very gentle way, say: "I give you permission to take me to the place that I have earned, for my greatest spiritual unfoldment."

And then silently or out loud, continue to chant HU, or God, or a holy word. Try to visualize yourself walking into the inner worlds, and know that the individual who comes to meet you is a dear friend.

DRAWING BACK THE CURTAIN

Imagine a curtain hanging in front of an individual who is looking for truth. He is able to see well enough on this side of the curtain. This is where he finds only the most apparent, shallow, superficial truths which occur in one's everyday life.

Through the Spiritual Exercises of ECK, he begins to draw back the curtain. This allows him to see how the greater part of life operates on the other side.

This curtain is not pulled back in one fell swoop. The individual does not get a great gust of instant Self-Realization (which comes at the Soul Plane) or God-Realization (which comes at one of the higher planes). Rather, it's as if the curtain that hides the true laws and mysteries of life is actually made up of many different layers of cloth.

DEGREES OF REALIZATION

As each layer of the curtain is pulled back, the individual is given another degree of realization. This is the point where he can say, "Ah! The things I have learned lately, through my own experiences, have come together. Now I understand a little bit more about the workings of life."

As each layer of the curtain is pulled back, the individual is given another degree of realization.

The experiences continue—some difficult, some happy and uplifting—until at some point he is able to go up to the curtain and draw back another layer of cloth. This time he sees even more.

Each layer he pulls out of the way allows him a fuller view of life as it is being manifested from the other planes of God down into this world.

As the dreamer, you are learning to walk through this curtain that separates the physical plane from the other worlds. As you enter the other worlds through one of the techniques of higher consciousness—dream travel, Soul Travel, direct perception, or beingness—you are able to see life in its greater format.

Tip: It Takes Practice

If the spiritual exercises don't work the first time, do them again and again. They are like physical exercises: Before your muscles grow strong, you have to exercise them a number of times; it doesn't always happen in one try. It's quite likely that if you take up an exercise routine for thirty days, you're going to be stronger than you were in the beginning.

It's the same way with the spiritual exercises. The purpose of the Spiritual Exercises of ECK is simply to open a conduit or a channel between yourself and the Holy Spirit. From the moment you begin chanting and looking for truth in this particular way, whether you are conscious of it or not, changes are being made in you.

THE REALITY OF THE INNER WORLDS

The inner planes are as real as the world out here.

The Dream Master wants to teach you how to begin to create a better life for yourself, both here and in the inner worlds. Because when we leave this world, we will still continue our explorations of all creation.

The inner planes are as real as the world out here. They are populated with individuals who are on missions, just as you are here. The second, third, and fourth heavens are filled with people who are still trying to find the way to God. They too are engaged in one activity or another, whether a profession or a field of art. They too are gaining experience so that they may become better and more compassionate instruments for the Holy Spirit and God.

This life provides the experiences needed to become the very best—not in a mechanical, mental way, but spiritually. In the process, you may become very good at your profession or some other facet of life, but what you are really doing is learning to open your heart to love.

Spiritual Exercise: For Direct Knowingness

Those who have Soul Traveled may now want to go to the higher state of direct knowingness, without having to go through the intermediary stages. Dreams and Soul Travel are helpful and important, but at some point you outgrow them.

Simply chant the words *divine love,* letter by letter. Originally I was going to give it as L-O-V-E, but some people would mix it up with human love. The word *divine* takes it beyond human love. Divine love brings you all forms of love, including human love. To limit it to the usual definition of love is like working from the bottom, instead of working from the top of spirituality.

So, chant D-I-V-I-N-E L-O-V-E. This means you seek the highest form of love, which brings all blessings to you.

SPIRITUAL GEOGRAPHY

The Dream Master is one with the Outer Master. It is the Outer Master who provides the books and teachings of Eckankar so that you can gain some understanding of the geography of your inner worlds. He does this so you are not caught off guard when something happens on the inner planes, even if it is not exactly as described in the ECK books.

You have enough information to say, "I have a

The Dream Master is one with the Outer Master.

feeling I was on the Mental Plane," or, "I went into a setting that was definitely from a past life. I was operating from the Causal Plane."

The ECK teachings give you enough spiritual geography to explain where you have been and why. This allows you to put your mind to rest. The reason people without this background are often upset by their inner experiences is because they have no way to fit them into anything society considers normal. They cannot relate them to what those in Eckankar know is spiritually normal.

Through the dream teachings of ECK, we learn that we can belong, but now it is with a higher order of beings.

When an individual has an experience that places him outside the herd, that makes him feel separate from the masses, he feels uncomfortable. It is human nature to want to belong.

Through the dream teachings of ECK, we learn that we can belong, but now it is with a higher order of beings. We can belong to a group of spiritual beings who operate both in the physical and the invisible worlds.

If you can just get down a few notes, maybe two or three sentences to trigger the memory, to give you a key, this will provide a focus so that during the day you can try to recall what happened.

3

Beginning Your Dream Study

A man told of a recent dream that gave the reason he was not remembering his inner experiences. In the dream, he and his wife were on a Ferris wheel that rose higher and higher into the sky. Soon he realized they were no longer on the amusement ride, but were passing from plane to plane in the inner worlds. Ever higher they flew. He was still in the seat, but more than a bit afraid of the great height. Finally, unable to take it any longer, he covered his eyes.

His wife said, "You can't see like that." To which he replied, "I know, but I'm afraid to look."

When he awoke, he found the dream experience amusing. And now he knows why he cannot recall many of his inner experiences: He is afraid to look. It is a good start toward understanding.

A man told of a recent dream that gave the reason he was not remembering his inner experiences.

OVERLOOKING THE COMMONPLACE

When we travel in the physical world, we're often in a greater state of awareness than usual; everything is strange and different enough for us to take notice. But back at home things are more commonplace.

49

We follow the same routine for so many years: get up at a certain time, take a shower, stumble out the front door, and go to work. If somebody were to ask you to describe the house on the corner of the third block from your home, you probably couldn't do it. It's too commonplace; there is nothing to strike the mental screen to make it stand out and cause you to remember.

It's the same way with the inner worlds. Many people fail to remember their experiences because when you're there, it is so natural that the inner and outer blend into each other. As you wake up and become conscious, you figure it's not worth the trouble to record the dream because it seems like something you always do. By the time you're finished showering, you've forgotten.

Tip: Study the Details

What can you do to remember your dreams and other inner experiences? You could write them down, but that's a hard thing to do. Sometimes you don't feel like writing. Another way to remember is to study the details of the experience while it's happening.

For instance, if you're at a baseball game in your dream, you could study the uniform of one of the players on the other team. See what kind of shoes he's got—cleats or whatever—and what color shirt he has on. Even notice the stitching on parts of the shirt.

Become aware of the little details. Notice a tree, a cat, and the cat's ears, how he twitches them. This will help you remember your dreams.

Become aware of the little details. This will help you remember your dreams.

DEVELOPING YOUR DREAM MEMORY

If you can just get down a few notes, maybe two or three sentences to trigger the memory, to give you a key, this will provide a focus so that during the day you can try to recall what happened.

Some people develop their memory of their dreams by keeping a notebook and pen at the bedside. But it takes a remarkable amount of self-discipline to rouse oneself from a deep sleep, turn on the bed lamp, and scrawl down notes for ten to fifteen minutes in a cold room. Not everyone is up to it.

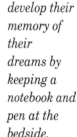

Some people develop their memory of their dreams by keeping a notebook and pen at the bedside.

 Spiritual Exercise: The Golden Cup

An ECK initiate told me about a spiritual exercise he uses to remember dreams. As he goes to bed at night, he visualizes a golden goblet on his nightstand. Then he says, "When I go to sleep and have a dream experience, the ECK (Holy Spirit) is going to fill this cup with the Light and Sound of God."

In this way, each dream or inner experience the dreamer has fills the cup a little bit, then a little bit more.

Upon awakening in the morning, he does another short spiritual exercise. He visualizes himself drinking liquid from the cup on his nightstand. The liquid is the Light and Sound, and he drinks it all. He imagines that he is drinking in the experiences. It is a conscious way of saying, *I want to remember what I'm doing on the inner planes while my body is asleep.*

After he used this visualization technique for a while, he began to notice that the cup became increasingly brighter every day. It seemed to have more life.

In contemplation he asked what this meant. The Mahanta, the Dream Master, answered: "The golden cup is Soul. As you put more attention on drinking from the cup, it takes on a life of its own. It grows brighter. The more the ECK flows in and out of the cup, the more Soul shines of Its own Golden Light. You, as Soul, become an ever-brighter vehicle for the Holy Spirit."

You, as Soul, become an ever-brighter vehicle for the Holy Spirit.

THE EXPANSE OF THE INNER WORLDS

Another reason it is hard to recall dreams is that although the mind on the physical plane seems like it has a great capacity to remember, there are a tremendous number of experiences happening in the inner worlds.

The physical mind is limited, like a little bucket. The inner experiences you have on all the spiritual planes are like the vast ocean. It is useless trying to pour the ocean into the mind's little bucket. The scope of action is much greater than the recall ability of the dreamer's mind.

Here is a way to understand the variety of inner experiences: As Soul, you can run a number of bodies at one time. For instance, the Astral Plane (the next level of heaven) has about 150 distinct levels, or heavens, in it; Soul may materialize a body in any number of those subplanes. The Causal Plane (above the Astral) is described as having many more levels than that.

It's as if Soul experiences what hundreds of people in a town do on a certain day. The mind, meanwhile, can only recall a few experiences at a time.

Tip: Nap Time—An Easy Start to Dream Study

Rather than disrupting your life through an all-out assault on your dream worlds, in the beginning just put a little attention on them. Instead of trying to record your dreams every day from now until forever, pick one day of the week that is most likely to offer a few minutes rest. You can begin to study dreams during a nap. When you feel tired, set an alarm for twenty minutes and have a notebook handy. Put your attention upon the Mahanta, the Dream Master. Do this in a light, easy way—almost as an afterthought.

Now tell yourself that you will have a peaceful nap and that you will remember a little of what occurs in the other worlds when you awaken. Then go to sleep.

When the alarm rings, jot down whatever you can remember, no matter how foolish it seems. In time, you may expand your study of dreams, because this method is easy to do even in a busy family.

MAP OF THE DREAM WORLDS

Soul inhabits the physical body but is not imprisoned in it. Therefore It can also move to the Astral Plane and take on the Astral body which is already residing there with some fragment of the consciousness of Soul.

The Astral Plane is the area where many of our dream experiences occur. There is also a delicate

Soul inhabits the physical body but is not imprisoned in it.

interplay—a tuning in to the unconscious mind, on the Etheric Plane—that deals with remembrances and the source of the impulses for the experiences which take place on the Astral Plane.

Soul can then move on to the Causal Plane, and then to the Mental Plane. It picks up one of the bodies stationed on each plane. There is always one body in each of these universes, and sometimes there are several, depending upon the individual's state of consciousness.

CLEARING UP DREAM MESSAGES

A dream usually applies very directly to what's happening in your outer life, often something right at the moment.

A dream usually applies very directly to what's happening in your outer life, often something right at the moment. So why isn't the dream message clear?

When you do the spiritual exercises, generally the Dream Master, which is the Inner Master, will begin to work with you in the dream state. It often starts out this way.

If you were to begin by working directly with Soul Travel, it might be too much of a shock for you. The dream state is the preparation for it. But in the beginning the dreams are often jumbled and distorted, and it's hard to make heads or tails out of them. You might think there's no point to writing something down in your dream journal that you can barely remember.

So, how do you work with this?

DREAM CENSOR

The Dream Master is trying to get a message to the human consciousness. Unfortunately, this pure message of truth has to go through a series of checkpoints in the Mental world, and this function of the mind is called the dream censor.

When the Dream Master tries to get this message to the human self, the dream censor acts like a doting mother who is very protective of her child. The Dream Master gives the straight truth, but the dream censor stands between truth and the human consciousness.

"Oh, no," it says. "That would shock the human self. It can't handle that."

So the dream censor, like the good mother, dresses up the message and makes it nice. Unfortunately, by the time the message gets to your waking self, it's so jumbled that it often no longer resembles the original. The censor thinks the logical order of truth itself might knock you over.

The function of the dream censor—those checkpoints built into the mind and the subconscious part of ourselves—is to prevent the pure truth from coming through as Light. If the Light comes through too strongly and directly, one can get burned.

The Dream Master gives the straight truth, but the dream censor stands between truth and the human consciousness.

FORGETTING THE DREAM

The censor may make you forget the dream. This accounts for the times you wake up knowing that something happened, that it was important, but you can't quite remember what it was.

It's like a writer struggling to come up with a certain word or a musician trying to find the right note—you know it's there, but you can't quite get it. In the same way, you cannot quite grasp the dream experience you know you had.

Tip: Writing to
Slip Past the Censor

What we are trying to do in the ECK dream teachings is to show you how to get past the dream censor. If the dream censor puts up a block, you learn how to slip past it to start reading the hidden meanings behind your inner experience. The way to begin doing this is to keep a dream journal.

What we are trying to do in the ECK dream teachings is to show you how to get past the dream censor.

Start by writing down anything that happens. Write down the experience as well as you can remember it, and try to fill in the gaps.

If you wake up in the morning feeling unsettled and upset, especially if you don't have a way to work this out, it can undermine your courage. It doesn't matter that you don't remember exactly what happened in the dream state; you can write whatever you do remember. Because once you start, you begin to work it out through the writing. This is one of the functions of the dream journal.

Soon you'll notice that the dream messages begin to make more sense. When you see an earthquake in the dream state, you'll come to realize this inner experience doesn't mean the earth is going to have a big earthquake.

The message might be that a big change is coming in your own world. All too often one likes to start reading the grand picture before he has even solved the problem of the little world.

Start by trying to relate the inner experience to your everyday life. It's not trying to tell you how the United States and Russia are going to fare in the next decade. It isn't concerned about the big world problems.

The Rest of the Story

I have a spiritual exercise to help you deal with the occasional bad dream that leaves you feeling unsettled when you awaken. The person who sent me this exercise is a student of ECK who likes to listen to radio commentator Paul Harvey's "The Rest of the Story." Harvey might start a story by giving a synopsis of a little-known incident in history. Then he breaks for a commercial. When he comes back, he says, "And now, here's the rest of the story," and continues in more detail.

In one instance, he told a story about a certain man's life, beginning from childhood. You didn't know who he was talking about at first. He described how, as a child, the person was very slow in school. "Your son is retarded," his parents were told by the teacher. "He belongs in a special school." But his mother felt the teacher was wrong. Her son had an interest in mathematics and science, fields that his teacher never suspected the boy knew anything about.

After Paul Harvey had recounted all these little details about the individual, he ended the story by saying, "And that was the life of Albert Einstein."

The ECKist decided to adapt a similar format to help her work out disturbing dreams. She starts with the assumption that there was a gap in her dreams, a part of the story the censor has not allowed to come through. By the time she works through the four steps of the exercise, she has a greater understanding of the dream.

I have a spiritual exercise to help you deal with the occasional bad dream that leaves you feeling unsettled when you awaken.

Spiritual Exercise: The Rest of the Story

This is a four-step spiritual exercise, and the steps are very easy.

Starting with the assumption that you do not know everything that happened in the dream, the first step is to go into contemplation. Visualize turning on the radio, and listen for the Sound in the form of the narrator's voice.

Second, listen to the narrator relating the details of your dream up to the time you awakened. Imagine that he is giving you a synopsis of your dream.

Third, take a commercial break, and while it's going on, chant HU. At some point, the voice returns and says, "And now, here's the rest of your dream."

Finally, imagine the voice of the narrator taking your dream to the next step.

There is a conflict of opposing forces going on in the inner worlds just like here in the physical world.

NIGHTMARES AND SPIRITUAL OBSTACLES

If a spiritual message is coming through from the Dream Master to you in the human consciousness, the lower Etheric mind, which normally acts as a censor of high spiritual truths, might let it come through as a nightmare.

There is a constant battle going on between the spiritual and the negative powers. The Dream Master then must try to undo the damage of this nightmare, caused by the censor scrambling an inner experience and letting it come through to frighten you.

There is a conflict of opposing forces going on in the inner worlds just like here in the physical world.

For example, say you have a goal to buy a car. Before you know it, all sorts of obstacles come up to oppose your desire to buy the car. Perhaps you have a teenager in the family who says, "Oh, boy, I can't wait to get behind the wheel to see how fast it can go!"

Now you have serious misgivings about having a new car in the family. It looks like you may never get to use it, and you fear that it will get scratched up with your teenager at the wheel. That is one conflict, one opposing force, that goes into motion as you try to reach what you feel is the positive goal of buying a car.

Other opposition may also occur. You have just enough money saved for the down payment. You go to the car dealer and try to make a deal. He suggests you apply for a loan through the bank, which sometimes presents a whole new set of obstacles.

All of a sudden the water heater bursts or the roof starts to leak. The money you had set aside for the down payment on the car has to be used for this essential repair. Setback! Now you either have to wait several more months until you can save up more money, or you have to depend on more creative financing.

In other words, here in the physical world, Soul—which means you in the human body—has a desire. You want something in order to be happy. So you set a goal, make plans to achieve it, and then everything that possibly can get between you and your goal occurs.

The same kind of opposition happens in your dream state. The spiritual force constantly tries to come to you through the direction of the Dream

The Dream Master wants to bring you insights for your spiritual benefit, to make you a greater and better person.

Master. He wants to bring you insights for your spiritual benefit, to make you a greater and better person. On the other hand there are the negative forces which may be, among other things, your subconscious fears from past lives.

Negative experiences are the testing ground of Soul. They are there purposely for you to overcome.

Negative experiences are the testing ground of Soul. They are there purposely for you to overcome. The Dream Master can overcome some nightmares for you, but he may not always take care of the entire nightmare. In some instances, you may be facing a karmic debt that you created many years ago. It is better to work it out in the dream state than to have this karmic debt appear in your physical life.

DOWNSIDE OF EXPECTATIONS

Another reason you may not remember your dreams is if you start out with certain expectations about the dream worlds and heaven.

If you were to have an inner experience that showed you the true nature of the other worlds before you were ready, you might feel the truth was too much to take. This could put you into a state of imbalance. The Dream Master often pulls down the curtain to spare you from having to make such mental adjustments.

The mind will always try to turn the inner experience into something nice and neat. If you learned too suddenly how the other worlds are run, you'd probably find that it's not the way you expected it to be.

"Heaven can't be this way!" you'd say.

Without having any experience, most people still have very strong ideas about what heaven should or should not be. To have opinions on things we know nothing about is a natural inclination of the human race.

Yet once you begin to work with the Dream Master and begin to accept the fact that you are Soul, you are opening yourself to a new level of spiritual understanding. In time you may begin remembering your dreams. They may be very jumbled at first, and there will be a lot of symbolism to wade through. But stick with it.

The dream message that's coming to you in the human self—as you wake up in the morning and rub your eyes and wonder what the dream was all about—is from you (Soul) and the Mahanta, the Dream Master. He is helping you remember an experience in the other worlds. The message goes through different layers of consciousness, is scrambled before it reaches the human self.

The higher self, Soul, is trying to get a message through to the human form. The higher part is trying to speak to your lower self to uplift you spiritually. To make you become more aware in this lifetime.

The higher self, Soul, is trying to get a message through to the human form.

Tip: Drawing the Curtain of Memory

Not everyone is conscious of experiences on the spiritual planes while living in the physical body. The curtain must be drawn across the memory at certain times in order for the dreamer to retain a balance in this physical world. Others are quite aware of the Sound and Light of ECK, the Holy Spirit.

Personal Habits as Obstacles

Sometimes people say to me, "I'm not able to see the Dream Master, so I cannot make this connection to all the wisdom that's available in the dream worlds." And the person who's saying this is a smoker.

One of the spiritual principles is this: the Dream Master does not give the deep secrets to someone who smokes.

One of the spiritual principles is this: the Dream Master does not give the deep secrets to someone who smokes. It's a very negative habit. It's destructive not only to the smoker but to the people around them. It cuts off the individual's spiritual connection with the inner worlds.

So when people who are smokers say to me, "I'm just not having any inner experiences with the Dream Master," I usually don't say anything. This is something they have to figure out for themselves. I'll mention it in a talk where they can pick it up themselves if they have the will or the desire to do so. But the next step requires a lot of spiritual self-discipline.

A person who smokes—or has any other habit that is detrimental to their health—feels it's an important part of survival. Sometimes a cigarette is a friend when there are no other friends. Otherwise the individual would have given up the habit long before.

I'm not here to judge. I just let people be themselves. When they're ready to give up a crutch and receive true spiritual help, they will do so. They will give up the crutches, the bad habits, whatever is detrimental to them spiritually. They'll give up these things themselves.

Tip: Three Steps for Better Dreaming

How do you sleep properly to get the most out of your dreams? There are three main steps I recommend. First, arrange your schedule to get as much sleep as needed to be fresh in the morning.

Second, for a few minutes before sleeping, read from any of the Eckankar books to signal Soul of your intent to pursue spiritual activity during sleep: for example *The Eternal Dreamer, The Dream Master, The Shariyat-Ki-Sugmad, The Spiritual Notebook,* or *Stranger by the River.*

Third, contemplate upon the face of the Mahanta, the Living ECK Master at bedtime. Do this in either a seated or prone position. Give an invitation to the Dream Master like this: "I welcome you into my heart as into my home. Please enter it with joy."

Then go to sleep as usual, but leave the eye of Soul alert to the coming of the teacher. Look for me, because I am always with you.

FASTING CAN REMOVE BLOCKS

One way to remember the dream state is through a practice in Eckankar known as the Friday fast.

There are times a block in our spiritual lives prevents us from entering the next spiritual plateau. It is possible to do a fast of some sort to remove this block. Not everyone is able to do this, and it should always be done with the advice of a physician. The fasts are to be done under a doctor's care if there is any physical problem.

Briefly, the three fasts are: the mental fast—

One way to remember the dream state is through a practice in Eckankar known as the Friday fast.

keeping attention completely upon the Inner Master; the partial fast—only one meal, or else fruit juices and fruit; and the water fast for a twenty-four-hour period.

Tip: On Fasting

When the dream memory stops for a period of time, new efforts in a new direction may be necessary to break through. At one time I would go on a juice fast for a day, then regular food the next day, then juice again for the following day—and alternate between solid food and juices for several days.

But I never did it too long at first, since our health is not always able to withstand the strain. This is an individual matter that I cannot recommend unless your doctor says it is all right.

Once you recognize that you are Soul and you know how to sing HU, your dreams will begin to have significance in your life.

Once you recognize that you are Soul and you know how to sing HU, your dreams will begin to have significance in your life. I say it this way purposely: Your dreams will begin to have significance. It doesn't mean you're going to understand them right away. At first, dreams can be wonderfully jumbled.

Tip: Recalling
Your Inner Experiences

Some people naturally enjoy vivid recollections of their dream state, but those who don't can develop the skill. There are several things one must do to remember dreams.

First, there must be a great desire that is love and goodwill at the heart center. Keep a happy thought of some past event or the like. Keep a notebook and pen by your bedside, and make a resolution to wake—even in the middle of the night—to record any memory of the dream state, no matter how trivial it seems.

The following statement is a way to seek help from the Inner Master at bedtime: "I give you permission to take me to that Temple of Golden Wisdom I have earned or wherever you wish." This is usually successful after some time.

"I give you permission to take me to that Temple of Golden Wisdom I have earned or wherever you wish."

RECORDING YOUR DREAMS

One of the reasons I recommend keeping a dream journal is that if these inner experiences are not recorded when they happen, most of them will be forgotten. Even if an experience doesn't seem to mean much now, at some point in the future you might look back at it and recognize its spiritual significance.

Another benefit to recording your dreams is that as you study and check your dream journal, you're going to find that you remember your dreams better and better.

One of the ways to begin working out the inner tangles and knots, where the communication lines between the higher worlds and the physical have been twisted by the censor, is to work with the dream journal. And as you write, you will find that the tension in your stomach goes away. If the dream journal can help to do this, it's done something.

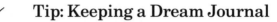

Tip: Keeping a Dream Journal

The first rule in keeping a dream journal is to write simply. Writing complex ideas in everyday language is hard work. A dream may have so many details in it that you can become sidetracked from the point.

To overcome this, write the dream out in full. Then put it away. At the end of the month, review those inner experiences that stand out. Condense them. Make believe you are an editor on the staff of *Reader's Digest*.

Dreams are another face of reality in the same way that our everyday life is another face of reality.

Not every dream will predict the future or give some insight into your life. Dreams are another face of reality in the same way that our everyday life is another face of reality. For some people, their waking life is just part of a dream.

Their dreams, visions, and inner experiences are so real that they don't separate them from everyday life. They are able to integrate and weave their inner and outer lives into one whole unit of spiritual existence.

The potential for the future is the other side of the present moment. As Soul stands on a promontory in the present moment, It can look at the past or future.

4

Uncovering Your Past Lives through Dreams

pilot for a commercial airline found that he had a very severe malignancy. One night he had a dream that fit with his life. He saw an airplane that was painted red, white, and blue, and he had the sensation that he was flying in it and yet was above it. He saw himself in the pilot's seat, but for the first time in his experience, he was standing back as Soul, observing the scene as well as participating in it.

Without warning, the plane went into a dive, heading straight toward the earth. He was certain that this was the end. His life flashed before his eyes. And just when it seemed that the plane must surely crash into the earth, it suddenly nosed up and started to climb.

He had an experience in the Soul consciousness. He saw how quick and easy it was to approach the veil of death, and more importantly, that life continues. After the plane pulled up, it went into a victory roll and flew off into the sky.

The pilot described it as a resurrection. He said this experience in the dream state gave him more

He saw how quick and easy it was to approach the veil of death, and more importantly, that life continues.

confidence than he had gotten from a lifetime in his religion. He was able to step forth as Soul, shake the fear, and see that death isn't even as substantial as a curtain. Realizing through his own experience that life continues, he found himself happy and uplifted.

ULTIMATE PURPOSE OF DREAM STUDY

Through dreams or inner experiences, the student of the ECK dream teachings is trying to learn to take responsibility for his actions.

Through dreams or inner experiences, the student of the ECK dream teachings is trying to learn to take responsibility for his actions.

There is no point in asking the Mahanta, the Inner Master, for certain experiences if you aren't going to benefit from them. We don't wait for someone else to come along and solve all of our problems. We look for an active way to take care of our own lives.

In a hotel I saw a sign management had posted for the benefit of the employees. The title was "Don't Pass the Buck." The sign read, "Blaming others is a bad excuse which keeps us from change and growth. Let's look at ourselves clearly and honestly. Only then can we improve and overcome our shortcomings." This refers to self-responsibility. It was very well stated.

The dreamer in ECK must look at himself clearly. He must understand that the circumstances he finds himself in today are those he created for himself sometime in the past. As the creative dreamer, he can take control of his life today and begin to change his circumstances into something that will make him happier.

To be the creative dreamer is to work with the creative principle of Soul. Soul is a spark of God. The creative principle that we are trying to learn to express is the creative power of God.

As one learns to express these creative abilities, he becomes a Co-worker with God. No matter what comes up, no matter how difficult the circumstance, he finds a way to make the situation a little bit better. He is able to come out of it a little bit happier than when he went into it.

Creative dreamers, whether they are on the path of ECK or not, are generally people who are responsive to their own dreams. They are highly successful in life and in their chosen profession.

Dream Insight for Our Lives Today

In the dream teachings of ECK, we learn to identify the problems that are plaguing us. The Inner Master begins to open up small scenes from our past. We sometimes perceive these as disjointed dreams. These dream experiences give us a way to start finding out who and what we are.

As we move into the higher states of consciousness, we become more aware of our responsibility—first of all to ourselves, but also to other people. Our responsibility to others is mainly to allow them the same freedom we want for ourselves.

The experiences you have in dreams are to give you another perspective on your life today.

People occasionally have a dream about a past life with another person. Misunderstanding its purpose, they may use it to try to put a hold on that person, who has no recollection of the mutual past life. It becomes a control factor.

When the Dream Master shows you a karmic picture from a past life, it is mainly to give you an insight into yourself as you are today—the most

The Inner Master begins to open up small scenes from our past. We sometimes perceive these as disjointed dreams.

perfect spiritual being you have ever been in all your lives. That is who you are today.

By the same token, if the Dream Master gives you an experience about a future event, the aspect about the future is secondary. Again, it is really about today. If you keep this in mind, you will interpret the experience in a way that will give you more perspective about your present life and how you can live it better.

> ## Tip: On Past-Life Study
>
> To awaken past-life dreams, make a note of what things you greatly like or dislike. Do that also with people. Then watch your dreams. Also note if a certain country or century attracts you. There is a reason.

To awaken past-life dreams, make a note of what things you greatly like or dislike.

VISIT TO THE OLD AMERICAN WEST

One time I was visiting the Mental Plane. I had made an appointment to meet with an ECK initiate on a certain street on the Astral Plane. So at the appointed time, I left the Mental Plane and came straight through to that particular place in the Astral Plane.

The initiate was waiting when I arrived. We greeted each other and started walking down the street. Suddenly we passed through an invisible curtain to a higher plane. Nothing seemed to change, but there was a slightly different sensation, like going through an energy field. The initiate didn't notice it.

As we continued our walk, the familiar twentieth-century scenery changed. We found ourselves in a setting right out of the old American West. Up ahead we saw Conestoga wagons—the covered wagons used by the settlers when they moved out West to establish new homesteads.

Soul always works in the present moment, and the past and future are all contained in the present. We think of the past as something that is gone, a dead image. This is so in a way, but at the same time, the past is still occurring in the Causal memory. When you get there, it looks as real as anything you normally consider to be in your present.

Soul always works in the present moment, and the past and future are all contained in the present.

The potential for the future is the other side of the present moment. As Soul stands on a promontory in the present moment, It can look at the past or future.

The initiate and I had gone through an energy field, and at this point we were on the Causal Plane. "We have to establish the time frame of this experience," I said, observing the covered wagons and pioneers prodding their oxen down a rutted road. *Probably the Oregon Trail,* I thought.

Experiences on the inner planes rarely come with signposts that announce the exact date. Nor can you count on someone running up to you and saying, "Hi, how are you? It's 1865." If you are interested in finding out how to fit into the framework of the experience, you have to use your wits and creativity to figure out what's going on.

Off to the right a grizzled old man stood in front of a ramshackle storefront. He had on a slouch hat and raggedy clothing, with a worn pipe hanging from his mouth. *He looks like one of those settlers who came west from Kentucky,* I thought.

I waved at him as we passed by. "Seen a lot of those wagons going by lately?" I called out. It was a subtle way of trying to find out the year.

"Yep," he said. "Folks didn't use 'em as much before the war."

War? He must mean the Civil War, I figured. That was a point of reference for many years after it was over.

"But you see a lot of 'em these last fifteen years," he continued.

The Civil War ended in 1865, I thought, *and according to the old settler, fifteen years had passed.* "This must be about 1880," I said to the initiate.

I pointed out that we had to be careful about the way we asked questions of these people. "Our clothes look the same to us as they did before, but to them we appear to be dressed like everybody else. They would not feel too comfortable around you if you were to ask outright, 'What year is this?'"

We said good-bye to the old man and continued down the road. After a while we came to some caverns. I led the initiate inside and showed him an underground city—an entirely different setting than the one we had just left.

The other worlds have various regions and cultures too, just as we have here on earth.

The other worlds have various regions and cultures too, just as we have here on earth. Sometimes they are so different from each other that the traveler can't tell where he is. It would be similar to an alien landing in an Eskimo village, then going to New York City. He would probably wonder if he was on the same planet.

I guided the initiate along an underground walkway that took us back to the Astral Plane. From there he was able to wake up back in his physical body, but he wasn't aware that anything had taken place.

I'm always a little disappointed when a person

who has an experience like this writes and says, "I can't remember my dreams. Is there something you can do to help?" I'm tempted to write back and just say, "1880."

Tools for Unfoldment

Many Christians believe that life begins at birth—as if the creation of Soul takes place at the birth of the human body—and ends at death, and then continues in heaven.

In the teachings of ECK we learn, sometimes through past-life experiences in the dream state, that we have lived more than just one life. We have lived thousands of lives.

In each life we gather talents, tools, and lessons which help in our spiritual unfoldment in subsequent lifetimes, including this one. Christianity's arena is limited to this one physical lifetime; in ECK we gain a broader vision. We recognize that Soul enters many different bodies throughout Its journey in the lower worlds.

In each life we gather talents, tools, and lessons which help in our spiritual unfoldment in subsequent lifetimes, including this one.

The ECKist learns that the reason he is reborn again and again is to learn how to love, to overcome those traits which prevent him or her from becoming a Co-worker with God. In each life we learn a little bit more. There is, of course, the grace of God which brings us to the Light and Sound and to the Mahanta; but at the same time, there is just as much effort required on our part.

Self-Responsibility versus Faith

Faith is fine, but the belief that someone else is going to pay for your debts is untrue. A broader understanding of how life really works comes with the recognition that self-responsibility is more important than faith.

When a person has a certain illness, we learn it's probably a condition brought forward from a past life. The individual chose to come into this life with that condition in order to learn a spiritual lesson.

In Christianity, there is no real understanding of why things happen. "Why do children die?" they ask. "It's not fair." The questions arise because the theology isn't broad enough to encompass the spiritual truth of God.

When an ECKist makes a mistake spiritually in his day-to-day living, it creates karma, a debt. When a Christian makes such a mistake, it's called sin. How is sin taken care of? Christians are told that Jesus, the redeemer, takes care of it. Believe in him and ye shall be saved—this sort of thing.

In the ECK teachings we realize that, in one way or another, the person who created the debt is going to have to repay it. Somehow it is going to have to be balanced in his own ledger book.

Faith is a starting point on the path to God. But faith in Eckankar is based on knowledge, and knowledge is based on experience. Experience brings awareness, and awareness leads to a greater trust in the ECK, the Holy Spirit.

Faith is a starting point on the path to God. But faith in Eckankar is based on knowledge, and knowledge is based on experience.

GUILLOTINE DREAM

A good example of how experience brings awareness came from a gentleman in Canada. He had the following dream.

Some years ago, as he began to study the dream teachings of Eckankar, he lay down on the couch after a hard day's work to watch TV. Soon he fell asleep. He woke up to find an old black-and-white movie about the French Revolution just coming to an end.

Still groggy from sleep, he watched the final scene: A group of nobles were being led to the guillotine. Some lived up to their nobility, not even blinking an eye, while others screamed, kicked, and cursed their way right to the end.

Mentally he began to play with the idea of himself in that role. If he had lived during the French Revolution, how would he have dealt with being dragged to the guillotine? It was just an idle thought.

That night in the dream state, the Dream Master, who is also the Inner Master, began showing him the same black-and-white film he had seen while he was awake.

"In a second you're going to be in that movie," the Master said.

"But I don't want to be in the French Revolution," the man protested.

"You have to go there," the Master said. "But you will understand later."

Suddenly the dreamer found himself a participant in the movie, a condemned noble being dragged to the guillotine by two revolutionaries. A part of him felt ashamed at the realization that he was kicking and cursing every step of the way. They forced him up the steps to the platform where he was to be beheaded and locked him in place. The blade made a whistling sound on its way down.

Just before the blade struck his neck, he found himself out of the body standing next to the Dream Master.

Suddenly the dreamer found himself a participant in the movie, a condemned noble being dragged to the guillotine by two revolutionaries.

"Whenever you have a thought," the Master said, "It has life."

Tip: Thoughts Have Life

People generally don't realize that without the protection of divine love, even the most idle thought creates a karmic situation that needs to be resolved sometime later.

In Eckankar, we learn to protect ourselves by singing the holy word *HU*.

If you have one of these thoughts and you're aware of it, just say, "Whoops, I really don't need that experience," and sing HU.

People constantly pick up these little bits of karma that have to be worked out at some point in their daily life, either in this lifetime or in another. One of the advantages of being in Eckankar is that you can work out much of the karma in the dream state. Then you don't have to go through the wear and tear out here in the physical body.

ARE YOU AWARE OF YOUR DREAM KARMA?

People can create karma in the dream state.

People can create karma in the dream state. Yet most are unaware that they do so, even as they are unaware of karma they make every day.

Each of us is like a power station. We generate energy all the time, energy that can either build or destroy. If we let unworthy thoughts or desires leave our power station, they pollute everything around us. That is bad karma. Our mind is like a machine, able to issue contaminants around the clock. Our thoughts even run on automatic at night, when we may unconsciously try to control others or harm them in the dream state.

The problem is a lack of spiritual self-discipline.

 Tip: Avoiding Unconscious Karma

To avoid making karma, while either awake or asleep, sing HU. Sing it when you are angry, frightened, or alone. HU calms and restores, because it sets your thoughts upon the highest spiritual ideal.

To avoid making karma, while either awake or asleep, sing HU.

A LABOR OF SISYPHUS

Some of you may be familiar with the phrase "a labor of Sisyphus," which generally refers to an unending task. It is based on a story in Greek mythology.

The greedy king of Corinth was condemned in the afterlife to repeatedly roll a great stone up a steep hill. Every time he got it to the summit, the stone would slip away and roll to the bottom of the hill. Over and over he would have to trudge back down, find the fallen rock, and once again start pushing it up the hill.

As you unfold spiritually, you often experience little incidents—the car that won't start, the light that burns out—that feel like a labor of Sisyphus. No matter how hard you try to get something accomplished, the stone slips away and you have to start all over again.

"Master, how long can this go on?" you ask. Actually, quite a long time.

There is a spiritual lesson incorporated in the

story of the king of Corinth. Soul keeps pushing the stone up the hill, trying to reach the spiritual heights. As soon as It gets there, It finds the stone is too heavy, the load is too great. Soul loses Its grip and then has to start all over again.

This is called reincarnation. And it's a slow process that we would like to do without, as soon as possible.

By Hard Experience

I was having lunch with some friends a few years ago. "What's happening to the video arcades?" I asked them. "I've noticed in the last few years that not as many people go to these places."

"More people are buying home computer games," one of our group said. "They are very instructive and a lot of fun. Some really good games are available now. One is called Zelda II: The Legend of Link."

The hero in this early home computer game is called Link. Link goes from level to level, through many worlds, meeting all kinds of opposition. One of his obstacles is a bush. By using the right tool, he finds the secret passageway that takes him to another level.

In each incarnation we pick up tools—we learn a particular lesson or develop a certain skill.

Even if you can't use the tool on a certain level, you keep it for possible future use. Eventually you realize that you can't get past level three without a tool picked up on level one. You learn by hard experience, by playing the game again and again.

Soul's Total Experience

It is very much the same as the spiritual experience in reincarnation. In each incarnation we pick up tools—we learn a particular lesson or develop a certain skill. But the problem is this: As we go into succeeding lifetimes, we forget what we have learned before.

If we only knew how to tap into our total experience as Soul, we could look to the past and draw upon a tool once mastered but now forgotten. We could bring that tool into this lifetime and use it to solve a problem that is holding us back on the spiritual path, a problem that is preventing us from going to the next level.

PRESENT TOOLS

If we only knew how to tap into our total experience as Soul, we could look to the past and draw upon a tool once mastered but now forgotten.

People not on the path of ECK generally get these tools by continuing to reincarnate—a very slow process. In Eckankar we want to take a more direct route. This is why I teach dream and Soul Travel techniques.

If you run into a block that keeps you from getting to the next level, you can go back; pick up the tool, talent, or lesson from a previous lifetime; and bring it into the present. You can then use it to help you walk the spiritual path to God today.

The creators of these computer games often have a deep insight into how life works. The games are constructed almost like a self-taught course in spiritual principles. Of course, the games give you only a secondhand, electronic experience. The best way to learn is to go out into the world, at least part of the time, getting your own experience.

THE ROLE OF KARMA

When people seem to be coming at you from all directions, sometimes you can't help wondering, *Why do I have to go through an experience like this?* But because the ECK dream teachings take into consideration the role of karma, eventually you come to a greater understanding of these things.

Many of the contemporary dream teachings, trying to work from a Christian background, do not recognize the effect of karma, so they ignore it. Their explanations disregard the feelings and impulses that have been created in the past, sometimes in the far, distant past of another lifetime.

Any study of dreams that is based merely on the happenings of this lifetime or on a product of the mind such as symbols, without taking into account past lives, is superficial. Most dream teachings of contemporary western culture are shallow and have very little to offer people besides glitter.

The teachings of ECK, which include the study of dreams, are the advanced teachings. We continue where the others leave off.

A number of people who work in these fields would respond, "Yes, but even with the limitations, one can learn to understand himself a little better than he did before he began to study his dreams under our methods and techniques." And I would have to agree with them. There is an elementary stage to the study of dreams, and this is the area that these people are covering.

The teachings of ECK, which include the study of dreams, are the advanced teachings. We continue where the others leave off. But we continue in such a natural, low-key way that other people may not recognize that we have something special, something unique. Nothing that you or I can say will convince them that there is a unique feature to the dream teachings of Eckankar.

INSIGHT FROM A PAST LIFE

Study of the ECK Dream teachings can bring us insight into who and what we were in a previous life. This can lead to a better understanding of who we are today and why certain things are happening to us.

A woman had an experience many years before she ever heard of the ECK teachings. As a child of seven, she had felt useless, unloved, and unwanted. Then one night in her dreams the ECK Master Yaubl Sacabi came to her.

She found herself standing in a desert with him, near a small encampment. A dust storm blew up, and people ran for shelter. Nearby she saw a little man trying to get some camels to move, but they wouldn't budge. First he cursed the camels, and when that didn't work, he began to curse his son.

"Where's that useless son, Yaubl?" he shouted. "I hoped he would take over the family business and make something of himself. But he's always off with his head in the clouds."

The seven-year-old girl stood and listened to Yaubl Sacabi's father call him useless. Yaubl then turned to her and said, "Everything I have I will always give to anyone who needs it." It wasn't until years later, when she read similar words in *The Shariyat-Ki-Sugmad,* the holy book of Eckankar, that she made the connection and understood what he was saying.

Yaubl spoke to her many times after that in her dreams during her childhood, always above the angry scolding of his father. It was in this setting that he explained the spiritual wisdom of ECK to this little girl who also felt useless and unwanted. On the inner planes, the ECK Masters come to each individual in a way they can relate to at that moment, regardless of their age.

On the inner planes, the ECK Masters come to each individual in a way they can relate to at that moment, regardless of their age.

DRUMBEAT OF TIME

The girl grew up, became a member of Eckankar, and soon began to study the *ECK Dream 1 Discourses.* Shortly after she tried the spiritual exercise in the first discourse, she started to hear a drumbeat, not only during contemplation but in her outer life too. She also heard an unusual kind of flute music.

The Sound is one of the ways that the Holy Spirit, the ECK, speaks to people.

The flute music and the drumbeat were actually forms of the Sound of God. The Sound is one of the ways that the Holy Spirit, the ECK, speaks to people.

About this time, someone gave her son an audiocassette of synthesized music. The first time she sat down to listen to it, she heard a flute playing in a certain way, combined with ocean sounds. It was very much like the melody she had heard inwardly during contemplation after she began to study the *ECK Dream 1 Discourses.*

That song ended and another began, this one with a familiar drumbeat. She closed her eyes to listen more closely. Soon the drumbeat carried over into a contemplative state, where she again met with Yaubl Sacabi.

This time he took her out into space. Nothing was visible in the absolute empty space except for a ledge. Then she saw tall, thin, pale men, walking back and forth along a pathway on this ledge. She knew they were masters.

Suspended in space was something that looked like a huge sundial with a series of big cogwheels and gears. Occasionally one of the masters had to go out there to make an adjustment. He would simply head in the direction of this assembly of machines, and a rock would appear under his feet for him to walk on. The rock stayed under his feet long enough for him to walk out there, make the necessary adjustments to the time gears, then return to the ledge.

This ECKist was getting ready for her Second Initiation in Eckankar. Years ago, when I was about to receive the Second Initiation, I went to this very same place.

Yaubl Sacabi explained to her, "This is where the time of the universe is kept."

She heard a steady drumbeat, much like the drumbeat on her son's audiocassette, coming from the clock mechanisms. "It sounds like the drumbeat on a Roman galley," she said.

Immediately she found herself on one of those Roman ships. There was a tall, strong man with reddish hair, reddish beard, and sunken eyes. First she saw him from the outside, but an instant later she found herself inside this man, experiencing everything that was going on from his viewpoint. He was an oarsman. She was seeing herself in a past life.

Yaubl Sacabi explained to her, "This is where the time of the universe is kept."

LESSONS FROM THE PAST

The first thing that struck her was the smell. It was musty, as it would be from the bodies of the other oarsmen below deck with her, rowing and rowing.

The only light below deck came through the holes where the oars poked out. Through those same oar holes also came frigid ocean spray. It was a cold, dark, miserable existence.

There was no hope of life in the sunken eyes of the man she had been. He was so thirsty. But rather than ask the cruel overseer for a drink of water, he would wait until the next one came on duty.

Down the walkway came the cruel overseer. The very sight of him inspired overwhelming hate and anger. Though he looked different, she knew immediately that this man was her husband in this lifetime.

A few days later her husband noticed her reading an ECK discourse. Her husband, who is not a member of Eckankar, asked her, "Well, what are they trying to teach you now?"

"They're trying to teach me how not to hate you," she'd answered. And she understood how true this was.

People rarely understand why they are drawn to certain relationships.

People rarely understand why they are drawn to certain relationships. As a couple they get along all right. He doesn't abuse her; he doesn't act like an overseer. But between them there is an opposition, a tension. It was brought here from the past.

What she didn't see, of course, were the lives in which she was in the role of the overseer and he was the oarsman. Life gives you an opportunity to scorch your iron from both ends.

GROWING IN UNDERSTANDING OF YOURSELF

The woman who met Yaubl Sacabi and went into the past had many of these experiences long before she came to the dream teachings of ECK. As a child, she had no idea what they meant. The first time she heard the Sound of God, she feared she was losing her mind.

Some of the people in her Satsang (spiritual discussion) class have said, "I'd do anything to have your experiences."

"Experiences are not why I stay in Eckankar," she tells them. "I stay because of the understanding I'm gaining through the Eckankar teachings of what those experiences mean."

THE INNER WORLDS AND PAST LIVES

Soul came from the high spiritual planes into the lower worlds. The lower worlds include the Physical Plane as well as the Astral, Causal, Mental, and Etheric Planes. The Astral Plane is the plane of emotions on the subjective side. On the objective side, certain parts of it are known as the area of ghosts, flying saucers, and things of this nature.

The subjective side of the Causal Plane is memory. It is an area of your mind that retains all the events of the past.

Beyond this is the Mental Plane, the area of the mind that works in the present. Unlike the remembering faculty, this is the active area that you work from to make plans, analyze, and solve problems as they arise in the present time.

Then comes the Etheric Plane, which is the unconscious, or subconscious, area. It is the high part of the mind that houses unconscious attitudes, some of which were acquired through karmic experiences in past lives. This often accounts for why we have certain talents or why we are instinctively drawn to one person and repelled by another.

At a certain stage in our spiritual unfoldment we may be shown, through dreams or Soul Travel, a past-life experience that explains a present love, hate, or fear. There is a particular reason, for instance, why some people have a fear of heights.

At a certain stage in our spiritual unfoldment we may be shown, through dreams or Soul Travel, a past-life experience that explains a present love, hate, or fear.

Fear has many faces. Each face has a specialized reason. Usually—though not always—it is based on something that happened in a past life.

INQUISITION DREAM

A woman had been afraid for many years. She was especially afraid to talk about Eckankar with other people. She could never understand this fear, but whenever she tried to share the joy she felt, something inside her closed.

She wondered, *Is there something wrong with me?* No matter what she tried to do she couldn't talk with others about Eckankar.

One night the ECKist had a dream. The Dream Master took her back on the Time Track to Spain during the time of the Inquisition. In that lifetime she was a man. Two people were very interested in her philosophy of life, which was a primitive form of Eckankar being taught at that time. And since they were interested, she told them more and more.

The next thing she knew, she was in a dungeon. Chained to the wall, she was beaten and died. She died because she had shared something close to her heart with seemingly sincere people who were really trying to trick her.

Each person has experiences from the past. Some of them are good, some are bad. Put together, they make each of us a unique individual.

Each person has experiences from the past. Some of them are good, some are bad. Put together, they make each of us a unique individual. The wheels of life are set in motion, and the experiences we need to manifest our state of consciousness come about. Very slowly we come to the understanding that we ourselves are responsible for all our actions at any time.

When this happens, the Dream Master begins

to open up small scenes from our past. Without these dream experiences, we wouldn't have a place to begin to find out who and what we are.

A Fuller Understanding of Past Lives

Regressive therapy involves hypnotizing someone to help them see past lives or remember events from their childhood. It's OK for people who are in a crisis. By all means, go to a psychotherapist if that's who you feel can give you the help you need. Psychotherapy is another way that Divine Spirit has provided for healing.

For a person who is well balanced, I would suggest doing the Spiritual Exercises of ECK. One or more examples of these exercises are in each chapter of this book.

Undertake the self-discipline to learn how to go into the other worlds with the Inner Master, the Mahanta. And with his guidance, see your past lives. This will give you a fuller understanding of the experience than hypnotherapy.

Undertake the self-discipline to learn how to go into the other worlds with the Inner Master, the Mahanta.

Regressive therapy works like this: A person has a problem with alcohol or perhaps a phobia such as fear of heights, fear of going outside, fear of men, of women, this sort of thing. So he goes to a psychotherapist who uses hypnotism to take him back to a past life. The images then bring about some realization—"Ah! The reason I hate Uncle Jim or Aunt Helen now is because they abused me in a past life."

In many cases, then, the patient of the psychotherapist has gotten a degree of healing. He can say, "Oh, I feel much better now that I know why I can't stand Uncle Jim or Aunt Helen."

What the patient may not realize is that when the psychotherapist hypnotizes him, neither he nor the hypnotist has control over which past lives come forward on the screen of the mind.

The censor is in charge.

The censor is the part of the subconscious mind that has taken it upon itself to decide what's good for you and what's not. It is also the dream censor.

If anything in your past lives would show you how to break away from the bonds of Kal, the negative power, the censor won't let you see it. The censor has a stake in this: being a part of the lower mind, its job is to keep Soul trapped in the lower worlds.

The dream censor is not going to tell you what you need to know to advance spiritually.

In some cases, the psychotherapist may also have a bias. He has a mortgage, a car payment, and a desire to live the good life. So even if he suspects the cause of your problem, he may not want to tell you any more than the censor does. He may not want to say, "You abused people before, and that's why you're abused now."

If he were to lay it on the line, the patient might not come back. How does the therapist make the mortgage and the car payments then?

What I'm getting at is that sometimes it's not a level playing field when a past life opens up under hypnosis by a psychotherapist.

There may be exceptions, of course, but in the case histories I've read, where someone glimpses a past life and sees incidents in which they were the victim of abuse, the person comes out of it feeling very self-righteous. Very, very seldom does psychotherapy reveal a past-life experience that makes a patient say, "The reason I was an abused child in this lifetime is because I caused it first."

I'm not saying this makes it right. When people abuse children, there is a law to pay, and this is as it should be. These laws keep the social balance here on earth, which is also part of the spiritual structure.

The social framework is part of the polishing of Soul. You cannot take advantage of others in the spiritual worlds.

Victim Consciousness

Just because you go to a psychotherapist and experience seeing a past life, you don't necessarily have the full answer. It's doubtful that you would see all the lifetimes in which you abused others. Because you couldn't handle it.

People who adopt the attitude "I'm a victim, I'm abused" might as well be running around in a dark room with their eyes shut.

They're so self-righteous, so right; the only reason their life is bad is because of somebody else.

The social framework is part of the polishing of Soul. You cannot take advantage of others in the spiritual worlds.

Self-Responsibility

The bottom line is, they refuse to take responsibility for themselves.

I find fault with any healing method that says, "We have healed you," yet does not explain at the same time that you are responsible for your life, not someone else. The abuse you endured is the result of the time that you once abused this person.

Again, this does not justify their actions under the social laws. Abusers pay. But spiritual law decrees that you can only get out of life what you have put into it.

Why does someone need the ECK dream teachings if
he or she already has vivid dreams? Regular dreams do
not come with the key to spiritual understanding.

5

Dream Glimpses of the Future

*W*hy are dreams so important? They are one way the ECK, or Holy Spirit, gives us Its guidance regarding the past, present, and future.

Nearly all of his life, a man from Ghana, West Africa, has had a recurring dream to show him coming fortune. In the dream, he is always crossing a flooding river: The bigger the flooding, the greater his wealth. Recently, such a prophetic dream revealed that he would gain a large sum of money. Soon after that he did, almost to the exact amount.

A woman from Washington State has universally prophetic dreams. Such dreams go beyond the personal life of the dreamer and take in world events.

In one of her dreams, she foresaw the volcanic explosion of Mount Saint Helens three years before it occurred in May 1980. In another, she witnessed the destructive earthquake in San Francisco a few years before it happened in October 1989. She does not pursue these dreams; they just come. They warn her to steer clear of the immediate areas of danger.

What do the above dreamers hold in common? Both are members of Eckankar. Both have studied

A woman from Washington State has universally prophetic dreams.

the ECK dream discourses, monthly lessons on the spiritual workings of dreams.

The ECK dream discourses tell you how to understand your dreams. People who appreciate the spiritual value of dreams study them to find peace of mind. That alone makes the ECK study of dreams every bit worthwhile.

DREAMS CAN SPEAK IN SYMBOLS

A college student had a dream that connected her physical and spiritual life. It all began with what looked like two strokes of luck.

Dreams had intrigued her since childhood. They were always vivid. When she related them to her friends and family, they would laugh and say, "You and your dreams." Her dreams were very real to her, but she could never understand the meaning they held.

One day she was in the college library, looking for a book to answer questions she hadn't yet put into words. She wandered aimlessly among the stacks, searching for a title to catch her eye. Then by chance she saw a book on Eckankar by Paul Twitchell. Though she had been to that area of the library many times before, she could not recall seeing that particular book. Quickly, she skimmed the first few pages, then literally skipped to class.

By chance again, an acquaintance gave her three more books on Eckankar. She had read a few chapters of one, when she had a dream with a white falcon. She was watching the bird with her fiancé. In the dream he was skeptical about her claim that the white falcon felt an attraction for her. To prove her point, she held up her right hand, and the falcon flew down to perch there.

In her mind, the falcon embodied wisdom. Whenever she voiced a question to which the answer was yes, the falcon would fly toward her. When the answer was no, it would fly away.

Once during the dream she asked the white falcon a question about witchcraft. This time it remained on her hand, but bent down and pecked her finger. This was as if to say, Witchcraft can only bring you pain.

She remembered only a fragment of that dream upon awakening. Later in the day, upset by mounting problems, she was losing control. Then the white falcon flashed into her mind, and her tension eased considerably. The ECK, or Holy Spirit, had brought comfort to her on the wings of this white falcon.

KEY TO UNDERSTANDING DREAMS

Why does someone need the ECK dream teachings if he or she already has vivid dreams? Regular dreams do not come with the key to spiritual understanding. And what is the key? It is a little-known name for God, HU, which was mentioned earlier. It will be referred to many times in this book, for it helps us awaken spiritually.

One way to open yourself to the wisdom of your dreams is to sing HU.

Spiritual Exercise:
For Higher Dream Awareness

The word *HU* is an ancient name for God that has a unique ability to lift one into a higher state of awareness. This dream exercise centers around this special word. One way to open yourself to the wisdom of your dreams is to sing HU. Sing it either softly or silently, for a few minutes before bedtime. This sacred name for God will charge you spiritually. Then go to sleep as usual.

Whenever you have a dream, jot it down in a notebook. Right after describing the dream, write down your feelings as to what it may mean. Some keep a tape recorder by their bed. Others awaken at night and merely fix one or two points of their dream in mind and record it later.

If you put any time at all into this dream exercise, you will begin to see how the Holy Spirit is using your dreams to bring you spiritual understanding. The spiritual program of ECK dream study can help you find peace of mind.

The spiritual program of ECK dream study can help you find peace of mind.

DREAM BIG, WORK HARD

One night, on the inner planes, I went to a local college football game. As usual, the home team lost. And in accord with its dismal win-loss record, the team had turned in a completely uninspired effort. So the locker room was a gloomy place after the game, even though it was full of people—the many friends and family of the coach and players.

The coach was a strict disciplinarian. He got on well with his players, but they could not win for him. The coach and I had little in common. So I mostly avoided him, because we lived and worked in two different worlds.

This evening was to be different, though. The crowd was still thick at a refreshment table inside the locker room when he called me over.

"I had a dream," he said. "Could you tell me its meaning?"

INTERPRETING A DREAM

A dream interpreter must always allow for the chance that his interpretation might be wrong, so he leaves an opening for the dreamer should the news look bad.

The coach briefly told his dream. For the second time within a few days, he had heard an orchestra play an enchanting piece of music. The musicians did not finish the song either time. Yet the music was of such haunting beauty that he wanted nothing more than to hear its conclusion.

Unknown to him, the heavenly music was exactly that: the Music of God. It comes from Divine Spirit, the Voice of God. Its purpose is to call Souls that are ready and show them the way home to Sugmad—another name for God, the Ocean of Love and Mercy. As the ECK texts put it: Soul has heard and is yearning to go.

But from all appearances, this coach did not work on a very high spiritual level, so he would not have understood an interpretation that spoke of this Music of God.

Yet a dream interpreter has a duty to speak the truth. That is not to say that he must be unkind, because it is a kind spirit who leaves an open door for a dreamer in case the analysis is wrong.

Before I could say anything, he spoke. "I think my two dreams are trying to say that I've reached the end of my career in this lifetime."

Unfortunately, that was my first impression too.

"I'll never get to coach at the state level," he added, looking closely at me for confirmation.

Then the ECK let me see the options of possibility.

"Dreams aren't final," I said. "I can't tell the times a dream appeared to point out failure to me, but I refused to accept the verdict. A dream about failure usually means that using the same methods

The coach briefly told his dream. For the second time within a few days, he had heard an orchestra play an enchanting piece of music.

as in the past will continue to lead to failure. But if a dreamer can break old habits and try something new to solve problems, it's a new ball game."

The coach was catching on.

"You mean my career's not over?" he stated, half in reply and half in question.

"There is a lot of power in the human spirit," I replied. "If you could unlock the spirit of your team, you'd see miracles. There is a power in people who dream big and who try hard."

There is a power in people who dream big and who try hard.

HOW TO GET HELP

Then two young players from the team returned to the locker room, which had cleared of most people during our conversation. They drew the coach aside to ask a favor. Immediately, he went to a metal toolbox and began digging around inside it. I mistook the action. I assumed that he had plans of game strategy in the box that he could not wait to show his two star players. They just happened to return to the locker room during the height of his excitement.

In fact, the situation was very different. Their car had a flat tire, and they were late for a post-game school dance. So the coach was not trying to dig out and explain next week's strategy.

I called to him on my way out. "By the way," I said, "something else always helps. That's to listen to the ideas of others when all yours hit the wall."

With a quick thumbs-up sign, he shouted back, "You mean, let them mount the tire?" His excitement was no longer about his own dreams of aspiration. He had put them aside to help his young players fix the tire and get to the party before it was over. He remembered his youth.

I knew that he now had the right idea about winning. Go for success in life, but not at the expense of other people's dreams. Help them meet their dreams, and they will help you meet yours.

Another student walked with me to my residence some three or four blocks away. The sidewalk ran up some small hills and down again, like a rising and falling wave of the ocean.

"As we get older," I said to him, "these little hills become like mountains. Even though it requires more effort to accomplish our dreams, we must always follow them."

END-OF-THE-WORLD DREAMS

Occasionally people have a dream that tells them the end of the world is coming. Individuals not familiar with the ECK teachings have been known to take the dream literally. A few have even gone to a printer and spent their last dime on posters and brochures that proclaim "The End of the World Is Coming!" With doomsday so near, what else do they need the money for?

A woman had a dream like this, but fortunately she was on the path of ECK. Though she didn't understand what it meant at first, she knew that the Inner Master was trying to teach her something.

In the dream she was listening to the news. Suddenly a scientist interrupted the newscaster to announce that the world was coming to an end. "The sun is moving closer to earth," he explained. "Four days from now it's going to explode, and everything in the world will be burned to a crisp. The sun will then begin to cool down, but the earth will be no more than a cold lump of matter, floating

Occasionally people have a dream that tells them the end of the world is coming. Individuals not familiar with the ECK teachings have been known to take the dream literally.

aimlessly through space."

"I've got four days left," she said to herself. "How do I want to spend them?" Being a sensible woman, she decided to take off from work.

"The scientists predict it's going to be like a huge nuclear explosion," she told her husband. "If there's no way to avoid the destruction, I might as well enjoy these last few days. And when the explosion comes, I'm going to watch it for as long as I remain in this physical body."

On the last day, she and her husband stayed in their home. Through the window they watched the sun grow larger and redder. "Oh, what a beautiful sight!" they said.

Just then the first explosion came, knocking out all the windows. They ducked and tried to avoid the flying glass, but the woman got a cut on her knee. "Let me get you a Band-Aid," her husband offered.

Just as her lifetime on the other plane came to an end, she awoke from the dream.

"Don't be silly," she said. "Let's just watch this while we can." Just as her lifetime on the other plane came to an end, she awoke from the dream.

STRENGTHEN YOUR WEAK POINTS

The dream stayed with her for quite a while. She was pleased to notice that she hadn't reacted to it with fear, as she might have done before coming to ECK. Still, she tried to interpret it in terms of her daily life. Was it a warning that something catastrophic was going to happen in four days? A family crisis? Her health?

Driving in her car later that week, she thought about all her problems. She began a mental conversation with the Inner Master about the many things that were bothering her. "Mahanta, can you please take these troubles away from me?" she asked.

The answer she got from the Master was very interesting: "You just had an experience in a dream of losing everything, even your own life. Nothing in this present life should ever trouble you again."

The answer gave her a new perspective on her troubles; they didn't seem so big anymore. She realized that this dream of apparent catastrophe was actually meant to strengthen her in her daily life.

NIGHTMARES

In the ECK dream discourses which come with the first few years of membership in ECK, I explain many of the different aspects of dreams—what they are, where they come from, how to deal with them.

Often I get a letter from a parent who says, "My child doesn't get any sleep because of nightmares. What do I do?"

Nightmares may be caused by a number of different factors. One possibility is an intrusion by someone on the Astral Plane who is able to enter the dreamer's world.

Nightmares may also be caused when memories of past lives come through in the dream state. In one or more of those lives, the individual may have faced torment, torture, sickness, death, fear of animals, or fear of any kind.

There are a lot of reasons why people have nightmares. The most essential factor for children, however, is that they are remembering incidents from one or more past lives. Usually it's from a past life that pertains directly to this one. They remember themselves as adults. Children often talk to their parents about a past life. If the parent has no

She realized that this dream of apparent catastrophe was actually meant to strengthen her in her daily life.

grounding in reincarnation or doesn't believe in it, the child is dismissed as having a wild imagination.

My parents dismissed me that way, saying, "Oh, he has such an imagination." Of course, I did, but that shouldn't invalidate my experience.

When your child has nightmares and you want to help, show him or her how to chant HU. It's a simple, effective way to help. People who chant HU open themselves to the Light and Sound of God, which is divine love.

People who chant HU open themselves to the Light and Sound of God, which is divine love.

GOLDEN-TONGUED WISDOM

The physical world as well as the inner planes can all rightly be considered the dream world. Truth reveals itself to us constantly, even here in the physical world. But how many people are aware of it? Not too many.

Occasionally something occurs that I call the Golden-tongued Wisdom, where the Mahanta warns you to watch out for something about to happen in your everyday life. The warning gives you the opportunity to be alert so you can protect yourself.

An ECKist went to the store to buy milk. She took her time, carefully examining the freshness date stamped on each carton. Just then an old man came over and stood next to her. "You MUST check the freshness date!" he said. When she didn't respond, he became very vehement about it. "You absolutely MUST check that freshness date!" That's exactly what she had planned to do, until someone told her she *had* to do it.

Glaring defiantly at the old man, she reached into the cooler and picked up a carton that had the second freshest date. Nobody was going to tell *her* what to do.

The next morning she got up early to make breakfast for her family. As usual, she turned on the radio to listen to the news as she cooked. One particular report suddenly caught her attention. The health department had issued an alert: certain cartons of milk had been found to be contaminated and should not be used. The report went on to identify the cartons in question.

The woman immediately went to the refrigerator and took out her carton of milk. Sure enough, the one she had bought—with the second freshest date—was contaminated. She was given a second chance to catch it before she served it to her family.

This is one example of how the Mahanta works through the Golden-tongued Wisdom. The ECKist was given a warning through the words of the old man, who for no reason at all felt compelled to tell her, "You must check the freshness date."

The Mahanta works through the Golden-tongued Wisdom.

PROPHECY FOR THE MOMENT

The Golden-tongued Wisdom comes in many other ways. For example: Something is weighing heavily on your mind, and you are wondering what to do about it. All at once a voice pops out at you from the radio or TV, as if someone just turned up the volume. The words or the phrase may seem completely out of context with what the speaker was saying before. But for you they have a spiritual context that tells you exactly what to do.

The words may carry a simple message from the Master that tells you, "Persevere, continue in what you are doing. You will see the reason for this

problem in a very short time. Your spiritual unfoldment will benefit from it."

Or you may be walking down a crowded street,
minding your own business. All of a sudden a person nearby speaks a few words to someone else in
what seems an abnormally loud voice. The rest of
the conversation is a mumble, but what he said at
that moment was clear enough to stand out.

This is what I call the Golden-tongued Wisdom.
It is part of the ECK-Vidya, the ancient science of
prophecy. Its purpose is to give a prophecy for the
moment or an insight into a personal situation.

YOUR OWN PATH TO GOD

The Golden-tongued Wisdom doesn't come only
to members of Eckankar. This happens to people all
the time, but not very many are aware of what it
means. Nor are many aware of the meaning of their
dreams or experiences in their daily life that could
be considered waking dreams.

But there is no reason to feel you are falling
behind someone else just because you can't understand everything. If you can understand just a little
bit, every so often, you are doing well.

*You are on your
own path to
God. There
isn't any hurry.*

On the other hand, if you do gain some insight,
there is no reason to feel you are more spiritual
than anyone else. You are on your own path to God.
There isn't any hurry. If you think in terms of being
slower or faster than someone else, then you are in
a race. That is not the path to God.

When you are walking your own path to God,
you recognize the message in the kernel of truth
that is given to you. The recognition usually comes
subtly at first, where you say, "Oh, I see." You may

understand the full impact of the message at that point, but more likely than not, it will take longer. Maybe a couple of weeks later, after you have forgotten about it, something else will happen to bring it back into your consciousness, and it will build on the earlier experience.

TAKING A CHANCE ON LIFE

When we're young, we like to take a chance on life. There is this joy in just being alive.

I know I took chances on life years ago. I would trust the Inner Master, or the Dream Master, and I would travel here and there and everywhere—going someplace without a job simply because I trusted the goodness of life to let me survive another day and lead me into a better life.

I trusted the goodness of life to let me survive another day and lead me into a better life.

It's a frightening thing, but when you do this you find you are truly alive in a way that you have never been before.

Some experiences practically scare you to death. But when you're through them, you say, "I sure don't want to do that again. But the colors were more vivid, the sounds were more vibrant, and basically I had more love because I was aware of every little thing that was happening to me."

WAKING DREAMS

A young woman found the teachings of ECK back in the late seventies, and she found a great joy in telling others about the Light and Sound of God. She would give them Eckankar books. And in her own way, while she was trying to make a living, she would travel for ECK. She just wanted to.

In 1983, after she'd been on the path of ECK for a while, the woman was living in Seattle, and she

got a nudge. Something inside her said, "Go to
Alaska." Well, she didn't really know anything about
Alaska. So one day she was driving with her brother,
and she asked him, "Should I go to Alaska, or
shouldn't I?"

Just then, he turned the car up an alley, and
they passed an open garage. In the garage were two
cars. The license plate on one car said GO NOW.
The license plate on the other car said ALASKA.

That's an example of the waking dream. An
inner nudge comes through from some source, in this
case from the Mahanta, the Living ECK Master
who is also the Dream Master in Eckankar. Sometimes people aren't very receptive in a sleeping
dream, so this guidance comes through as intuition
or a nudge.

The young woman went to Anchorage. When she
got there, she knew she had to make a living somehow, so she took all the money she had and invested
it in a small business.

But her real purpose for going to Alaska was to
be a missionary for ECK, so she decided to set up
some introductory lectures on Eckankar at the library.

The woman was very short on money. She had
put all her money into trying to start her business,
and at times she didn't even have enough to buy gas
for her car. One particular day she had to get to the
library to finalize the plans for the talks. So she
began to walk to the library, which was on the way
to work.

Walking along, deep in thought, she suddenly
realized she had walked right past the library.

In a sense, this woman was at a crossroads in
her spiritual life. *Should I just keep walking to my*

An inner nudge comes through from some source, in this case from the Mahanta, the Living ECK Master who is also the Dream Master in Eckankar.

business and hope to make a little bit of money so I can put some gas in my car and get around? she wondered. *No, my first purpose in coming to Alaska was a spiritual one. It was to tell other people about the Light and Sound of ECK. So I'd better go back to the library and finish making the arrangements for the series of talks.*

And as she turned around, she saw a big sign that said Trust in God with All Your Heart. Another waking dream.

Another Waking Dream

After she'd been in Anchorage for a while she moved back to Seattle for a couple of months. One day she found herself repacking the boxes which she had just unpacked after arriving home from Alaska. She started laughing.

"What am I doing this for? I just got here," she said to the Inner Master.

At that moment another nudge came through: the young woman got the feeling that she was to go to Chicago.

"There are a couple of problems with this," the woman said to the Inner Master. "Number one, I don't really know where Chicago is. Number two, I don't have enough money to get there, and three, I don't have a job if I do get there. I'm going to need some kind of sign to prove to me that this is really what I should do."

She stood up, walked over to the TV set, and turned it on. On the television program, a young woman was throwing everything she had into a suitcase. And the sister of this TV character said, "Where are you going?"

Of course, you know what she said. "Chicago."

As she turned around, she saw a big sign that said Trust in God with All Your Heart. Another waking dream.

It's another example of a waking dream. I'm trying to make this very clear for you so that you get an idea of the waking dream. When I first brought out the concept of the waking dream it was very difficult for people to grasp. Things would happen in their life, they got nudges, they responded to intuition, and sometimes they would have a dream where they would see the Dream Master come to them and say something, but they needed confirmation.

Confirmation in the physical world of some inner direction is what we call the waking dream.

This confirmation would come to them in their daily life in the outer, physical world. Confirmation in the physical world of some inner direction is what we call the waking dream.

Now it becomes a matter of trust. How much do you trust this inner guidance from the Mahanta, the inner teacher?

A MATTER OF TRUST

The young woman arrived in Chicago after three days on a bus. She had sold her car and her possessions so she'd have enough money to get there. When she got in at six o'clock in the morning, it was the start of a hot and humid day. Chicago, set on the shores of Lake Michigan, can be very uncomfortable in the summer.

But the ECKist wasn't worried. She looked in the newspapers and called a few places to find work and a room. Near the end of the day she saw an ad in the paper for a place to rent. When she called the number, the landlord said, "Yes, come by, I have a place for you."

But when she went to see it, she found a note on the door: "This place isn't for rent anymore, sorry."

It was the end of a long day, and she hadn't slept

very well on the bus. She was hot and tired, and there was no place to clean up. During the day she had gone to the YWCA, and she thought, *In a pinch I could stay here,* even though the rooms were all small, dismal, dark, and dirty.

At a loss as to what to do next, the woman went back to the bus station. She went into the rest room, into a stall, leaned against the wall, and cried. "I trusted you," she told the Inner Master. "I trusted you."

"Try again," he said. But she didn't know where to try again. So she went back to the YWCA.

TRY AGAIN

The young woman dragged her bags up the stairs to the reception desk, a lot more humble than she had been that morning. "I'll take one of your rooms now," she said. The man behind the desk looked at her very proudly and said, "We don't have any more rooms. This is the first time in five years we've been sold out."

She left her bags right there in front of the desk and walked off to one side of the room to have a little conversation with the Mahanta, her spiritual guide. "I trusted you," she said. "I traveled to Chicago, and here I am. But you've stranded me."

All she heard was, "Try again." So she turned around and went back to the desk.

The first man was gone and another man came out of a back room to help her. "Don't you have just one more room?" she said. "Well, yeah," he said. He was holding an envelope in his hand, and there was a key in the envelope.

"Take this to the room that's marked on the

envelope," the man told her, "and if you like it you can have it."

The woman felt really sick at heart; she had seen all these dark, dismal rooms earlier in the day. But when she went to this room and opened the door, she found a clean corner room with two windows. Beautiful evening light was coming in. "This is great," the woman said. "I think I'll take this one."

When she went back down to the desk, the second man was gone and the first one was back. She said, "I'll take the room." He said, "What room?" She said, "The room that goes with this key." He said, "Where'd you get the key?" She said, "From the other man who was here." He said, "What other man?"

So the desk clerk began to look for the other man. The woman began to look for the other man. He was gone. *Wow, this stuff really works,* the woman thought.

"This isn't one of our envelopes," said the desk clerk, "and what about the woman who's already in that room?" And the ECKist said, "There wasn't anybody in the room. Now can I check in please?" So the desk clerk checked her in.

The woman went upstairs to the room, and the room was so filled with love that she felt this vibration that is part of the Sound of God.

The Sound and Light of God are the appearance of God's love in your daily life in a very real way.

APPEARANCE OF GOD'S LOVE

The Sound and Light of God are the appearance of God's love in your daily life in a very real way. Sometimes you'll feel a vibration, sometimes you might hear the music of a flute. These are both manifestations of the Sound of God.

People see the Light of God inwardly as a white

light, a blue light, a pink light, a green light, sometimes in the form of a lightbulb, sometimes as a fire, sometimes as a lamp, or just as a globe that glows—It can be any form, any color.

The Light and Sound of God is a part of God's love that few people know about. And It's one of the mainstays of the teachings of ECK. The Light and Sound of God are the twin pillars of God's love.

This woman stayed in her room that night very happy and filled with love. She was ready to meet the new friends that she knew awaited her in this once-strange town. She knew that the love of the Master was with her.

INTERCONNECTED WHEELS

Through the stories in this book and the Spiritual Exercises of ECK, I'm trying to help you develop your spiritual awareness, to bring you to the realization that all life is a series of interconnected wheels. Very little can happen to you that isn't known by you beforehand. All you have to do is learn to be aware.

This is how our awareness goes—up and down, up and down— hopefully always moving toward greater awareness.

This is not as easy as it sounds. It doesn't happen overnight; we don't go straight upward in our awareness. We may do very well for a while, then all of a sudden we go into a downward cycle. But there is no reason to get discouraged. Eventually the cycle takes a turn again, and we come back stronger in our awareness than we were at the last peak.

This is how our awareness goes—up and down, up and down—hopefully always moving toward greater awareness.

A DREAM OF DEATH

An initiate in West Africa learned about the truth of the ECK dream teachings through an experience he had with his friend, Lewis.

An initiate in West Africa learned about the truth of the ECK dream teachings through an experience he had with his friend, Lewis, who is also an ECKist.

One day Lewis, a twenty-five-year-old bachelor, came to the ECKist and said, "I just got a very good job with an oil-drilling company. I'll be working on a sophisticated computer."

An interesting point is that out of the hundred applicants for that position, Lewis was the only one who did not have a degree in higher education. But he did have the quiet certainty that he could do the job. He went on to tell his friend the rest of the story.

One of the members of the review panel had tried to dissuade the others from considering Lewis. "Since he doesn't have a higher degree, we ought to disqualify him."

But another review panel member, an American, said, "No, let's give him a fair chance. He's here, he's had three months of training on another computer, and he has shown some expertise. Let him take the test." The rest of the review panel finally agreed to let Lewis take the test. Each candidate was given fifteen minutes to work out a series of complex problems. Lewis got busy, worked everything out, finished before the fifteen minutes was up, and ended up with higher marks than any of the other candidates.

When it was announced that he had been chosen for the job, one of the other candidates came over to chat with him. She said, "Throughout this entire review, I have noticed how calm and confident you were; you have a happy countenance." Lewis responded pleasantly, but he didn't elaborate.

Later, after he finished telling all this to his ECKist friend, he said, "I have two more things to tell you. First, the reason I did so well on the computer is that the Mahanta has been teaching me how to run it on the inner planes. When it came time to take the test on the physical computer, it was very easy."

Then he said, "The second thing I have to tell you is that I had a dream, and I'm going to translate [die] very soon."

The ECK initiate just about fell over. He couldn't believe that he was hearing these words from Lewis, a young man standing at the threshold of a promising and brilliant career. "You must have mistaken the meaning of your dream," he said.

"You must have mistaken the meaning of your dream," he said.

Lewis shook his head. "No, I went back to the Inner Master and asked for verification. The Master said that the dream was true, that I would translate in six weeks."

But Lewis had some things to take care of that would require more than six weeks. "Could the timing be postponed for a little while?" he asked the Master. "Of course it can," the Inner Master said. And so a postponement was arranged.

Lewis began to get his outer affairs in order. For the first week or two after the dream, he wore a worried look on his face. He had become attached to his human body, to his friends, and to his life in general. And, for a brief time, the teachings from his Christian past came creeping in. But the worry soon passed, and once again he was able to show his confidence, his loving nature, and his good will.

One day he said to his ECKist friend, "The company has decided to send me to the United

States for additional training. I'm supposed to leave within the next month." The date of the trip was scheduled very close to the predicted date of his translation.

A few days later the two ECKists went to a lawyer so that Lewis could have his will prepared. Lewis then bought some gifts and took them back to his hometown. He confided his dream to a few close ECK friends, gave them his gifts, and had a very happy supper with them.

That night he went to bed, and very quietly during the night, he translated. His health condition was unknown to most people, and so his death was totally unexpected to all but a few. But he had been given time to prepare, and he used it to give his love to other people.

The ECKist who remained in the physical body learned many things about the truth of the ECK dream teachings and the spiritual laws of the Holy Spirit. The sharing of the experience was Lewis's gift to him.

He had been given time to prepare, and he used it to give his love to other people.

RECURRING DREAMS

A few years ago we were in a restaurant. There were stairs leading to other businesses on the second floor. The place seemed vaguely familiar. Later we decided to go up the steps.

I noticed the brass railing as we walked up. When we were almost at the top, I suddenly had the feeling that I had been there before. To the left there was a white door, shut and locked. I walked past and didn't think much of it.

Two days later we went back to the restaurant, but by then I had forgotten about the feeling I'd had the last time we were there. Again, we went up the stairs, and as I reached the third step from the top, suddenly I got the same feeling: *I've done this before. And not just the other day but a long time ago.* A vague memory of an old dream came back to me.

We returned to the restaurant a third time, and as we went up the stairs, I noticed that the door to the left was open. It was a private office. You wouldn't just walk into the office if you didn't have any business there. But with every step, I became more curious to see what was inside the room.

Looking through the doorway, I saw that it was a computer room. The walls and floor were all white. All around were computers, monitors, printers, and other machines.

The setup looked very commonplace to me except that I suddenly remembered the rest of the dream.

I'd had it back in the 1960s, when I first came into Eckankar. At the time it was a recurring dream, so real that I woke up very upset each time it came. I couldn't understand what I was seeing.

In the dream, somebody opened a white door and I walked into a small, roundish-shaped room. Everything was crisp and clean. There were numerous monitors that looked like television sets but smaller, and I knew there was something different about them. In front of each monitor was a keyboard, and nearby was a large printer. This was several years before computers, video monitors, and printers were everywhere. Because I couldn't relate it to anything I had seen on earth, I figured the dream must have been about a spaceship.

The computers and monitors in the dream room were humming, and the printer made a muffled,

Suddenly I got the same feeling: I've done this before. And not just the other day but a long time ago. *A vague memory of an old dream came back to me.*

clattering sound. "What are all these strange noises?" I had asked. You hear it all the time now, but back then I had never heard machinery make those particular sounds before. It felt all wrong.

The experience at the restaurant demonstrated once again that life is more than a random occurrence. There is something that connects the invisible worlds to the visible worlds.

Life is more than a random occurrence. There is something that connects the invisible worlds to the visible worlds.

PROPHETIC DREAMS

In Australia a number of years ago a young boy was looking forward to seeing his first movie. An uncle and aunt had come into town, and they said they would take the two children to a comedy.

The boy was so excited. He'd never been to a movie before. But he was so excited that he got sick right before they were going to leave for the movie.

"If you're sick, you can't go," his mother said. At this, the boy threw a classic temper tantrum; he screamed and he shouted in his room until he fell on his bed in total exhaustion. Then he had a dream.

In the dream, he found himself walking in front of their house. Four houses down the street was an old Federal-style building. On one side of this old house was a door that should have led to the basement. In the dream, the boy walked to the building and opened the door, but instead of a basement, he saw a huge auditorium with blue and orange seats.

The room was filled with people, and the people seemed to know him. They waved to him and invited him to come in.

There was someone on the stage, but the little boy didn't understand what the man was saying. He was too young to understand. But a feeling of love came over him, and it was a good feeling. He stayed for the entire talk, and when it was over he went back out through the door, walked back to his house, and woke up in bed.

The boy kept having this dream over and over, until one day in the physical he went out of the front door and walked over to the Federal-style building. He opened the front door and saw a dirty, dark old basement.

After that he never had the dream again. He never again dreamed of this wonderful auditorium where all the people were full of joy and this person onstage was giving a talk.

He forgot all about this until 1992. At the end of November there was an ECK seminar in Sydney, Australia. By now this man had married, had two children, and was a member of Eckankar. He was sitting in the audience at the seminar, just enjoying everything that was going on, when suddenly this scene from his childhood opened up.

The man remembered the auditorium. It was the same one as in his childhood dream. He realized that as a child, long before he knew about Eckankar, he had been at an ECK seminar. In fact, he had seen the future, he had seen the 1992 ECK South Pacific Regional Seminar.

The auditorium was the same one as in his childhood dream. He realized that as a child, long before he knew about Eckankar, he had been at an ECK seminar.

ABOVE THE TIME TRACK

People wonder, *How can this be? How can the future happen in this way?*

Although it seems to be a startling concept, it isn't. There really is no separate past, no separate present, and no separate future. We talk about them as such: we look at past lives that we have spent in some other time, we speak of different things we've experienced. We speak of all that as in the past. But past, present, and future are really one.

We just see things sequentially because the mind is constructed to see things in a linear fashion, along a straight line.

But people who have a particular talent in dreaming or prophecy can get off this linear Time Track. They can get above it in the Soul body. And they can see the past, the present, and the future all in the present moment because they are above time and space.

Dreams can help you in your daily life. They can help you see what's coming, they can help you see why things are as they are.

One of the preliminary steps to coming to this spiritual ability, this spiritual state of consciousness, is dream study. This is why we put so much emphasis on dreams in Eckankar.

Dreams can help you in your daily life. They can help you see what's coming, they can help you see why things are as they are. You'll find you were a key player in the circumstances that brought the situations you find yourself in today.

As we begin the path of ECK, generally within the first year comes the experience on the inner planes known as the Dream Initiation.

6

Eight Types of Dreams, Part 1

*A*photographer once pointed out to me that people are reluctant to have their pictures taken because they don't like to see the aging. I understood what he meant.

A photograph cuts through the illusion of who and what we are. Like it or not, we get to look at ourselves a bit more honestly than we do in the mirror, and this cracks our personal image of how we appear to other people.

The eternal dreamer starts to see himself more clearly, and often he doesn't like what he sees. He can then either resist who he is—or better yet— accept who he is. This is when he can say, "I am what I am, and I will be that with as much grace as I can muster at this time."

Eternal in the true sense means not being limited by time or space. The eternal dreamer obtains his experiences here in the physical world as well as in the inner worlds.

The eternal dreamer obtains his experiences here in the physical world as well as in the inner worlds.

EIGHT TYPES OF DREAMS

In the dream teachings of Eckankar, we put a different slant on the subject than is found in

121

psychology or through other sources: We learn to identify the different areas of the dream life as they relate to our own spiritual life.

There are eight categories of dreams that I would like to discuss. Examples will be given to help you recognize them, both in the waking state and during the sleep state. You can then try to see how they advance your own spiritual understanding. The list is not complete, but it will serve as a starting point in learning the ECK definition of what happens in your own dream world.

The eight categories are (1) daydreams; (2) initiation dreams; (3) dreams of intrusion; (4) dreams of release from fear; (5) the waking dream; (6) the Golden-tongued Wisdom, which is part of the ancient science of prophecy, the ECK-Vidya; (7) dreams of understanding; and (8) dreams with the Mahanta, which include experiences with the Light and Sound—the essence of the ECK teachings.

DAYDREAMS

The first type of dream is the daydream.

The first type of dream is the daydream.

I read a story in *Writer's Digest* about a writer who diligently plugged away at his craft. Every day he wrote and wrote, but he didn't sell much. He practiced every technique he felt a successful writer would use: When he found a topic of interest, he'd research it, write an article, and mail it to a publisher.

After eighteen months, he tallied up his earnings. They amounted to only seven thousand dollars—a long way from being enough to support himself and his family.

Totally dejected, he sat back in his chair. Soon he was involved in a daydream in which he was the editor-in-chief of a large New York magazine. From this top position in the organization, he began an inner dialogue: "You know, this magazine could use a few articles." All of a sudden, with an amazing degree of clarity, he saw all the different subjects that the readers of the magazine would like.

Snapping out of his daydream, he picked up a pencil and made a list of all these topics. He selected one to start with, then reviewed past issues of the magazine. Sure enough, the subject had not been covered: How to get a cab in New York City when you want one.

He did some quick research and gathered information from cab companies. After he wrote an outline of his ideas, he called the magazine. "Would you be interested in an article about what to do when you need a cab in Manhattan?" he asked one of the editors.

The editor was not only interested, he was willing to work with the writer to develop the article. When it was completed, the magazine bought it for several thousand dollars—all for one story.

He no longer limits his writing to subjects *he* thinks are important. Instead, he has learned to assume the viewpoint of the person who knows what the readers want. He went on to write many other articles for major magazines, and his financial picture improved greatly. Through his daydream, he found a way to build a successful career for himself.

The second type of dream is the dream of initiation.

DREAMS OF INITIATION

The second type of dream is the dream of initiation.

As we begin the path of ECK by studying the

ECK discourses, generally within the first year comes the experience on the inner planes known as the First Initiation, or the Dream Initiation.

The Mahanta, who is also the Dream Master, escorts you into one of the inner heavens, a plane very close to earth, to give you an experience that fits your spiritual unfoldment at that time. Mainly it is to provide you with proof that you are Soul, that Soul exists beyond life in the physical body, and that as Soul you can conquer death.

You are not given the Dream Initiation as soon as you walk in the door. Someone new to the teachings of ECK needs time to strengthen his spiritual legs.

This inner initiation is a preliminary linkup with the Holy Spirit.

This inner initiation is a preliminary linkup with the Holy Spirit. The full linkup is given at the Second Initiation, which generally comes after two or more years of study in Eckankar.

REMEMBERING INITIATION DREAMS

Whether the dreamer remembers the experience or not, this is an important point in his spiritual life.

Whether the dreamer remembers the experience or not, this is an important point in his spiritual life.

One ECKist reported this dream. He was a child playing in the street with friends. The setting was tropical, much like Hawaii. Suddenly he looked up and saw the Mahanta coming down the street. As the Dream Master walked past, he looked directly at the dreamer. The Master then entered a nearby house. The dreamer was close enough to watch him pick up the phone, dial a number, and carry on a conversation.

All the while the Master's gaze never left the dreamer. Finally the Master hung up the phone, nodded and smiled at the dreamer, and walked away.

The ECKist awoke with the memory fresh in his mind, and he immediately realized the importance of the experience. Through the image of making a call on the inner planes, the Dream Master was letting him know that the connection had been made with the ECK. The Mahanta had made the linkup between the chela and the ECK, the Holy Spirit. This initiate was fortunate; sometimes one cannot even put into words the realization that comes with the initiation experience.

While the First Initiation in ECK takes place entirely in the dream state, the Second through Eighth Initiations occur in two parts. The first part comes on the inner planes, and some time after that an ECK Initiator, acting as a channel for the Mahanta, gives the outer initiation.

DREAMS OF INTRUSION

The third type of dream is the dream of intrusion.

To understand this category of dreams, we must assume the viewpoint of the dreamer, whether asleep or daydreaming.

Let's say you are having a dream in which a certain friend, love interest, relative, or other acquaintance appears. Normally any of these people would show up in your dreams in a predictable way, acting pretty much the same as they do in their everyday life.

But all of a sudden you have a dream experience where things are topsy-turvy; the people are acting out of character. This could be a sign that someone—whether close to you or outside your circle—is unconsciously projecting his or her thoughts into your dream world. This is a dream of intrusion.

The third type of dream is the dream of intrusion.

If that person has an aberration of some kind, or perhaps thinks of you as a playboy or playgirl, those feelings may be projected into your dream state and affect the actions of the characters in your dream. Naturally you are going to wonder what is going on. If misunderstood, it could cause jealousy and other problems in the outer world.

For instance, say an old girlfriend of the dreamer has been thinking about him a lot, unconsciously wanting to break up his new relationship. Her thoughts and hopes intrude in his dream life. When the dreamer wakes up, he misinterprets the dream and says, "My current girlfriend is not being faithful to me—I've seen it on the inner planes." And so jealousy arises.

If you have a dream in which someone who has shown up repeatedly in the past is suddenly acting out of character, look for certain traits.

If you have a dream in which someone who has shown up repeatedly in the past is suddenly acting out of character, look for certain traits. Then look around you in the physical world. There may be someone who either has those traits or, more likely, imagines that you have those traits. Through this method, you may be able to identify the person who has been sending these signals into your dream world.

SCREEN OF PROTECTION

What do you do now? Do you confront the person and accuse them of sending you psychic attacks?

Frankly, it is a cop-out to put the responsibility for our inner worlds on other people. Even if somebody is able to transmit or broadcast a wrong signal into your dream life, it is your responsibility to shut it off at this end. The only reason they are able to get in is because somehow, in some way, you haven't put up a screen to stop that kind of intrusion.

The creative part of the eternal dreamer must figure out a way to do this without causing problems out here in the physical world. This can be tricky. But imagine what would happen if you went up to the person and spouted off: "You have been intruding in my dreams. I want you to get out and never come back!" He would be completely astounded. He wouldn't know what you were talking about. Since he is working from the unconscious level, he probably has no idea that he is invading your space.

Tip: Cut Back on Contact

If the dreams of intrusion become a problem, you can begin to cut back your contact with that person. This includes meetings, phone calls, and correspondence. The way to protect yourself is to begin shutting down the pipeline of negativity that is being fed into you.

LOSING CONFIDENCE IN YOURSELF

Another kind of dream of intrusion can cause you, the dreamer, to lose confidence in yourself.

Another kind of dream of intrusion can cause you, the dreamer, to lose confidence in yourself.

Usually you are in charge of what is happening in your dream world, just as you are out here. When you're cleaning your house, you don't have someone else telling you how to do it. In other words, you are not the servant in your own home.

But occasionally you might have a dream in which there is a turnabout of roles. Throughout the entire experience, you seem to be behind the eight ball. Someone else is telling you how to do this, how to do that. No matter what you do, it's wrong. Before you finish a certain task, they'll say, "Let so-and-so do it—he can do it better." If you make a suggestion, one of your dream characters will say how foolish it is.

By the time you wake up in the morning, your security and self-confidence are shattered. Doubts about your ability set in. You begin to wonder if you're really as good at your job as you thought. You can't seem to make decisions with your full creative power. You are in a reactive mode, almost apologetic about whatever you say or do.

And you won't get any help from those around you, either. Sensing that you are in this reactive, apologetic mode, they become like healthy fish in an aquarium with the sick fish: they give absolutely no mercy. All this happens simply because someone with a negative opinion about how you live your life or do your job has intruded into your dream.

The solution, again, is to try to trace the attitudes that are being expressed during this dream of intrusion. Then use your inner direction to find out who among your acquaintances has a similar attitude about you.

As much as you can, keep away from people who disrupt your life.

 Tip: Take Precautionary Measures

Once you know who is rewriting your dream script to impose their own disturbing thoughts into your inner worlds, take precautionary measures. Watch your conversations around this person or group of people. Start backing off from being friends with them.

As much as you can, keep away from people who disrupt your life. They can only do it because at this time you do not have the strength, the force field of love, or the spiritual stamina to overcome their intrusion.

DREAMS TEACH YOU STRENGTH

Rather than being all bad, these dreams of intrusion teach you to become a stronger individual. You grow more aware of the sources of such attempts to dethrone you. This is essentially what is happening: Someone is trying to dethrone you from your spiritual position. Whether or not you allow this is up to you.

Keep in mind that you are always led into a higher state of challenge. When you become strong enough to face one level of obstacles or intrusions, the ECK raises you to the next level.

Once again, you have to figure out how to meet the greater challenges.

Rather than being all bad, these dreams of intrusion teach you to become a stronger individual.

CREATING YOUR OWN PROTECTION

A dreamer wrote to me stating that he became aware that members of a religious group he used to be involved in were still trying to get him under their influence. Besides outer ways—mail and phone calls—they were appearing in his dreams. He wanted to know how to protect himself from them.

Tip: Protection Techniques

There are several means of protection that are possible to use against those who intrude into our state of being. One simple method is putting a reversed mirror between yourself and the harm. This is done by imagining a mockup of a mirror that reflects back to the sender all unwanted thoughts and forces.

Another form of self-protection is to put yourself in a white circle of light. Then look out from this center at whatever is disturbing you. You may also imagine a wall that shields you from the psychic enemy.

First, use the inner techniques given in the tip above. Also do whatever is necessary on the physical level. In case they are able to bother you physically, it may be necessary to ask the legal authorities for protection. When the force is all subtle, consider calling competent counseling and tell them what is troubling you. Ask what, if anything, can be done for you. The local hospital ought to be able to give you the names of licensed counselors.

The Holy Spirit often works through professional medical people to help us out when we're in trouble.

The Holy Spirit often works through professional medical people to help us out when we're in trouble. After all, all healing comes from Divine Spirit, no matter what It chooses as Its instrument.

METHODS OF THE BLACK MAGICIAN

A black magician has a degree of knowledge as to how invisible energies split from the Audible Life Current, the Holy Spirit, but he bends them toward darkness and destruction.

With power to invade dreams, he can bring terror through nightmares. The dreamer quakes, wondering what has suddenly unbalanced the delicate scale of his affairs. Monsters appear, forces tear at the Astral body, and strange, awful phenomena confront him.

Fear grows, and with it, the disarming influence of the magician steals over the victim. In the initial phase he scatters the individual's serenity so as to control the mind. Craving raw power, the magician cares not a whit for Soul's freedom.

A trick used to breach a victim's psychic home is done through a dream where the victim is told to expect a letter from the magician. When he opens the envelope, a posthypnotic suggestion is triggered that enforces the black magician's original dream contact. The individual is duped and unknowingly gives up a little corner of himself to an outside force that is not at all concerned about his welfare.

The black magician creeps into his prey's life, step-by-step. Every emotional trick is used to bind the two ever more closely together.

Tip: How to Survive a Psychic Attack

To survive a psychic attack may take several approaches: (1) A conscious closing of the emotional door against the intruder. Any photos, as well as memorabilia, of a disruptive personality must be put out of the house. (2) The constant chanting of HU or the initiate's personal word. (3) An actual fight on the inner planes whereby the trespasser is driven off by martial arts or some weapon at hand. (4) Getting plenty of rest each night.

The old law of protection is this: "Nothing can hurt us unless we ourselves allow it!"

People under psychic attack must make a decision whether to follow the Lord of Light and Sound, or the lord of darkness. Hesitation creates a split current of energy within one. I've had reports of people who suffered heart attacks because they let their emotions pull them in two different directions at the same time. Forgo the worship of Moloch, the worship of personality. The price is too dear.

The old law of protection is this: "Nothing can hurt us unless we ourselves allow it!"

Spiritual Exercise:
The Mountain of Light

Try this technique if you feel in need of spiritual protection. Shut your eyes at bedtime, and see yourself standing before a gigantic mountain of light. From the mountain flows the most enchanting melody of the Audible Life Stream.

Now visualize yourself walking up the sidewalk to a huge door that guards an entrance into the side of the mountain. The door's mighty construction can withstand a thermonuclear blast.

Enter and pull the door shut behind you. Notice how easily it swings, despite its great height and massive construction. With the door shut and you safely inside the shelter, lock the door securely. Snap the padlock, set the dead bolt, and drop the bar into place. Then turn around and walk directly into the worlds of Light and Sound.

In extreme cases it is perfectly all right to create several outer chambers inside the entrance. Each chamber is likewise protected by an enormous door; all are secured against the night.

Be aware of one thing: The door of protection is made from the ECK Itself. Nothing can get through It!

The door of protection is made from the ECK Itself. Nothing can get through It!

USE YOUR OWN RESOURCES

When handling a dream of intrusion or some other complicated situation, life can seem like a poorly written play. The ancient Greek playwrights used a tactic known as *deus ex machina*—god from a machine. Another way of saying it is *god from the sky.*

The writer creates a drama around a character. The character performs all sorts of heroic feats. At some point, the writer paints his hero into a corner and doesn't know how to get him out. The solution? Have a deity swoop down from the sky—by way of stage machinery—pick up the hero, and take him away to safety.

Instead of having the character figure his own way out of the situation, the writer brings in a celestial being to rescue him. Nowadays this would be considered poor plotting.

Whenever I watch an episode of the old *Star Trek* TV series, I look for some element of *deus ex machina*.

A recurring theme finds the starship *Enterprise* rushing through space to a specific destination. Suddenly a call for help comes in from some planet off the beaten track. The problem is, if the *Enterprise* doesn't reach the original destination on schedule, there will be a great catastrophe in the universes.

Captain Kirk makes his decision: "We will go off course and find out what's happening on this out-of-the-way planet." He and other crew members then proceed to the transporter room, where they are beamed down to the planet. And in record time, all communication with the *Enterprise* is cut off.

So Captain Kirk and the others are trapped on this planet, captive of either enemy aliens or some mysterious force. How will they ever get themselves out of this fix?

This is where I watch for the writers to cheat. Before Captain Kirk can figure a way out of the problem with the tools at hand, will a rescuer suddenly beam down and blast the bad guys away? In most of the episodes I have seen, the writers don't take the easy way out. They make the crew work out a solution even before the starship reestablishes communication with them.

Sometimes your life seems to flow like a well-written script. You can handle the story line. If a problem arises, you can solve it by yourself. It's your story, you're the star, everything's going great, and the world loves you.

Then you come to a chapter that seems to have been devised by a very poor scriptwriter. Problems come up with your health, personal relationships, job, finances, or anything of this nature. All of a sudden, you can't handle it. This is when you say, "Mahanta, help me!"

Develop Your Creativity

There is nothing wrong with asking for help, but we must remember that our purpose for being on earth is to learn how to arrive at the correct solution to our own problems.

There is nothing wrong with asking for help, but we must remember that our purpose for being on earth is to learn how to arrive at the correct solution to our own problems. We have to write the script and—as well as we can—figure out how to untangle the plot.

If we can't get ourselves out of the fix, there is always *deus ex machina*. This divine intervention is a true, spiritual quality of the teachings of ECK. It is the essential element.

An equally essential part of the teachings is to develop your creativity. Then you can learn to resolve your own problems. Remember, they are problems that you have made for yourself. Out of the factors that made these problems, surely there must be solutions.

Beam Me Up, Scotty!

An ECKist felt that his relationship with the Inner Master was such that anytime he had a bad experience, he could simply say, "Mahanta, please fix this." And the problem would be magically resolved.

One night the initiate had a dream. He was playing the role of Captain Kirk of the starship *Enterprise*. Enemy Klingons are holding him captive on a strange planet while the starship circles above.

The Living ECK Master, in the role of Scotty, is in charge of the transporter. The dreaded Klingons have taken away Captain Kirk's communicator. Luckily, he has a little electronic device hidden in his back pocket. He uses it now to signal the starship in Morse code: "Scotty, beam me up!" Over and over he sends his distress signal to the starship, but things are getting tense.

Off in the distance the dreamer sees a battered little truck, raising a dust cloud behind it as it chugs its way toward him. Behind the wheel is the Living ECK Master, playing the role of Scotty.

Scotty slams on the brakes and jumps out. He grabs Captain Kirk, pushes him in the back of the truck, and takes off driving back down the road in the direction he'd just come from.

The dreamer calls out to the Mahanta, the Living ECK Master, "Scotty, beam us up!"

"Listen," the Living ECK Master says, "I drove for thirty-five hours to get here. We're not going back the easy way!"

The dream helped the initiate to realize that he had a problem: He was being held captive by the passions of the mind. Until he could be free of them, he wouldn't get back to the starship, which symbolized the spiritual freedom to travel the worlds of God.

Out of the factors that made these problems, surely there must be solutions.

DREAMS OF RELEASE FROM FEAR

The fourth type of dream is the dream of release from fear.

The fourth type of dream is the dream of release from fear.

Many of the habits and karmic patterns that we acquired before coming to the ECK dream teachings can be limiting. They can even prevent us from rising in consciousness toward the spiritual freedom which is the birthright of Soul. These limitations often stem from the fears instilled by the religion we followed in the past.

They can also be caused by people from our former church attempting to pull us back to the old ways which no longer suit us.

One woman came from a strong fundamentalist Christian background, but her religion had never addressed her spiritual questions. The God she had been taught about didn't fit her spiritual needs or expectations. Did that mean there was no God, or just that she would never know for sure? For several years she wavered between being an atheist and an agnostic.

After she joined Eckankar, she had a dream where she found herself in an unusual church with her parents. The pulpit stood at floor level, and the pews were elevated on risers that ascended to the back of the church. There were very few people in attendance.

The atmosphere of the church was so heavy and oppressive that the woman became drowsy. She decided to stretch out on the pew to rest. When her parents objected to this display of disrespect for their church, she sat up and made an effort to keep her eyes open. But soon she grew sleepy again, and before long she was lying down.

Suddenly crowds of people poured through the

doors. She had to sit up to make room for them. As the service began, she felt very uncomfortable. *Why am I here?* she wondered. *I feel so out of place.*

The minister's voice droned on in a dreary sermon. After he finished, the congregation rose and began to sing a song. It was as depressing as the sermon. *Oh, no,* the woman thought. It was a communion hymn. She did not want to take communion with the others.

Then her attention was drawn to the high, tremulous voice of a female singer several rows behind her. She turned around to look. Just to the left of the singer was the Mahanta, wearing a dark blue suit. Though he was standing up with the rest of the congregation, he was not singing. The Dream Master looked at the dreamer, then smiled and winked.

At that moment the woman knew that the church and all its doctrines no longer had any hold on her. She felt very happy as she turned back to the altar. She was ready now to go up there, just so her parents would not be displeased.

As quickly as she had that thought, the singing stopped and the congregation broke up. Everyone headed for the door. The minister got very upset that the people were leaving his church right in the middle of communion. First he threatened them, then begged, then tried to bribe them into coming back. But they all left anyway.

The woman awoke in the morning with a new outlook. She realized that her fears about the church and Christianity had been taken away. At the same time, she was able to recognize the role her early religion had played in her life and how it had brought her to ECK.

At that moment the woman knew that the church and all its doctrines no longer had any hold on her.

UNEXPECTED RESCUE

A Catholic man in his early thirties was having a hard time sleeping at night. He had a recurring nightmare where he was both a participant and an observer at the same time. It frightened him because he had no idea what was happening.

The Catholic man had heard about the word *HU* from one of his friends who is an ECKist. They had gone to a twelve-step program together, and this friend had told him, "Whenever you have a problem and you don't know what to do, just sing HU silently to yourself. It's a sacred name for God."

That night the dream came again. He was in a barnyard with a strange creature. It had a snake's body and a head like a turkey. The turkey's head was a deep, dark blue.

This creature came up to the dreamer and began conversing. Somehow the man knew he had to tap the turkey-headed snake on the forehead with his fingers every few moments to keep from being harmed. So every few minutes he reached out his hand and tapped the ghastly looking creature on its head.

The Catholic man knew he was asleep in bed, yet the dream was so real. He was terribly frightened because he couldn't wake up. Then he remembered what his ECKist friend had said: When you're in trouble, sing HU.

In the middle of the nightmare the man began singing HU. Suddenly the whole scene—the barnyard, the turkey-headed snake, everything—just vanished into midair. The man woke with a pounding heart. He knew he wasn't as afraid anymore.

Sleep came again, and the man found himself

This friend had told him, "Whenever you have a problem and you don't know what to do, just sing HU silently to yourself. It's a sacred name for God."

in the barnyard with the turkey-headed snake once more. *What do I do now?* he wondered, and right away he knew to just sing HU. Again, the scene disappeared.

The Catholic man told his friend about the dream and thanked him. He was very grateful that the secret name of God was available for people of all religions to use.

He explained that the prayers he knew as a Catholic were much too long and complicated to remember in a dream. But HU was simple; he could remember HU.

He was very grateful that the secret name of God was available for people of all religions to use.

Often the Holy Spirit gives us warnings about something soon to enter our lives.

7

Eight Types of Dreams, Part 2

$\mathcal{S}$oul is working on a number of different planes at the same time. It's just not possible for the physical mind to contain everything that takes place, even on just the Astral Plane. You have all this pouring in and boggling the little physical mind, so you have to be selective.

You will have many different kinds of dream experiences. Some are routine, day-to-day kinds of things, which are not highly interesting. Others will seem disjointed and won't make logical sense. There are also the spiritual dreams, which are the important ones, and you can make a discipline of learning to remember these. Some will occur in your waking, daily life; others in the dream state.

NATURAL WAY TO REMEMBER DREAMS

Some people are very good at learning in the dream state, and some are very good in contemplation. I can work with you in the dream state a little bit more. The dream state is generally a very easy way for the Inner Master to work with Soul because the fears are set aside.

The dream state is generally a very easy way for the Inner Master to work with Soul because the fears are set aside.

The gentlest technique that I know is one that I used to use fairly often when I'd run up against a wall: I'd still do the contemplation every day, same as always, but before going to sleep at night, as an inner thought I would just give permission to the Inner Master to take me to the place I had earned. I'd say, "Mahanta, I give you permission to take me to that world or to that Temple of Golden Wisdom which would be for my benefit."

Then I would go to sleep and not be concerned about it. Next day, I'd see if I remembered something.

So often when we first wake up, the inner experience is fresh, but the reason we forget is that it is so commonplace. If you can develop the discipline to write down whatever happened in the dream state immediately upon awakening, then within an hour or two you'll be quite surprised at what you find written in that notebook—and much more so after a month.

WAKING DREAMS

The fifth type of dream is the waking dream.

The fifth type of dream is the waking dream.

As mentioned earlier, the waking dream is usually an outer experience given by the Mahanta. Its purpose is to point to a spiritual lesson through an example in your outer life.

The waking dream could happen just as easily in the dream state, where the meaning might be as clear as a bell. But because it takes place in the course of our daily life, we tend to overlook the spiritual significance. We are so involved in the experience that we can't step back and see what the Inner Master is trying to show us about the dream of life.

FATEFUL BUS TRIP

An initiate from Canada wanted to go to an Eckankar seminar in Washington, D.C., but found herself short of money. When other ECKists in her area hired a bus to take them to the seminar, she decided to join them. She really preferred to fly, but the bus was much more affordable. Besides, with the air conditioning, it would be a comfortable ride.

The woman didn't get a wink of sleep the night before they were to leave. Since the trip would take twelve hours, she looked forward to sleeping as they traveled. But as soon as the bus left Montreal, a series of problems began.

First the air conditioning stopped working, and then the toilet backed up. The bus grew uncomfortably warm and the air turned foul, but the woman was so tired that she tried to rest anyway. Just as she was on the verge of sleep, the other ECKists decided it would be fun to sing all the way to Washington.

To top it off, the bus driver took a wrong turn and got lost. Unfamiliar with the route, he ended up exploring mile after mile of scenic side roads that nobody cared to see. The trip took sixteen hours. By the time the woman stumbled off the bus, she was very upset.

She wanted to enjoy the seminar, but she had a hard time keeping her attention on the speakers or participating in the workshops. She kept thinking about that horrible bus ride. It was the most awful trip she had ever experienced in her life—and to an ECK seminar of all places! She couldn't stop stewing.

That evening she was standing in the hall,

waiting to get into the main session, when one of her friends from Canada tapped her on the shoulder. She immediately blurted out all the ordeals she had suffered on the bus trip —"no sleep, the toilet backed up, the air conditioning broke, the trip took four extra hours from getting lost, and everybody sang like hyenas!"

The other ECKist listened patiently to her sad tale. When she finally wound down, he said, "What an interesting dream!"

The woman almost had a fit. "I don't believe you understood me," she snapped. "I didn't say this was a dream. It was my bus trip from Montreal to this seminar!"

"But think about it," the other initiate said. "At this seminar, the attention is on dreams."

The woman stared at him for a minute, and then her anger faded. "Why, of course," she said. "It was a waking dream."

The woman stared at him for a minute, and then her anger faded. "Why, of course," she said. "It was a waking dream." Suddenly she saw the spiritual story behind that fateful bus trip and knew that the Master had given her the experience to teach her something about herself.

The bus symbolized herself as Soul, and the trip was a parallel of Soul making Its journey home to God. She compared the broken air conditioning to what happened when she lost her patience and got hot under the collar. The backed-up toilet represented the problems she experienced when she ate the wrong foods. The constant noise on the bus reminded her of the times she talked when she should have listened.

The woman now saw the entire bus trip as a journey to a greater spiritual understanding of herself. She knew that the inner teachings had been given to her even before she arrived at the seminar. With this realization, the cloud that had hung over her seminar experience went away, and she was able to enjoy the rest of the weekend.

LOCKED OUT

An initiate was interested in becoming a distributor for a computer software package and sat in on a sales presentation at a local hotel. As he left the meeting, he thought, *This is pretty good. I think I can hitch my wagon to this star and make quite a profit.*

He went out to the hotel parking lot and reached in his pocket for the car keys. They weren't there. As he looked through the window of his car, he saw his keys in the ignition. He was locked out.

The ECK was trying to tell this man that the business opportunity, the investment, was a lockout. This was his first warning.

The hotel management had a special tool to unlock his car, and within minutes he was inside. He thought, *That was bad luck, but now I'm in my car.* And he turned the ignition. But the car wouldn't start; the battery was dead. The hotel management helped him start his car. As he drove away, he said, "These things happen," and never realized that the Inner Master was trying to get a second warning across to him.

Next he tried to get a loan to finance his distributorship. He kept running into blocks and delays, one after another. It never occurred to him that the ECK was giving him still a third chance to back off.

Right about this time, the man had a dream. He found himself on top of a huge corporate building. The height made him dizzy, and he had the feeling

The ECK was trying to tell this man that the business opportunity, the investment, was a lockout. This was his first warning.

that he didn't belong up there. It was much too high for him. Somehow he had to find a way to get down to the street level again, and he didn't know how to do it.

It turned out that his distributorship failed. Now he has to try to work himself out of a deep hole. He said it was a very expensive lesson, but he learned something.

Often the Holy Spirit gives us warnings about something soon to enter our lives.

Often the Holy Spirit gives us warnings about something soon to enter our lives. We can miss the warnings if we have our own plans so strongly in mind that we don't like to be moved off track. It's when we become so sure of the power of the mind and our own plans for material riches that we forget to listen to the warnings and directions that are given.

COPPER COINS

A woman was nearing retirement in a company she had been with for many years. She had about a year left but wondered if she should work extra years to put more money aside.

One day in contemplation she said to the ECK, "Please give me a sign about my retirement. Three weeks before I am supposed to retire, show me a little copper coin with a hole near the edge." She had selected an item that was not too common, yet something that you possibly could expect to see.

A week later she saw an unusual pair of earrings made of two copper coins. The coin on each earring had a hole punched near the edge. The woman laughed to herself at the coincidence, thinking earrings didn't count. So she tried to put it out of her mind.

Three weeks after that, however, her employer

offered certain employees early retirement, complete with a cash bonus so that they could afford to do it. Though it came eleven months earlier than she'd expected, she realized that the Holy Spirit had given her an insight into the best course to take, in a way that she could understand.

Waking dreams such as this happen constantly, and not only in the life of an ECKist. They come more often if you are looking for these insights because you realize this is how the Holy Spirit works in everyday life. You know that the kind of miracles reported in biblical times still happen today, all the time.

All you need to do to recognize and benefit from these gifts of the Holy Spirit is to open your consciousness.

In ECK, of course, we open the consciousness through the Spiritual Exercises of ECK, such as singing HU.

CONTACT LENSES

A woman who had worn glasses since the age of eight suddenly began to lose her eyesight. The decline took place over a period of three months. Then her right eye started to ache. She tried switching back and forth between her glasses and contacts, but her vision continued to worsen.

"I'm losing my eyesight," she told the optometrist.

"No, you're not," he assured her. "The only thing wrong is that your contact lenses are worn out. After we replace the contacts, your eyes will start to heal. The pain will go away, and your vision will return to normal."

He was right. But the experience had caused

In ECK we open the consciousness through the Spiritual Exercises of ECK, such as singing HU.

her enough worry to catch her attention. She had a feeling there was a deeper meaning behind it. During contemplation she had a conversation with the Mahanta, the Inner Master, on the inner planes.

"What was going on in your life when your eyes began to give you trouble?" he asked.

"I was having a number of difficulties," she said. "Things were not going very well."

"When these difficulties arose, did you have a hard time letting go of something?" he asked.

"No, I don't think so." But as she thought it over, she realized that she had been attached to the way certain things used to be. The more she resisted the changes, the uglier life looked to her. Because her physical eyes now saw life as ugly, her Spiritual Eye began to close. And as the inner vision shut down, her physical eyesight started to fail. It went hand in hand.

The Inner Master tried to get the message to her through the optometrist, who said, "Your contacts are worn out." In other words, your old way of looking at life is wrong; it's worn out. By replacing her contacts, or releasing her attachments to the things that had changed during those three months, she would be able to see clearly again. Spiritually, she could get back on the right track.

The Mahanta used an outer action to give a spiritual lesson—a waking dream.

The Mahanta used an outer action to give a spiritual lesson—a waking dream.

WALL HANGINGS

An ECK initiate was trying to make wall hangings for a home. When he ran short of money for supplies, he had to improvise. First, he constructed a wooden frame. Then he stretched the wall hanging over his handiwork, using temporary tacks to hold it in place until he could do it right.

Later he went back to replace the temporary tacks with sturdy, industrial-grade tacks. This would secure the wall hanging to the frame permanently.

He removed the first tack and, poking blindly through the burlap, stuck the permanent one in place. Somehow he managed to hit the same hole that the old tack had been in. *That's unusual,* he thought. *How often can you do that?*

He removed another tack, reached for a permanent one, and again, he hit the exact same spot where the old tack had been. The odds of this happening twice were so astronomical that it gave him pause. He began to wonder, *Is this a waking dream? If so, what does it mean?*

Since the ECK arranges the waking dream to give the individual a spiritual insight, there is a way for him to find the answer for himself.

The ECKist began to look over the situation: Is the waking dream trying to tell me that I'm doing things wrong or right? If I'm doing them wrong, does it mean I'm in a rut? Am I putting my new efforts into the same old pattern?

On the other hand, he thought, *could it be that I'm doing things right? Does hitting the same holes twice mean I'm right on target?*

Suddenly he knew that this was the case. The feeling of rightness that came with the experience told him that he was right on target. Through an outer action, a waking dream, the Mahanta had given him the spiritual insight to know that he was moving in the correct direction on the path to God. It was not a dramatic experience. But even the little events in life can have an important meaning.

Since the ECK arranges the waking dream to give the individual a spiritual insight, there is a way for him to find the answer for himself.

GOLDEN-TONGUED WISDOM

The sixth type of dream is the Golden-tongued Wisdom.

The waking dream and the Golden-tongued Wisdom are two different categories of experience. Sometimes it is hard to tell which is which. Whereas the waking dream usually involves some kind of action in the outer world, the Golden-tongued Wisdom normally involves voice.

The Golden-tongued Wisdom is the voice of the Mahanta that jumps out to impart spiritual insight. It might come through words spoken by another person, or even in a short printed message. The Golden-tongued Wisdom is usually an outer experience, but it may also come on the inner planes. These works are all a part of you.

GLASS ETCHINGS

In the dream state, the Mahanta, the Inner Master, led an ECK initiate down the street to a store with a large glass window. The Mahanta then began to engrave scenes and images on the glass, one after another. The dreamer watched in silence.

"It is best to use images in telling stories," the Mahanta explained as he worked. "The person who is hearing the story can see through the image, just as you can see through the pane of glass. By seeing through the image, the person is able to find the spiritual truth or principle demonstrated by that image."

This was the voice of the Master on the inner planes. The spoken words, along with the images of a mocked-up scene, were used to get a point across to the ECK dreamer.

Fortune Cookie

This next story is another example of how the ECK may speak to an individual through the Golden-tongued Wisdom.

An ECKist went out to lunch with a friend. As they ate, his friend told him a joke about a fat couple who sat in a booth next to him in another restaurant. The ECKist, thinking that was really a funny story, filed it away in his head for retelling at a later date.

The next evening he met a business associate for dinner at a Chinese restaurant. They finished their meal and asked for the check, which the waitress placed on the table along with two fortune cookies. As the ECKist picked up his fortune cookie, a large couple came in and took the next booth. Reminded of his friend's story, he wondered if this might be the same couple. The thought struck him funny.

He broke open his cookie, then leaned over and began to whisper the story to his associate. He unfolded the little piece of paper as he talked. He glanced down to read it. The message from the fortune cookie said: "When one speaks only good about others, there is no need to whisper." The ECKist stopped the story in midsentence.

In ECK we learn to keep our spiritual eyes and ears open. As soon as he saw what was on the paper, he knew that the Mahanta was giving him a very different message. He also knew that it was for his own good.

In ECK we learn to keep our spiritual eyes and ears open.

"Go on with the story," the other man said. "I want to hear the rest."

"I'd rather not," the ECKist said.

"Why not?"

He showed him the piece of paper, and the man caught on right away. "Yeah, I guess I don't want to hear it, either," he said.

DREAMS OF UNDERSTANDING

The seventh type of dream is the dream of understanding.

The seventh type of dream is the dream of understanding.

An ECKist had a dream where she and another person were in a dimly lit room. There were glass doors covered with heavy, lined drapery that reached from the ceiling to the floor and kept the room in almost total darkness.

The dreamer went up to the drapes and grasped the cord at the side, drawing the drapes open to let more light into the room. Behind the heavy drapery was another curtain; this one was thinner and more sheer. She found the cord for the second set of drapes and pulled on it. As the curtain opened and more light came in, she was able to see just a little better than before. But now she noticed that there were several more layers of drapery behind this one.

"This is crazy," she said. "I don't want to go through all this trouble to pull back the rest of the drapes that are between me and the light. I did the heavy one and the sheer one, but that's enough."

She was very upset when she awoke and remembered the dream. She thought, *I had a chance to see the Light of ECK come through clearly in Its pure form, but I didn't open all the drapes.*

At this point she remembered a talk I had given during a recent ECK seminar. It was about the many veils that stand between the human consciousness and the higher states of spiritual awareness. We have to be in a higher state of consciousness to see the pure, clear forms of Light or to hear the greater Sound of God.

At our present level, we can handle a certain amount of the Light and Sound, but before we can take in more, we have to reach a higher state of consciousness. To take in more than we are ready for could be harmful. In ECK this is never allowed.

The woman didn't realize that the person with her in the dream was a representative of the Mahanta. She would not have allowed the ECKist to open any more layers of the sheer draperies.

After thinking it over, she understood why she had refused to open all the drapes. Instinctively she had recognized that she could not take all the pure Light that would have come through. She could accept just so much Light and no more. This was a dream of understanding, which can also be called a dream of realization.

Instinctively she had recognized that she could not take all the pure Light that would have come through. She could accept just so much Light and no more.

A BEACHED WHALE

Another dreamer found himself arriving at a seminar on the inner planes. He entered the dream hotel, walked all the way through to the back, and opened the door. The ocean was so close that the water lapped at the edge of the hotel rug. From the doorway he could see whales as they swam back and forth in the bay. Everything was so pretty.

Then he noticed that a small whale was lying on the sand. It had no way to get itself back into the deep water.

One of the bigger whales swam in close and managed to nudge the little one back into the water. Together they rejoined their companions, and they all swam away.

The dreamer understood that he was like the small beached whale, out of his natural element. The big whale symbolized the Mahanta, who had come along to push him back in the water. He was now back in the spiritual waters of life.

A dream like this shows the individual that he is making progress spiritually, and that there is protection and help. This is very important, because sometimes one can feel he is alone in a desert. A dream of water, especially the ocean, represents the fullness or the fulfillment of life. It was reassuring to the dreamer to see a greater creature helping one who was not yet able to fend for himself.

A dream of water, especially the ocean, represents the fullness or the fulfillment of life.

GOLDEN SEEDS

An ECKist dreamed that he saw a large sack hanging on a beautiful, ancient tree. The sack was filled with water and golden seeds. A perfectly formed hole in the sack began to open, allowing the water to flow out. But the seeds held back, not wanting to be first. They were afraid of what might happen if they went through the hole with the water. Finally many went, but many stayed.

The golden seeds that went out through the opening with the water were bold and adventuresome. They had no criticism or reproach for the others. Accepting life openly, they went into the ground and were watered and nourished by Spirit. They flourished and bore fruit in another season. They trusted the ECK and prospered. But those who stayed behind withered and died.

This was a highly spiritual dream. What flowed from the sack was the water of life. The seeds were Souls—those who were willing to go with the flow of ECK and those who were not.

The seeds that stayed were fearful of what they might lose if they allowed the water of life to carry them through the opening to another world. And so they held back. But those who went forward found they were now free of the small, old world that once enclosed them. They entered the soil of a grand, new world, where the water allowed the seeds to blossom and grow. Again, this was a spiritual dream of understanding.

REPAYING A DEBT

The play of karma underlies all human relationships.

The play of karma underlies all human relationships.

In this next story, a young man we'll call Nick gets to balance the scales of justice from the past. He needed to repay a victim from a previous life, but the Mahanta sent a dream to prepare him for the necessary, though painful experience.

Nick had a dream in which a beautiful young woman came to the office. She was trying to use the phone on his manager's desk. Nick and the girl felt an immediate attraction for each other in the dream, and soon they began a passionate romance. But, to his frustration, it led nowhere.

Then he awoke.

Some weeks later, a young student came to the office to get work experience. Nick loved her from the start. He did everything in his power to win her heart, but she coyly brushed aside his passion with promises. Later, always later. Soon everyone in the office was talking about their relationship.

Then the sky fell in.

Through the office grapevine, Nick learned that this young woman had been having a secret love affair with his best friend at work. It had begun nearly the first week that she had arrived there. Worse, Nick had set the stage. One night that first week he had to work late, so he asked his good friend to take her home. That was the beginning of the end.

Only the ECK, Divine Spirit, kept Nick from losing his mind when he learned of the secret love affair. But he turned sour on life. Why had this beautiful young woman come—to purposely bring him grief?

In his anxiety and anger, he even forgot about the spiritual love of the Mahanta, the Living ECK Master.

Then came a second dream. The Mahanta took him on the Time Track and showed him a past life in which he had been a woman. Married to a wealthy man, this individual had two house servants, both of whom suffered due to Nick's misuse of position and authority. One was this student.

"You made that karma," the Mahanta explained. "That debt stands between you and God's love. Pay now and be done with it."

In the end, Nick recognized the hand of karma and the long, outstanding debt that he needed to settle. It took awhile for the crushing pain to subside, of course, but now he's happy he settled the debt. After the pain had finally gone, Nick felt a new sense of freedom and lightness. God's love could now shine more directly into his heart. That obstructing block of karmic debt was gone.

The eighth type of dream is those with the Mahanta.

DREAMS WITH THE MAHANTA

The eighth type of dream is those with the Mahanta.

The ECK, or Holy Spirit, can be known through Light and Sound. An inner experience with either of these two aspects is actually the presence of the Mahanta, in visible or audible form. When the Light and Sound combine, they form into a single matrix which shows up on the inner planes as the Mahanta, the Inner Master.

An ECK dreamer had often met the Mahanta on the inner planes but avoided him out of shyness and fear. One night in the dream state she attended a HU Chant in a large hall. People were going to be gathering to sing HU together, the ancient love song to God. Chairs were being set up in several areas, and the people were able to sit where they chose.

The woman selected a certain area and headed in that direction. When she got there, she found the chairs arranged in very disorderly fashion. People were scattered about, sitting here and there; everything was in chaos.

The HU Chant wasn't ready to begin yet, so she decided to leave the hall for a few minutes. As she started to cross the street, she met a few of her friends. They all got into a gondola, the kind used to transport skiers up a slope.

She felt the sensation of being lifted from the ground, and soon the vehicle was gone. In fact, everything was gone. She continued to move very high, very fast, but now there was a noticeable increase in vibration.

This vibration was the Sound of ECK uplifting this person. What started as a dream had turned into a direct experience with the Sound, which showed Itself as vibration.

A few minutes later she found herself back in the body on the plane where the dream had begun.

When the Light and Sound combine, they form into a single matrix which shows up on the inner planes as the Mahanta, the Inner Master.

What started as a dream had turned into a direct experience with the Sound, which showed Itself as vibration.

She returned to the hall in time for the HU Chant, but this time she went to an area where the chairs were arranged in an orderly circle. All the seats were taken, except for one, and she knew it was hers. She sat down, and the HU Chant began.

RECOGNIZING THE MAHANTA

In the circle was the Mahanta, the Inner Master; but because of her old fears of unworthiness, she kept her eyes down. Then something made her glance up. Looking his way, she suddenly had a feeling of recognition: She had known the Master before, in many lifetimes. She even recollected that he had once printed her wedding invitations.

Rather than an outer marriage, she knew the invitations had been for Soul to be linked up with the ECK. The image actually symbolized an inner marriage between Soul and the Holy Spirit.

For the first time in her experiences on the inner planes, she looked directly into the Master's eyes, and the fear went away.

For the first time in her experiences on the inner planes, she looked directly into the Master's eyes, and the fear went away. She had reached the degree of unfoldment that allowed her to surrender to the divine principle which operated within her at all times.

SOUND EXPERIENCE

Another dream found two ECK initiates being escorted by the Inner Master through a Temple of Golden Wisdom on the inner planes. As they walked along, suddenly they heard the chanting of HU, sung like a Gregorian chant. The sound went on and on, filling all space.

The two initiates met several other people in the temple, but none were able to hear the sound of HU. To the ECKists it seemed deafening enough to drown out all outer noises. Yet, when the other people spoke, the ECKists could hear them just fine, even over the loud chanting of HU.

This was a direct experience with one of the sounds of God. To hear a number of ECK Masters chanting HU on the inner planes is one of the higher experiences an individual can have in the dream state.

To hear a number of ECK Masters chanting HU on the inner planes is one of the higher experiences an individual can have in the dream state.

River Run to God

A woman went to sleep and woke up on the inner planes. In the dream state she had a raft, and she was using a pole to push it along in the shallow water, before moving into the current of a wild river. She was just ready to push off when the Mahanta came along.

"What are you doing?" the Mahanta called.

"I'm going down the river," she answered.

"Would you like some help?" he asked.

"Sure."

"I mean, do you really want help?" he asked again.

"Yes, I really would like to have some help," she said.

"All right," the Mahanta said. "If you really want help, we'll build a house on your raft."

"A house?" she said in alarm. "Won't the raft tip over with a house on it?"

"No," he answered, "it will give it ballast."

The woman hesitated. She had never heard the word *ballast* before. Later, when she looked in a dictionary, she found that it meant something that gives stability.

"But I don't know how to build a house," she said, finally.

"Don't worry, I'll help."

The Mahanta brought lumber. "I'll cut it to size, and you hammer it in place," he said. "I'll show you where."

They worked together floor-by-floor, wall-by-wall and room-by-room at her own speed, which was slow and unsure, until the house was finally finished. Then they climbed on board. "Let's go!" the Master said cheerfully.

She looked around the raft and felt comfortable, knowing that as she headed down the river, the Mahanta would be there to help her around the blind bends in the river.

As the woman began her study of the ECK discourses, she became more aware of the inner worlds. When she made the inner commitment to the path of ECK, the Master told her to build a raft on the inner planes for her journey home to God. When she was ready to push off, she was frightened of this voyage to forever, and so the Master helped her build a house, which would make the raft more secure. The house was the knowledge of ECK that she would need in order to survive the river run to God.

I research the dream state in an effort to find a thread of common experience for the eternal dreamer.

THE RICHNESS OF DREAM EXPERIENCES

I research the dream state in an effort to find a thread of common experience for the eternal dreamer. My research has barely begun. It doesn't begin to cover all the different areas that the dreamer may encounter as he travels the path of ECK.

These eight categories of dreams are by no means complete, but what was given here should provide some guidelines for your experience in the dream state.

Look at each dream in one of three levels. They are about our daily life, our emotions and thoughts, and, less often, about the pure spiritual side.

8

Understanding Your Dreams

$\mathcal{W}$ here do the beginners start to interpret their dreams? Do they begin in the bookstore, buying volumes of books that supposedly give the inside scoop on dreams?

No. That's not to say they won't learn something by reading books on dreams, because they will. They will learn the many ways that people approach the dream world: through symbols, the emotions, as outer causes, or as riddles. These only give a small part of the picture. If people have the wisdom and insight, and spend enough time at it, they can eventually piece all the odd ends together and come up with their own dream patchwork of sorts.

Yet it will still miss the beauty and wonder of living, in full consciousness, in your heavens of dreams.

BEGINNING TO INTERPRET

Dreams have a meaning at every step—the human, emotional, causal, mental, subconscious, and spiritual levels. They correspond to the six

Where do the beginners start to interpret their dreams?

planes of existence, spoken of so often in the ECK works—the Physical, Astral, Causal, Mental, Etheric, and Soul Planes. And each deals with a part of us. Each of our dreams comes mainly from one of these areas.

Our task is to keep the interpretation of dreams simple.

THREE LEVELS OF DREAMS

Look at each dream in one of three levels. They are about our daily life, our emotions and thoughts, and, less often, about the pure spiritual side.

Look at each dream in one of three levels. They are about our daily life, our emotions and thoughts, and, less often, about the pure spiritual side. So, simply put, there are dreams about our everyday events, our emotional well-being, and our relationship with God.

The beauty of dreams is that they go with you everywhere, no matter what. They are a portable treasure. You need only recall them, to recognize them as a divine gift to gain insight into your true spiritual nature. Never are you without your dreams.

Is it possible to go somewhere for the weekend and say, "Oh, I forgot to pack my dreams?"

No, they are always with you, because they are a part of you and you of them. They give a broader picture of yourself and the great spiritual potential that lies within you.

I would say that some figures of state, church, and science understate the value of dreams, for they often ridicule or punish those who speak too freely about the dream life. A dreamer is often an independent being. He looks inwardly, instead of outwardly, for the real answers to life.

Dream Symbology

The real importance of dream symbology is in how it relates spiritually to your daily life. An ECKist discovered this through a dream about his wife, who is not in Eckankar.

In their outer life, his wife appeared somewhat interested in ECK, but she wasn't quite sure that she wanted to become a member. At various times she had also considered either staying in her present religion or looking into some other spiritual teaching. She often discussed her dilemma with her husband.

One night the husband dreamed that his wife called him at home. She said, "I'm at a phone booth, but I don't know where I am. I'm lost. Can you help me get home?"

"If you know the name of the road you're on, or even a nearby crossroad, I can help you find your way home," the husband said.

"There aren't any crossroads around here," she said. "I don't know where I am."

"OK, get in the car and drive down the street very slowly until you come to an intersection. Then call me back and tell me the names of the two crossroads. We'll be able to figure out where you are."

The ECKist woke up wondering what the dream was all about. The experience on the inner planes had been so lifelike that he knew it was trying to tell him something.

Suddenly he realized it was an answer to his fear that he may have been pushing Eckankar on his wife. At times he thought she seemed truly interested in the teachings of the Holy Spirit. But

The real importance of dream symbology is in how it relates spiritually to your daily life.

he had often wondered, *Does she really care, or am I only imagining her interest?*

The dream had given him a spiritual understanding of his wife's position. She was in the car, and she was lost. This represents Soul's journey through the lower worlds as It tries to find Its way home. But until she had at least some idea of where she was, her husband couldn't help her.

All he could do in the dream was encourage her to go very slowly down the road until she came to a crossroad. This gave him the insight to tell her out here, "First you have to find out where you are spiritually. You have to know where you are before you can figure out where to go."

He recommended that she examine her own religion, other spiritual paths, Eckankar, and whatever else she wanted to, but to go very slowly. Eventually she would come to a point in her life that seemed significant. Then she could stop, take a look around, and see where she was. Her husband could then try to help her figure out her direction home.

She was in the car, and she was lost. This represents Soul's journey through the lower worlds as It tries to find Its way home.

CREATING YOUR OWN DREAM DICTIONARY

During important times in my life, one of the dream symbols I used to see was a field with a regular-sized baseball diamond. When everything on the field was aligned and in proper order—four bases evenly spaced, a pitcher, a batter, and two opposing teams—it meant that my life was in good order.

But sometimes the bases were at odd distances apart or the base path wasn't in a perfect square. Or the ball I'd hit might pop and blow feathers all over the place. Or I'd have to run into the woods to find first base. Second base might be closer in than usual; third base might be off in another direction entirely. In other words, everything about the game was wrong.

When I'd wake up after a dream like that, I'd often notice that something in my outer life wasn't going right. The sport had gone out of it. There wasn't any fun in it.

This was an indication for me to sit down and work out a plan to reorganize. In other words, I had to figure out how to get myself a real baseball field again—proper space between bases, correct number of players on each team, and so on.

Tip: The Dream Dictionary

Creating a dream dictionary can help you become familiar with your own dream symbols. Whether a baseball diamond, a bear, an eagle, or anything else, you'll know immediately what a particular symbol means to you.

In a section at the back of your dream journal, keep a list of the symbols that occur in your dreams. As you create your own dream dictionary of symbols, record the date next to the meaning of each symbol. This way you can keep track as the meaning changes. As you unfold, your dream symbols are going to take on different meanings, a fact not generally known by people who study dreams.

Creating a dream dictionary can help you become familiar with your own dream symbols.

DREAM GUIDANCE

Many ECK initiates are given guidance through the dream state. A situation may be mocked up by the Dream Master to simulate something that is causing the ECKist concern in his daily life. Through this dream, the ECKist is shown what he should or should not be doing if he wants to resolve the situation.

The ECK dream discourses can help you learn to work more effectively with the dream state. Many books on dreams rely on a specific list of symbols. They would have you believe that symbols like a pebble or a vulture mean the same thing for everybody. But it is unlikely that you will get your own truth out of someone else's interpretations. For this reason, I use symbols only as a way to show you how to interpret your own.

The ECK dream discourses discuss the structure of dreams and how they relate to your everyday life in the physical world.

The ECK dream discourses discuss the structure of dreams and how they relate to your everyday life in the physical world. More importantly, they show you how to make the connection between your inner life and your outer life. Bringing the unknown inner part of yourself to your outer consciousness can help you make your life better in every way, for your own spiritual good.

The discourses include spiritual techniques. These are used step-by-step, month-by-month to break up the ingrained thought patterns which are holding you back.

Translator Function

In chapter 3, I explained the role of the dream censor. Briefly, the Dream Master often works through the Etheric mind. A portion of the Etheric mind has an automatic function which operates as the censor. If the Etheric mind feels that a certain experience in the other worlds would be too much of a shock to the dreamer, the censor comes in, says,

"Shut it down!"—and wipes out the dream.

There is also a higher part of the Etheric mind, which corresponds to the high Mental Plane. This is the level at which the Dream Master works.

The Dream Master translates or converts an experience in the other worlds into symbols or words you can understand here. I call this the translator function.

Different languages or modes of communication are used on some of the other planes. As the communication comes through the Etheric mind, it is unscrambled and retranslated for your physical mind. All the ideas expressed in the other planes are then perceived in the language you normally speak here on earth.

There are modes of transportation in some of the other planes which we cannot fathom here. For instance, vehicles may be propelled without wheels, in ways that the human mind simply can't understand. Things like this are unscrambled and converted into something we can relate to.

The Dream Master gives you an experience in another world because there is a lesson for you to learn. It may have to do with a harmful habit or attitude you have acquired, such as anger. The Dream Master will guide you in the Soul body to another plane for an experience that will point out the harm your attitude is causing you.

The Dream Master gives you an experience in another world because there is a lesson for you to learn.

EFFECT OF INTERFERENCE

One of the initiates has a habit of interfering in other people's space, and she recognizes this. She isn't the only one with such problems. As we begin on the path of ECK and move into the higher stages, we have to keep our eyes open and learn to recognize in our own lives the spiritual principles that are being taught by the Mahanta.

Her lesson from the Dream Master came in two parts. In the first dream, she was the person who was offended; in the second, she was the offender. The Inner Master, or the Dream Master, was simply trying to show her the importance of allowing other people their spiritual space. This means that we do not interfere, eavesdrop, or any of those other things we feel we have the right to do. We do not have the right to meddle in other people's personal business.

In the first dream, she was seated at a table in a restaurant. The Dream Master was talking with a group of people nearby. At one point he leaned across the table and began to speak directly to her.

But as he was talking to the dreamer, giving her kernels of wisdom and truth, someone at the table interrupted him. She waited for the Master to go on, but instead he sat back in his chair and said, "Well, that's all I have to say anyway." But she knew better. He had stopped speaking because someone else had interrupted his message.

One can readily accept a dream like this, where someone else is the wrongdoer. She didn't quite connect it to her own habits yet. But a few days later she had another inner experience to show how she was often the offender.

In the dream world, she was standing near the front of a long line of people who were waiting to say hello to the Dream Master. Each person would shake the Master's hand, exchange a few words with him, and move on so that the others in line could have their turn.

The Inner Master, or the Dream Master, was simply trying to show her the importance of allowing other people their spiritual space.

The dreamer's turn finally came, and she shook his hand. But instead of moving on to allow others their chance to have a private word with him, she stood at his elbow and listened in on his conversations with the initiates he was now greeting.

As she eavesdropped and imposed her own opinions on several people who had each come to ask the Master for a spiritual healing, the higher part of the Etheric mind went into action. This is the part that translates inner experiences into graphic images that the dreamer will certainly remember and, hopefully, learn where he or she went wrong.

One of the initiates was holding some human organs in his hands. The Dream Master turned to the person who was being a busybody. "Touch that thing," he said.

The dreamer just looked at it. *I really would rather not touch that thing,* she thought, *but I guess I have no choice.* With great reluctance she reached out to touch it and immediately awoke from her dream.

She realized then what the Dream Master was trying to tell her. When she intruded in other people's business, some of their problems rubbed off on her. It was a very insightful dream.

The woman was given a lesson on the effect of interference from two different angles, which is often how the Dream Master gets a point across to an individual. The only purpose of these experiences on the inner planes is to make one a more spiritual being. This is why ECK is one of the best teachings on earth today. These experiences show us our weakest points and give us the insight needed to overcome them.

The only purpose of these experiences on the inner planes is to make one a more spiritual being.

A DREAM ABOUT HABITS

A woman had been running her life by the forces of power and control instead of love. Her inclination was to control other people, to tell them what to do. It was second nature to her. She realized she had developed some bad habits, but she couldn't pinpoint what they were doing to her life.

So the Dream Master gave her an experience about habits.

One night in the dream state, the Dream Master took her into a basement with a group of people. Crust-covered leeches were crawling all over the walls and floor. The basement was dark. The other people felt it was very important to keep plucking the leeches off themselves. They spent most of their time just sitting there, plucking and plucking.

Suddenly a door opened from the outside. Sunlight poured into the basement, and a second group of people came in. They seemed very unconcerned about these crusty creatures.

The first group tried to warn them, "Be careful of these leeches. Keep plucking them off, because they'll get all over you, and they stick! Get them off!"

The second group didn't seem to care. They were too busy laughing and enjoying themselves. The first group simply could not impress upon these happy people that leech-plucking was important enough to worry about.

The second group left the basement, and sunlight poured in through the open door. About this time, the dreamer awoke.

The dream was upsetting and left the woman with a feeling of discomfort. It showed her where she was coming up short. From this experience she

A woman had been running her life by the forces of power and control instead of love. So the Dream Master gave her an experience about habits.

was able to take a bad dream one step further, to a higher level, and raise herself spiritually.

HOW TO CHANGE A DREAM YOURSELF

In contemplation, the woman visualized herself walking out of the dark basement into the sunlight. She made an effort to dispel the frightening effects of the dream by moving from a lower, darker world into a higher, lighter one.

As she did this, she realized that the crusty things that hung on like leeches were actually habits. They were the habits of control, fear, power, and other practices that did not allow the people she was with to have their freedom.

The second group was concerned simply with living in the love of everyday life and loving the Holy Spirit, which is the ECK. They realized that this love was in the Light and Sound, outside in the greater worlds of God.

A definite effect occurs when you begin working to change your inner space, to uplift it from power to love.

A definite effect occurs when you begin working to change your inner space, to uplift it from power to love. Something happens out here. You begin to have brighter vision; you become more willing to allow other people as much freedom as you would like for yourself.

Spiritual Exercise: Into the Light

This technique will help you if you have a dream that you don't like. Close your eyes and go into contemplation for about fifteen minutes.

Begin by chanting HU—one of the most beautiful words in the language of mankind. After you have chanted HU for a few minutes, rewind the dream that upset you or that left you somewhere you didn't want to be. Run through the dream mentally, from the beginning up to the point where you awoke. Then try to take it one step further.

Perhaps the dream ended with you in a frightening situation—let's say a dark basement. In your spiritual exercise, take it to the point where you were left in the dark basement. Then use your imaginative faculty to get yourself out of there: Visualize an open door that leads to golden sunlight. Know that this golden light is the Light of Divine Spirit, the Light of ECK, the Light of God. Look to the Light, and listen for the Sound.

Remember, when you have a dream that you would like to change, you can go into contemplation and use this technique to take the dream one step further. Always take it to a higher level. Move it out of the darkness, out of the silence and loneliness. Take it to the Light and Sound of God.

Through the Spiritual Exercises of ECK, such as the technique above, you are creating for yourself an open door to a greater world. Soon you will find that you have established a new habit. When you run into dark and troubling times, awake or asleep, you will be in the habit of creating for yourself a brighter world in which you can be happier and more satisfied than you were before.

If you can achieve an improvement over yesterday, even a small one, then you have gained significantly.

If you can achieve an improvement over yesterday, even a small one, then you have gained significantly. You, with the help of the Dream Master, have done it yourself. You are taking charge of your own world because you are becoming a creator.

DREAMS OF FLYING

An ECKist who worked in the medical field for many years one day realized the computer age had caught up with her. She didn't have the necessary skills to compete in today's work force. Forty years after leaving school, she realized she would have to enter the classroom again to educate herself in computer technology. She was filled with doubts about her ability to meet these new challenges.

Around that time she had a dream in which a group of people attacked her. The interesting part was that they came after her with the tools and instruments of her profession—surgical knives and hypodermic needles.

She was terrified. She called for help from the Dream Master, but nothing seemed to happen. Suddenly a thought came to her: *I can fly! In these inner worlds, if I'm in trouble, I can fly. I'll fly higher than they can reach.*

And so she flew—above their groping hands and out of their grasp. As she sailed through the air, a woman dressed in white rose up behind her. "You can't come up here," the dreamer said. "You can't fly." The woman in white immediately fell back down to the ground.

When the dreamer awoke and thought over the dream, she saw that it was actually she who was cutting and attacking herself. She was doing it with her own attitude about her inability to learn what she needed to upgrade her skills. She was belittling herself, and in so doing, she was harming herself. It was a destructive mental action she had allowed. It would prevent her from making a better life for herself.

She recognized that the lady in white was also herself. When she said to the woman, "You can't fly," she was telling herself that she couldn't try to achieve the higher things in life. Because she had

She was belittling herself, and in so doing, she was harming herself. It was a destructive mental action she had allowed. It would prevent her from making a better life for herself.

convinced one part of herself that this was true, she had condemned herself to a lower level of performance that would eventually lead to a dead end in her material life.

Soon after this, she enrolled in a class and did very well. She was surprised. But just by taking that first step, she was able to develop her self-confidence; she was creating her own worlds.

Most dreamers can learn their own feelings or thoughts about a person by studying what the dream character does or says.

✳ Tip: Dream Characters

Human characters play leading parts in most dreams. They are often people who are close to us in everyday life. In many cases, they represent other things than themselves.

Most dreamers can learn their own feelings or thoughts about a person by studying what the dream character does or says.

If you wish to use this technique, write down not only the dream upon awakening but also your thoughts and feelings about it and the people you encountered.

IS IT REAL, OR IS IT A SYMBOL?

An initiate asked me an interesting question: *How can I tell whether the people I meet in the dream state are other Souls or just symbolic parts of myself?*

The dream world and its people are real. It is only our recall and understanding of it that are incomplete. Our link with the inner worlds is usually through dreams, but illusion can make our memory of inner events faulty.

What about the dream people who appear to be just symbolic parts of ourselves? Let's start with the waking dream. The Mahanta uses it to give someone a spiritual insight from an experience in his daily life. The Master draws on the individual's experiences with real people and real events to point out some personal truth.

Apply the principle of the waking dream to your dream world. The people you meet there are Souls, just like you. However, the Mahanta can turn your experiences with them into an open window of understanding, to unlock your desires, needs, and goals.

The Meaning of a Dream Marriage

Every so often someone will report having a dream about a wedding. If it's a man, he might say, "I dreamed of marrying a certain woman." Then he forms the mistaken conclusion that it means they are Soul mates. There aren't Soul mates in the teachings of ECK; that is an occult concept.

Each Soul is an individual and unique being. In the lower planes we have the two parts of our lower nature: the positive and the negative. When we get to the Soul Plane, we find that these two parts become one. This is called the self-recognition state, what Socrates referred to when he said, "Man, know thyself." Up until this time, knowing the self has meant merely knowing the ego, or the little self, rather than our true spiritual nature. Our consciousness changes when we reach the Soul Plane; we now have an outlook on life that is balanced.

In the dream state, marriage simply means that Soul is having an inner initiation where the two parts of Itself are drawn a little closer together. We

Apply the principle of the waking dream to your dream world. The people you meet there are Souls, just like you.

are looking for the linkup of Soul with the ECK, this Divine Spirit which comes from God.

Each time you see a marriage on the inner planes, regardless of the personality you perceive as your mate, it means a closer marriage with Spirit and with God.

Each time you see a marriage on the inner planes, regardless of the personality you perceive as your mate, it means a closer marriage with Spirit and with God.

INTERPRETING SPIRITUAL DREAMS

To help you develop the ability to understand your own dream symbols, here are a few dreams that I have been asked to explain.

I had a dream in which I was walking down a sidewalk with a friend at 9:00 p.m. I looked up in the sky and saw the moon, which looked huge. Beside the moon was a big planet with a ring around it. Everyone else in the dream seemed to take no notice but carried on as if it were just an ordinary day. I was excited and wanted to know why the moon and planet were there. Can you please explain to me what this dream means?

Yours is a spiritual dream.

The sidewalk is the path of ECK. Since it's your dream and your path, the lessons will be yours— not your friend's. Evening means the end of Soul's karmic day: this life is your gateway to spiritual freedom. Looking up into the sky indicates your high spiritual vision. The huge moon is the promise of a brighter life in ECK, here and now.

The big planet with the ring is a symbol for the great worlds of ECK beyond our own. You alone, of all the others in the dream, were thrilled at the sight of the moon and planet because of your appreciation for spiritual things. Overall, the dream means you may go with the Mahanta to the spiritual worlds of ECK.

⟡ ### Tip: Invite the Mahanta Along

If you would like to see the spiritual worlds of ECK, say at bedtime, "Wah Z, show me the wonder of Sugmad's creation." Wah Z is my spiritual name.

FEAR OF DEATH IN DREAMS

I have had a recurring dream ever since I was a child. I'm taking a bath, and a hand falls into the tub and grabs my toe. I usually wake up screaming, very scared and having trouble breathing. What does this dream mean?

Your dream about a hand falling in the bathtub and grabbing your toe is, oddly enough, a spiritual dream. It shows a deep fear of dying, even though outwardly few people would guess that of you.

Taking a bath sets the dream up as meaning: Be ready; this is a spiritual dream. For water often means something spiritual. Being in the bathtub means you're immersed in thoughts of a spiritual nature. But then the hand falls into the tub. It's not a normal hand, but a *disembodied* one. *Disembodied* here means death. The hand grabs your toe, the very end of your body. That means, "In the end death will get you."

Fear will lose its grip on you once you know yourself as Soul. The Spiritual Exercises of ECK can help you do that.

Fear will lose its grip on you once you know yourself as Soul. The Spiritual Exercises of ECK can help you do that.

> ### Tip: The Value of the Spiritual Exercises of ECK
>
> Once you understand that a frightening dream is a spiritual dream, you will find its power over you will lessen. The Spiritual Exercises of ECK will prove to you that Soul never dies.

Once you understand that a frightening dream is a spiritual dream, you will find its power over you will lessen.

SHARING DREAMS

My wife and son had a dream the same night about the same subject. Both were bitten on the foot: my wife by snakes; my son, by a monster. Is it possible to share the same dream? And what does it mean in the dream state to step on things like animals or to lose one's shoes? I've had dreams about misplacing my shoes and cannot start an important activity until I find them.

Two people can indeed share the same dream, especially when there is a close affinity between them. To your wife, the snake bites mean to watch for hidden or missing clauses in contracts that pertain to the building and furnishing of your new home. Watch for "snakes in the grass." The monster biting your son means for him to be aware of more obvious accidents around the home, such as the one he suffered recently. If attention is put upon the Mahanta, these minor irritations can be avoided, for they need never be more than that.

To step on things like animals means to be careful not to hurt the feelings of others by thoughtlessness. The image of animals, which are often thought to be inferior to man, means a lack of sensitivity to those on the perimeter of our own consciousness.

Misplaced shoes or articles of clothing that prevent one from keeping important appointments mean that one's inner life has outpaced his outer life. He must immediately set new goals in his daily life. This is so both worlds are brought into balance again; otherwise, he will be left with a gnawing feeling of misplacement.

Misplaced shoes or articles of clothing that prevent one from keeping important appointments mean that one's inner life has outpaced his outer life.

Soul's Freedom

I walked up into some hills, and it seemed like the Fourth of July. Thousands of people were sitting in the hills looking into the sky as if expecting fireworks. The sky was light blue and free of clouds.

I walked past the crowds until I was alone again and looked at the hills in the distance. They were like hard-packed sand dunes without vegetation. Suddenly, a flash of red went by and stopped long enough for me to recognize it before disappearing. It was me. That made me feel really old. Looking out over the ridge of hills, I saw that they had undergone a drastic change. They were much lumpier, and a huge boulder with green vines all over it had been raised ten feet into the air.

The dream felt very real. I had just gone through a doorway and was expecting a member of an ancient American race that I had just read about in a Louis L'Amour novel. But I woke up before he arrived.

This is what your dream means: Your walk up into the hills indicates that in the dream you were moving into a higher state of consciousness.

The Fourth of July is American Independence Day. The Dream Master used this image to evoke in you the ideal of spiritual freedom, which you can achieve in this lifetime if you set your heart upon it.

The thousands of people are your collective awareness—i.e., the sum total of your thoughts and hopes. You are awaiting the ecstasy of spiritual freedom. The blue sky signifies the Blue Light of the Mahanta. When you leave the crowds, it means you leave behind your worries and come to rest in Soul, the center of your being.

You are now in the Soul body and look back on the hills, which are nothing more than events in your daily life. From the lofty vantage point of Soul, your outer life seems to be a spiritual wasteland, especially when you let anger (the 'flash of red') flare up.

The image of the boulder is used in a double sense here. First, Soul studies the ridge of hills to see what harm anger might do, and It perceives "a much lumpier" life. Anger makes mountains out of molehills, or in this case, a huge boulder is raised ten feet into the air.

This dream gives a most exacting look at yourself. It shows how the Master may shape your dream to help you better understand yourself.

Second, green vines clinging to the face of the boulder show the power of envy or jealousy to undermine a relationship. Have you heard the phrase "green with envy"? The roots of the vines can, in time, shatter the greatest boulder, just as envy and jealousy can destroy the closest relationship, even one that seems "solid as a rock."

The member of an ancient American race whom you were expecting was the Mahanta, the Living ECK Master.

This dream gives a most exacting look at yourself. It shows how the Master may shape your dream to help you better understand yourself.

DREAM ADVICE

I have been having recurring dreams which involve me, my boyfriend, and another woman. In all the dreams, my boyfriend treats me like extra baggage and ignores me while paying attention to her.

We have been having difficulties in our relationship, and for some reason, I don't trust him. How can I tell whether my dreams are intuitive or simply represent my insecurities?

A relationship without trust won't last. What is the source of this mistrust? Does he look at other women when you are out together in public?

Dreams can prepare you for a relationship that may be coming to an end. They will tell you something is wrong. If your partner is showing less affection toward you, you must decide whether to try to patch up the relationship or let it go.

Think of your dreams as advisers. They may point out problems and offer solutions, but consider all the facts before deciding on any important issue. Especially watch people's daily behavior toward you. Your dreams may suggest what behavior to look out for, but don't break up a relationship without some physical evidence to back up your suspicions.

Think of your dreams as advisers.

No matter what happens with this relationship, try to be a greater channel for divine love. Love will overcome suspicion, which can destroy any relationship.

OVERCOME PROCRASTINATION

I have a recurring dream in which I'm back on campus. Suddenly I remember certain classes I have been forgetting to attend and will need to start soon to catch up and finish the term. Recently I had this dream again, but this time I was so far behind and the courses so difficult, I wondered if I could possibly make up the work. What do these dreams mean?"

The campus is at a Temple of Golden Wisdom connected with the Param Akshar Temple. The instruction is always an ongoing study of the Shariyat, the holy scriptures of ECK, but the significance for you in the physical world carries another meaning.

The Dream Master is saying that you have gotten caught up in procrastination. You are wrestling with its parent, *attachment,* a passion of the mind. This has kept you from the Spiritual Exercises of ECK and other spiritual pursuits.

You find it upsetting to be unprepared for these dream classes. Sit down with a paper and pen; and make a list of the material, financial, and spiritual parts of your life.

Straighten out the outer life, and your dream world will fall into place.

Straighten out the outer life, and your dream world will fall into place. One state reflects the other; it has to do with the waves of ECK that come and go.

Soul has actually wandered into a new region but has resisted picking up the ways and customs there.

This means that you have reached a new level of unfoldment inwardly, but the physical, mental, and emotional bodies have not kept pace. Set a new schedule of goals for yourself. Determine where you are today and where you want to be a year from now—then establish well-defined steps how you will get to that point.

This dream means: "Your mode of living life must be stepped up to keep pace with Soul. Set new goals and do this now!"

This will put you back in charge of your life again.

Tip: How to Interpret Your Dreams

Remember that dreams have a meaning at the human, emotional, causal, mental, subconscious, and spiritual levels. They correspond to the six planes of existence—the Physical, Astral, Causal, Mental, Etheric, and Soul Planes. Each deals with a part of you, and each of your dreams comes mainly from one of these areas.

Keep the interpretation simple. Look at each dream in one of three levels. Is the dream about your daily life, your emotions and thoughts, or about the pure spiritual side, your relationship with God?

Here, then, are a few tips:

1. Dream—get plenty of rest for a few days. Then go to sleep with the intention of remembering some of the places you visit while your human self lies sleeping. (It helps to write the dreams down as soon as you awaken.)

2. Interpret your dreams—ask the Dream Master (my inner self) to let you see each dream on three levels: the daily, the emotional/mental, and the spiritual.

3. Realize your dreams—take the dream lessons and apply them to your everyday life.

The ECK dream teachings can help you enter a better spiritual life through the doorway of dreams.

The ECK dream teachings can help you enter a better spiritual life through the doorway of dreams.

You can make this study of dreams as easy as you like. However, you need to give the ECK Dream Master permission to help you understand them.

Your consent can be as simple as saying, "Please, Harold, help me remember my dreams and understand them."

It's that easy.

My task is to help you become mindful of yourself in the real worlds, the dreamlands of God.

If you want your dreams to lift you into a higher state of awareness and joy, you have only to ask. My task is to help you become mindful of yourself in the real worlds, the dreamlands of God.

Sometimes a lesson derived from the dream state brings a healing.

9

Dream Healing and Help in Everyday Life

*V*ery often, dreams speak to us in specific detail. They show us what we need to do now to heal ourselves or better our lives.

In Germany, a woman on the path of ECK who hadn't been in the job market for eleven years decided to go back to work. Her husband was working but lately it was becoming more difficult to make ends meet.

The woman had been on her job search for a year. Every time she went on an interview, she faced rejection.

Interviewers told her, "No, you don't have quite the qualifications we're looking for." And every few days her husband would give her an ad that he had found in the newspaper in the employment section; he'd circle it for her and she'd call for an interview. But finally she didn't even call these places anymore because she was afraid of one more rejection.

Then she had a dream. In the dream, she and her husband were out for a drive when suddenly he pulled the car over to the curb. "My brother's over

Very often, dreams speak to us in specific detail.

189

there," he said. "I want to talk to him for a minute." So he got out of the car, and while he was off talking to his brother, along came two acquaintances of this couple, a mother and a daughter.

The wife leaned her head out the car window and asked, "Where are you going?" The mother and daughter said they were on their way home. "You can ride with us as soon as my husband comes back," the dreamer said.

As soon as the two women got in the car, they began to complain. The daughter complained about a broken necklace she had. She had tried to piece it together, but she just couldn't get it pieced together. So she just complained on and on about it. The mother complained that she had been looking for a frame for a certain picture for a long time. But she just couldn't find it.

After the couple drove the mother and daughter home, they took the daughter's necklace to a friend who was a jeweler and quietly had it fixed. It cost quite a lot. The husband brought it back to this young woman, but the young woman wasn't at all grateful. She just stuffed the necklace in her pocket without even a word of thanks.

Meanwhile, the dreamer's mother phoned around and finally found a frame for the older woman's picture. But the woman didn't really care for the frame, and like her daughter, she never bothered to say thank you.

She realized that the dream was about herself.

The dreamer woke up and wondered, *Why did I ever become friends with those two people? They are so ungrateful.*

The Inner Master said, "Look again." And then it struck her. She realized that the dream was about herself.

The necklace meant the need for something valuable—a job to bring money in—but it was broken. She tried in her own way to get the necklace fixed (find a job), but she couldn't. The second part of the dream was the picture frame that couldn't be found. This meant that the circumstances surrounding the job were never right.

She realized that when her husband cut out these ads for her—he'd been doing it for over a year—she was never even grateful.

After this dream, the ECKist realized that the Dream Master had spoken to her to let her understand something about herself. The dream helped her understand just where she wasn't facing up to her own responsibilities. She wanted to help with family finances, yet she wasn't willing to persist enough. But this dream gave her the motivation.

Letting Go of Fear

That Tuesday the woman called one of the ads her husband had just circled. It was an employment agency. The woman at the agency was not very encouraging. "It's a recession; it's hard to find jobs. I don't think I'll find you anything," she said. "But you can leave your name if you want."

On Thursday the employment agency called her and said, "You know, it's very interesting, but I think I have the ideal job for you. All you have to do is go to the company and take the interview." The woman who had the dream went to the interview. She got there early and sat out in the parking lot, very nervous.

"Don't worry," said the Inner Master. "Don't hang on too tightly. You've got to let go of your fears."

The dream helped her understand just where she wasn't facing up to her own responsibilities.

This is the meaning of detachment, she realized.

Detachment is
something we
know about in
the spiritual
life. It doesn't
mean not to get
involved; it
means to not
let outer
circumstances
throw off your
inner balance.

Detachment is something we know about in the spiritual life. It doesn't mean not to get involved; it means to not let outer circumstances throw off your inner balance. The ECKist heard this from the Inner Master through her inner feelings. She calmed down, and she developed the feeling of a child who expects only good from life.

So when the time came, she walked into this company, had her interview, and was hired. This was quite surprising because she had been out of the job market for eleven years.

The dream helped her recognize that she had been holding herself back from a better life.

DREAMS ABOUT YOUR HEALTH

Truth in the area of health matters is also taught through the dream state. These benefits come to the dreamer who has learned how to do the Spiritual Exercises of ECK and has made some degree of advancement on the spiritual path. The Inner Master will come and take the dreamer into some other world to give instruction in an area that needs improvement, so that the dreamer can walk around a physical problem and avoid a serious illness.

A woman visited the inner planes with the Dream Master. Together they walked into a large shopping complex. They entered a store and went up the stairs to a section that contained shelves lined with a colorful array of glass decanters for sale. Each one was filled with colored sugar water to make the display more attractive to the eye. She made her selection, and as they walked downstairs to the checkout counter, the Dream Master took the decanter from her and poured the liquid into a potted plant.

The manager, wearing a very impressive tuxedo, stood by the checkout counter watching the shoppers. It was a very high-class store; even the sales clerks were dressed in fine clothing.

The woman said to the clerk, "I'd like to buy this glass decanter."

The clerk said, "But what did you do with the liquid?"

The Dream Master replied for her: "I dumped it in a potted plant upstairs."

The manager got extremely upset. This was not in keeping with the style of the store. He and a couple of the clerks ran upstairs to see if any damage had been done to the plant, but when they came back downstairs, he said it was all right. The Dream Master stood there while she paid for the decanter, and then they left.

When she first woke up, she wondered what this dream was all about. Later she interpreted it to mean that sugar was bad for her, no matter how attractively it was packaged. The Dream Master illustrated this for her as a product in a store where everything was marketed with the greatest degree of class.

A certain aura of respectability had been given to this food by placing it in expensive glass decanters. But because it was actually bad for her health, the Dream Master dumped it out to show her that she had no use for it. She had been having health problems that she suspected were connected with sugar, and thus she was able to understand why the Dream Master used this example.

When she first woke up, she wondered what this dream was all about. Later she interpreted it to mean that sugar was bad for her, no matter how attractively it was packaged.

DREAMS AND DIET

A mother found that when her eldest son was in sixth grade, he was often sick on Monday mornings. The teacher concluded, "He's got school phobia; just send him to school." The doctor said, "Give him these medications, and send him to school." But the mother wanted to find out what the problem really was.

One night in a dream the mother got a nudge to begin checking her son's diet.

She recorded what he ate during the week and what he ate on weekends. And she found out he ate more ice cream on the weekends than at any other time.

The mother experimented. She found that when he didn't have ice cream or other milk products on the weekends, he was fine on Monday, ready to go to school. She concluded that he was sensitive to dairy products.

She could've been intimidated by the school officials, who were highly educated. They huffed and puffed and said, "Send him to school anyway." But she said no; she knew there was something else. Because the still small voice of the Mahanta was speaking to her and nudging her to look a little bit further, she found the food sensitivity.

Sometimes a lesson derived from the dream state brings a healing.

HEALING DREAMS

Sometimes a lesson derived from the dream state brings a healing.

An ECK initiate went to see her doctor about a certain health problem. He gave her two prescriptions which had proven helpful to other patients with the same condition. She took the medications faithfully for a few days but finally concluded that they were not going to work for her.

One night she had a dream—a very simple inner experience. First she saw a plain black screen. Then letters began to appear, one by one, each a different color, spelling out the word *Ornade*. She didn't know exactly what it was, but she had a feeling it was significant for her health. She woke up in the middle of the night and, while the experience was fresh in her mind, she got out of bed and carefully wrote down the word.

The next day she called the pharmacist who filled her prescriptions. "Is there a drug called Ornade?" she asked.

"Yes, there is," he said. "It's often used as a decongestant." As far as he knew, it had never been used as a remedy for her particular condition.

A few days later she went to see her doctor again. "The drugs you prescribed don't work for me," she said. "I would like to try Ornade."

"It won't help you at all," he said. "It's perfectly useless for your condition."

She felt foolish, but she told him about seeing the name in a dream.

She felt foolish, but she told him about seeing the name in a dream. She was very persistent about wanting to give it a try, and finally he gave in. "All right," he said. "I don't recommend it, but it won't hurt you."

He wrote her out a prescription. She went directly to the pharmacy to have it filled and began to use the drug that same day. In a short time she found that it worked very well for her, even though it was not intended as a treatment for her condition.

HEALING THE PAST THROUGH DREAMS

It is possible to get a healing for many conditions, like poor health, emotions, or mental stress. But not always.

The study of dreams in Eckankar begins with the fact of past lives.

The study of dreams in Eckankar begins with the fact of past lives. All conditions are due to karma, and some will last a lifetime, such as the loss of a limb. A study of dreams can help people learn the spiritual reason their life is as it is, and what they can do to improve their lot.

 Spiritual Exercise: How to Heal Yourself

A way to heal oneself begins with a spiritual exercise. At bedtime, sing the word *HU*. Softly sing this ancient name for God for five to ten minutes. Also create a mental picture of your problem. See it as a simple cartoon. Beside it, place another image of the condition as you feel it should be.

The second week, if you've had no luck seeing a past life, do this dream exercise for fifteen or twenty minutes. Take a rest the third week. Repeat this cycle until you succeed.

Keep a record of your dreams. Make a short note about every dream you recall upon awakening. Also be alert during the day for clues about your problem from other people. The Holy Spirit works through them too.

IF YOU DON'T LIKE IT, CHANGE IT

An elementary-school teacher taught students how to sing and play musical instruments. Lately she had found that teaching was taking a toll. She realized she was going to be exhausted unless she learned how to work with it.

One night in the dream state, she met the Dream Master. He took her into his office and held out a wastebasket. "Take your cares and worries, and put them in here," he instructed the woman.

So she put all the things that were bothering her into the Master's basket. When she awoke, she felt more rested than she had in days.

As the teacher went to work that day, the idea of dreaming was very much on her mind. In class, the children sang a song about daydreams.

The teacher suddenly asked them, "Do any of you try to change your dreams when you're dreaming?"

Most of the children raised their hands. "Yes, yes, we change our dreams," they said. They all wanted to tell their experiences of what they did in the other worlds.

The dreamer realized the Master's message: If something is unpleasant in your life, change it. You are the creator of your worlds, whether they are on the inner planes or out here. The Dream Master will try to show you how to make your life out here better because of what you learn in your dreams.

The teacher suddenly asked them, "Do any of you try to change your dreams when you're dreaming?"

Spiritual Exercise: Game of Chess

Lightly place your attention upon a situation in your life, then put your viewpoint as Soul above the situation. Look down on everything going on below as if it were a chess game—even though it might be in your imagination. You can look at a situation anywhere in the world from this viewpoint.

As you are gazing upon it, change the situation by simply rearranging your place on the chessboard. It's a successful device, and those who use it often make great changes around themselves.

OVERCOMING PANIC

Life sometimes puts you in situations that can cause you to panic. When this happens, you have to remember to calm down. To get yourself, Soul, back in control of the mind. That helps you think clearly enough to see what needs to be done. Then you can take care of the situation.

Patience and composure are among the attributes that help you take charge of your life. What can you do to develop these two qualities in yourself?

In contemplation ask the Inner Master what you can do to go slower.

In contemplation ask the Inner Master what you can do to go slower. Once you've figured out this secret, you can be patient. You can let the storms of life blow over you while you think of a way to find shelter.

Spiritual Exercise: How to Go Slower

One way to go slower is through surrender. Tonight, before you go to sleep, speak to the Mahanta, the Dream Master. Say, "I am a child of thine. Take me where you will, to show me the ways of God."

Soul—the spiritual principle, the creative spark of God—cannot work if you panic. Anxiety shuts down the creative centers. When you can't think, whatever you try to do becomes one blunder piled upon another. If you slow down, the spiritual principle can begin working through you so that you can figure out the solution to the problem that is bothering you.

Tip: Using Dreams to Understand the Outer Life

If I'm going through a particular problem in my outer life, I might try to use dream experiences to extract the meaning of that problem. An inner experience can give us an insight into our outer experience. The dream becomes like a play with hidden meaning, which gives us a clue about the outcome of our outer life.

From this level, I look at an inner experience for symbols. I know the experience was real, but I'll strain to dig out the symbology that will help me understand what to do to make my physical life work better.

An inner experience can give us an insight into our outer experience.

Dream Guidance: Plan Better

An initiate of ECK found herself with the Inner Master one night, and the Master was showing her a newspaper photo of a truck.

As she was looking at the newspaper, something jogged her memory. Three times in the past month she had seen a big truck driving down the road; each time the truck would suddenly go off the road, do a sharp U-turn, and get back on the road again.

The drivers hadn't even seemed to pay much attention to the near accidents.

When she woke up, she thought about the dream and the three trucks. She asked the Inner Master, "What do these three trucks mean?"

"I think that's something you have to find out for yourself," he answered.

This answer took her by surprise. So she began looking at her daily life and found she wasn't very careful about details. She drifted here and there, and the next thing she knew, she was off track. If she would plan more carefully, she realized, she wouldn't get off on all these sidetracks. She would stay on the road.

This woman is a very easygoing person who gets along well with others and is able to work with them. She was worried that she was not keeping on track, but she was actually doing very well up to that point. It was just that the Mahanta was saying, "It would be a little easier on you now if you made a plan and went for it, if you drove straight ahead and didn't wander off the road."

HELP IN BUSINESS

The dreamer was standing off to the side, watching as the accountants sat down and began to audit the books.

In his business a man had the responsibility of accounting for the funds of small firms. He hadn't kept his books up for a while, and one night he had a dream. In the dream, two young men came into his room and began examining the accounting books. The dreamer was standing off to the side, watching as the accountants sat down and began to audit the books.

When the man woke up in the morning, he immediately started catching up on his ledger accounts, straightening everything out. As he worked on this for a couple of mornings, his wife asked him, "Why are you taking care of the books when normally you'd be getting ready for work?"

"I don't know," he said, "I just have this strong feeling to do it."

On the third day when he went to work, two young men walked in the door. They were auditors; they had come to audit his books. And he was ready, all because he trusted the message he got from his dream.

Dream Help with Finances

In an African country where hyperinflation has taken over, an ECKist and his wife were having a very hard time making ends meet. They didn't know what to do. Some outstanding bills were about to come due, and the family needed money to pay them.

One night in the dream state the Mahanta came to the husband and in his hand the Mahanta carried a belt. Just a belt. He handed it to the dreamer.

The dreamer said, "What do you want me to do with this belt?"

The Mahanta said, "Tighten it."

So when they woke up in the morning, the man and his wife sat down and made a budget. They figured out where they were going to tighten their belts and cut expenses. And because they did this, they were able to cope with the inflation. They had taken measures to do it.

The dreamer said, "What do you want me to do with this belt?" The Mahanta said, "Tighten it."

Learning How to Help Others

A teacher in Sweden was in charge of young children in a public school. Lately she had been noticing the children quarreling among themselves; they seemed less happy than usual. And she wondered what she could do about it.

So one evening she went into contemplation and asked the Mahanta to show her if there was some way to help the children get along better.

That night she had a dream.
The Inner Master came to her and said,
"Talk about the happy things in class."

That night she had a dream. The Inner Master came to her and said, "Talk about the happy things in class."

The next day after lunch break, the teacher sat down with the children. "How many of you had a good time on lunch break today?" she asked. A number of hands went up. So she asked each of these children what they had done to make their lunch break a happy one. Some had jumped rope, some had played marbles, and some had played tag or another game.

When all these children spoke of their happy times at lunch, it left an impression on the children who didn't have a happy time. Then the teacher asked, "Who didn't enjoy themselves during lunch break?"

A smaller number of hands went up, and she asked them what had happened. Some of them said they were unhappy because someone had pushed them or hit them. The teacher then took the aggressor child and the victim child into another room, and she talked with them to find out why this happened. It was one reason or another.

Then the teacher said, "If you love someone would you do this to them?" She talked some more with the children. "Now can we be friends?" she asked them. And if the two agreed, they went back into the classroom with the other children.

As she spent more time talking with the children, they got along better and quarreled less. After a few days other teachers came to her and said, "The children in your classroom are behaving much better than our children. What are you doing?" And the ECKist was able to give this simple technique of discussing the children's lunch break with them.

This is an example of an enlightened person. She went to the source of wisdom within her and got what she needed to help her solve some of her everyday problems. You can do the same.

Tip: Don't Act Blindly on a Dream

If you have the ability to go into the inner worlds, you can find direction there. Sometimes it comes through dreams that tell you how to live your life better. Sometimes you'll get advice about what foods to look for, for your health. Other times it even helps you in things like investments.

But don't take this information from the dream world literally without testing it.

Just because it came from the dream state, don't drop everything and run off to Alaska, for example. Test the information you get as carefully as any scientist. It may not make any sense or maybe you wouldn't want to follow it, so don't.

If you have the ability to go into the inner worlds, you can find direction there.

Overcoming Fear of Death through Dreams

The dream world is an interesting one in that it has no beginning or ending. Sometimes you'll go to a certain house, again and again and again, but each time you go back, there may be different people there.

The dream world is a real world. It's a world you live in. It's a world you live in now, and it's a world you will live in, in full consciousness, when you leave this body.

That is why I feel it is so important for anyone who wants to overcome the fear of death to learn about the other worlds in the dream state. Because those are the worlds you're going to go to. But the distortions won't be there; you'll live there clearly. And they're usually lighter and happier worlds than here.

MEETING LOVED ONES IN DREAMS

A woman told me of an experience she'd had before she found Eckankar. She and her mother were very good friends, which is not always the case between parent and child. It's very heartening when two people have a close, warm relationship where the love and respect comes through.

One day the woman stopped in to visit her mother but caught her at a bad time.

"I'm in a real hurry," the mother said. "I have an appointment with the eye doctor." They only had a few minutes to chat.

The mother had always been afraid of death, wondering how it would come about. But on that particular day she said to her daughter, "You know, I've learned something over the years. Sometimes it's better not to know what's coming, because then you don't worry about it."

Two hours later she was killed in a car accident on her way home from the eye doctor.

As the daughter struggled to understand why

this had happened, a message kept coming gently into her mind: *Your mother will teach you more through her death than she did throughout her life.* The daughter didn't quite know what this meant.

Over the next two years she searched for answers. During that time she met with her mother in the dream state a number of times.

The experiences were so real that she knew she was there and her mother was alive, well, and happy. Every time they met, the daughter brought back a feeling of love and joy.

Still she kept wondering, *What is all this about? What is the meaning of life? Where is my mother? Why am I so happy when I see her, even though I don't understand what's going on?*

The woman enrolled in some courses on religion. One day in class the teacher announced, "We have a guest speaker today who is going to talk to us about Eckankar."

During the talk she began to get certain insights into what was happening in the dream state and how she was able to have actual meetings with her mother. She began to understand that Soul lives forever.

Soul lives forever.

Helping Others in Dreams

As you advance in the teachings of ECK and as love begins to enter your heart, you are able to work with individuals who are ready to cross the borders through death.

An ECKist changed jobs and moved to another city, promising to keep in touch with an older woman in her hometown with whom she had a long-standing friendship. At first the two women telephoned each other regularly, but as the ECKist began to build a new life and make new friends, she became less inclined to keep the ties with people in her hometown.

Several years after moving, the ECKist heard that the other woman had suffered a stroke. She felt a nudge to give her old friend a call. The two women had a very nice conversation. But the older woman sounded sad as she reminisced about the bridge games she used to enjoy playing with her sister Anna and two of their friends, all of whom had died. On the other hand, she said, she still found pleasure in watching the soap operas on TV every afternoon.

The ECKist had told her friend a little about Eckankar over the years. During their conversation she said, "If you like, we can visit in the dream state. All you have to do is ask the Mahanta."

During their conversation she said, "If you like, we can visit in the dream state. All you have to do is ask the Mahanta."

A few weeks later the ECKist got word that the other woman had died peacefully in her sleep a short time after their last conversation. The ECKist had a strong urge to converse with her old friend.

One evening while doing her spiritual exercises, she went into the other worlds and found herself in a setting similar to the physical plane, talking with her friend on the phone. The other woman said, "My sister Anna and our friends are here, and now we four can play bridge again." They talked a bit about the TV soap operas, and then the older woman said, "You know, I'm having a wonderful time here. It's a lot better than it was on earth."

The Christian concept of heaven is outmoded—frozen in time from two thousand years ago. People of the twentieth century are not going to see beings who walk around in robes and sandals; they are going to find themselves in a heaven with people who dress in a modern way. The consciousness of the human race has evolved in two thousand years, and so have the heavens.

THE POWER OF DREAMS

A member of Eckankar who worked as a counselor to students in various county schools awoke one morning feeling so tired and heavy that he couldn't get going. He thought about calling his supervisor to say he would be late, or better yet, not go in at all. After a while, he dragged himself into the shower, forced down some breakfast, and started to get dressed, but all he really wanted to do was go back to bed. By this time he was very late for work.

While he was trying to make up his mind what to do, he suddenly realized that his fatigue was gone. He finished dressing, then got in his car and headed for work.

As he drove down the street, he noticed a boy sitting on a curb, crying. He wondered what was wrong. The Law of Noninterference seemed to suggest that he should just mind his own business and drive on by. On the other hand, he thought, the Law of Love supersedes all.

He pulled over to the curb and called to the boy, "Do you want a ride?" Normally he would never encourage a child to accept a ride from a stranger, but this case felt like an exception.

The boy tentatively walked over to the car, tears streaming down his cheeks. The ECKist unlocked the door to let him in. "Let's go for a ride and talk," he said.

They drove along in silence for a while to allow

The Law of Noninterference seemed to suggest that he should just mind his own business and drive on by. On the other hand, he thought, the Law of Love supersedes all.

the boy a little time to compose himself. Finally the ECKist asked the boy, "Why are you crying?"

"I just got suspended from school," the boy said.

"Why?"

"The teacher told us to write a paper on a love relationship we have with someone. I wrote about my parents."

"Why would that cause a suspension?" the ECKist asked.

"My parents died in a car wreck four years ago," the boy explained. "But they come to me in dreams, and I know they're always with me. That's the only love relationship I have. That's why I wrote about it."

The ECKist was intrigued by this story. "What happened when you handed in your paper?" he asked.

"The teacher read it in front of the class and made fun of me. He said I hadn't adjusted to the death of my parents, and that I needed counseling."

Why would the teacher say such a thing to a boy in front of his classmates? The ECKist could imagine the effect that would have on a child.

The boy went on to say that he was sent to the principal's office, then taken to see the school counselor. Together they tried to convince him that the visits from his parents were not real, they were just figments of his imagination.

"That's not so," the boy protested. "I actually see them. It's just the way I wrote it."

"You're imagining the whole thing," they insisted.

"No, I'm not," he said. "It's true."

When he continually refused to admit that he had made up the story, they got fed up with him and sent him home on a three-day suspension. He had just left the school when the ECKist drove by

"My parents died in a car wreck four years ago," the boy explained. "But they come to me in dreams."

and saw him sitting on the curb.

"I bet you don't believe me either," the boy said defensively.

"Oh, I wouldn't say that." The ECKist knew in certain instances people who had left the physical body were able to keep in contact with loved ones, for the bond of love is stronger than death.

"Have you ever heard of Eckankar?" the boy asked. The question just came out of the blue, and the ECKist was taken completely by surprise. Without a word, he took his left hand off the steering wheel and held it out to show the boy his ECK insignia ring. The boy took one look and burst into tears all over again.

He began to tell the ECKist a little more about himself. He was ten years old and living on the West Coast when his parents, both ECK initiates, were killed in an automobile accident. Since there were no other relatives, he was made a ward of the state. Checking into his background, the California officials discovered that he was originally from the East Coast, so they sent him back to the state of his birth. He was placed in a foster home with a family of Seventh-Day Adventists, who constantly tried to convert him to their beliefs.

For four long years, this young boy had held fast to the ECK teachings he had studied with his parents, which his parents continued to impart to him in the dream state. But on this particular day, as he sat all alone on the curb, he wondered if the Mahanta had forgotten him.

"Would you like me to go back to school with you and try to straighten this out?" the ECKist offered. As a counselor for the county, he was acquainted with the principal of that school. The boy said yes,

For four long years, this young boy had held fast to the ECK teachings he had studied with his parents, which his parents continued to impart to him in the dream state.

he would like that very much.

They went back to the school and had a meeting with the principal, who confirmed the boy's story.

"This isn't a matter of lying," the ECKist said. "It's a matter of freedom of religion. Eckankar is this boy's religion, and it teaches that Souls are able to communicate in the dream state with their loved ones if they so choose."

The principal looked doubtful.

"Furthermore," the ECKist added, "I am a member of Eckankar, too, and I share his beliefs."

The principal quickly backed down. "There has obviously been some misunderstanding here," he said. "We'll get him back in class immediately."

Contact with the other worlds helps one lose the fear of death, and that removes the fear of living here and now, today. This is what we offer in Eckankar, by showing people how to have a conscious awareness of experiences on the other planes, both in the dream state and through Soul Travel.

Contact with the other worlds helps one lose the fear of death, and that removes the fear of living here and now, today.

These dream teachers, the ECK Masters, are often with people for their entire lives—long before they've ever heard of Eckankar.

10

Experiences with ECK Masters

*A*n ECKist on the East Coast put a listing in the local Eckankar newsletter so people could call a special number at her house for information on local events. She installed a separate phone and hooked up an answering machine to take the calls.

About 11:30 one night, a man called and left an unusual message. He had fallen asleep and had a dream. In it, a man he described as being on the thin side, dressed in a nightshirt, had told him, "Dial one for long distance, then these ten digits." The dreamer didn't realize it, but this was the Inner Master.

The dreamer was startled awake. Without knowing why, he had an urge to call the number right away. It turned out to be the information phone at the ECKist's house in a neighboring state. Since he hadn't left a number, the woman was unable to call him back.

A second call came the next night, about 3:30 a.m. In this message, the caller described himself as a simple farmer in North Carolina. All he was trying to do, he said, was get some sleep, but these

He had fallen asleep and had a dream. In it, a man told him, "Dial one for long distance, then these ten digits."

strangers kept interrupting, telling him to call the same number.

This time there were two men in the dream. "The man in the nightshirt was with another fellow. He had dark, wavy hair and appeared to be of Mongolian descent," the caller said. This, of course, was the Tibetan ECK Master Rebazar Tarzs.

A few days later he called again, and the ECKist answered the phone. The man had never heard of Eckankar, and he wanted to find out what it was all about. The ECKist told him a little about dream travel and Soul Travel. She also talked about the Sound and Light of God, and the word *HU*. The man began to open up to her.

While in the army, a near-death experience had frightened him very much.

While in the army, he said, he had gotten very ill. He'd had a Code Blue, a near-death experience that had frightened him very much. He had seen his deceased mother and aunt, who now lived on the Astral Plane. "There is a beautiful world here," they said. "We can show it to you if you want to come with us." The choice was his: stay on earth or come to this other world.

Inwardly he decided to stay; outwardly the doctors revived him. But he had been terrified of death ever since. Now, he said, the men in the dream were telling him, "If you want to get over your fear of death, call this number."

He said the men in the dream were telling him, "If you want to get over your fear of death, call this number."

On top of that, he was now having out-of-body experiences. "I'm worried that I'm losing my mind," he said, "because I seem to have this separation from the body. I'm not quite sure, but I think I'm going crazy."

"No," said the ECKist. "It's a very normal thing." She explained to him that there were quite a few people in Eckankar who had the very same experiences. "Once you get used to it, you won't find it fearful at all. You'll find it joyful to be able to move with such freedom, even while still here in the physical body."

The next time the man called, he said, "I've been Soul Traveling to your town." He accurately described the streets and a river nearby. "I find myself in these rooms where people are sitting in small groups, talking about spiritual things. At other times I'm in some sort of temple." He sounded less upset now, as if he was beginning to accept these new developments.

The next time the man called, he said, "I've been Soul Traveling to your town."

MEETING THE MASTER AGAIN

A letter came recently. It was addressed to Mr. Klemp from someone who's not a member of ECK. This woman went to an Eckankar open house in one of the southern states of the U.S. Her husband wanted to go and she didn't, but she went along anyway. Here are her words:

"When I first went in, I felt like I was among people I knew. I told myself it was because they were so friendly. Then I saw your picture, and I thought, *I've seen him, I know him from somewhere— must be TV or some magazine.*"

While she was at the open house, someone invited her to listen to a tape about HU, the love song to God. "I realized," she writes, "that I had dreamed all of it just a couple of nights before. I'd been there in my dream. I also realized that I knew you from my dreams.

"The first time I saw you, you were on a porch and you turned to face me as I came up to you. It startled me, for I didn't know you were there until you turned. Our eyes met, and I could tell you meant me no harm. And all my fears left me.

"You said, 'I can help you.' I said, 'No, you can't. No one can.'

"You again told me, 'I can help you.'

"We stood and looked at one another, and I could read you through your eyes. And I was aware that you could read me through mine.

"You told me a third time, 'I can help you. But you must accept it, you must believe me.' You smiled at me, and I thought, *But I know you.* And you said, 'Yes, you know me. But not as who you are now. I've been waiting for you to come to me.'

"And I asked, 'Where did you wait for me?'

"'Where I'm supposed to wait. You lost your way, but I knew you'd find it.'

"And I said, 'I almost know who you are. By what name are you called?' And as I tried to remember it, I woke up."

DREAM MASTER VISIT

"I'll probably never meet you in person. I'm writing you this just to share the experience I had with you in my dreams."

The Inner Master came to her again in another dream. She writes, "I was in a garden somewhere, and suddenly you were there and you said, 'See, I found you.' And we both began to laugh, and I woke up laughing. But I remembered your face; it was the same face in the photograph at the open house today.

"I'll probably never meet you in person. I'm writing you this just to share the experience I had with you in my dreams."

She goes on to say that she and her husband probably won't become members because her husband doesn't have the ability to visualize. A lot of times if a mate isn't ready, the other person says, "My mate's not ready, but I know about you and we can meet in the dream state."

I get these letters, but I don't often share them because its sounds immodest. And it probably is, highly so. I can't help it. If I don't tell you about this, who's going to? I'm simply doing it to give instances of the power of Divine Spirit working through the teachings of ECK, which are alive and dynamic, such as you won't find anywhere else on earth. This is a very direct path to God.

This is a very direct path to God.

✳ Spiritual Exercise: The Dhyana Technique

The Dhyana technique is simple: you gaze steadily at the shining face of the Living ECK Master on the inner screen of the mind. Keep this exercise to a half hour maximum unless you are getting results. These results should be that the Master steps into your attention and begins to lift you out of the body to start traveling into the higher worlds.

When you have your attention fixed on the Master's image, start singing his name. You can sing *Harji, Wah Z,* or simply *Z.* The Living ECK Master awaits you in his radiant form. He is always here looking for his beloved follower to arrive in Soul body.

HELP FROM ECK MASTERS

The ECK Masters sometimes work in the dream state, and sometimes they help more directly, if people are in trouble and need protection when something comes up very quickly.

These Masters are here to help you.

When the time is right and you need the help, you will find someone like Rebazar Tarzs or Paul Twitchell, who founded the modern-day teachings of Eckankar. They will come, and they'll help you.

You may wonder, *Why would these people help me, a stranger?* Sometimes people ask me about this, saying, "After all, I'm a Christian. I don't believe in ECK Masters." But remember that one of the principles in ECK is reincarnation. Nearly 99 percent of the people who come to ECK in this lifetime have been a follower of ECK in the past under one of these ECK Masters.

We provide pictures of the ECK Masters for this reason. Some of them are in our books; sometimes we have them available in other ways, like at the ECK centers. We do this for the new people, those who come to Eckankar for the first time, so that they may recognize one of their dream teachers.

These dream teachers, the ECK Masters, are often with people for their entire lives—long before they've ever heard of Eckankar.

These dream teachers, the ECK Masters, are often with people for their entire lives—long before they've ever heard of Eckankar.

HELP TO MOVE BEYOND FEAR

The Mahanta, the spiritual leader of Eckankar, is the Dream Master. His sole purpose is to help people find spiritual freedom, and he often comes to a person in the dream state to give love, wisdom, and advice as needed.

He and other ECK Masters often appear to a woman named Mary, who lives in New York. They have shown her what love is and what love is not. At work, Mary used to care too much about social acceptance, even if it meant staying at lunch far beyond the usual lunch hour. She often ate with the office gossip circle. This "in" crowd fed upon the latest happenings at work, but Mary grew more and more uneasy in that group, so she finally quit going to lunch with them. But to reach that decision, she first had to deal with her fear of being an outsider. Now she feels more in balance and at peace.

Then she had a dream about fear.

Lai Tsi, one of Mary's favorite ECK Masters, often appears in her dreams to teach about things like love and fear. She loves him for his strength and gentleness.

One night Mary had asked for his guidance and ended up with a potent yet frightening dream. She dreamed she had brought home an inmate. She never thought of him as a prison inmate, but simply as a human being in need of food, shelter, love, and care. Later, her suspicions about him began to mount. Why had he been in prison? As her curiosity grew, so did his anger and ill-treatment of her. Then he had his friends over, and they disrupted what little peace remained in her home.

She awoke in a panic. Angrily, she asked Lai Tsi how he could have allowed her to have such a frightening dream.

Then she understood its meaning.

Lai Tsi had indeed been loving to her. He stood by, giving her protection, though he let her have a traumatic look at how fear was destroying her life.

Who was the inmate? He was a symbol for the energy current of fear she had been carrying with her for a long time. Mary had housed it, nurtured it, and slept with it, not fully aware of its basic negativity. Once she took note of its sinister force, it gained momentum and began to avenge itself

Lai Tsi, one of Mary's favorite ECK Masters, often appears in her dreams to teach about things like love and fear.

upon her. Fear had always been a threat to her very existence and inner security.

All the attention she had showered upon fear had come back to her like a boomerang. It had been destroying her life. From that dream, she realized the need to get a grip on her fears if she ever wanted to find peace.

In the end, she was grateful to Lai Tsi for this dream.

SPIRITUAL PERSPECTIVE

When the time is right, one of the ECK Masters on the inner planes will give a person very clear instructions on how to find Eckankar. When this happens, an ECKist doesn't really have to do much more than direct them toward the ECK books, if they even want that. Because from then on, the Inner Master takes over and helps the individual on his own path home to God.

Some of these experiences also happen to people in other religions. If they don't have the spiritual perspective we learn in Eckankar, they become fearful and wonder if they're losing their mind.

Some of these experiences also happen to people in other religions. If they don't have the spiritual perspective we learn in Eckankar, they become fearful and wonder if they're losing their mind.

But others are more open to the guidance they are given on the inner planes. They will find their way to an ECKist, who will tell them about the Light and Sound of God.

SPIRITUAL EXPERIENCES AS A CHILD

A man had been visited by different spiritual travelers since he was a baby. It began one night when he was lying in his crib. He was about two or three years old, and he remembers looking out the window at some stars.

Then he noticed one star that began to move sideways, first left, then right.

Suddenly the star came zooming toward earth, right through the boy's bedroom window. It became two stars, a blue one and a white one. An instant later two spiritual travelers stood there in the bedroom. They glowed with light and goodness. They were ECK Masters who work on the inner planes to teach Soul.

One of the spiritual travelers looked at the child. "Don't be afraid," he said. "We came to you because of your love."

The boy climbed out of his crib and went to wake his parents. As he was walking toward their bed, he heard one of the spiritual travelers say, "He's not ready yet." Then they were gone.

The next time this young person ran into an ECK Master was when he was living in Indiana as a college student. He was on his way to the library when a very tall beggar approached him. The beggar with very clear eyes looked at the young man and said, "Excuse me, could I borrow two dollars?"

The young man had ten dollars on him, "Here, have three," he said. "I only need two," the beggar replied. Then the beggar looked carefully at the young man. "In case you're interested," he said, "Paul Twitchell is giving a talk in town tonight."

"Paul Twitchell," the young man said, not recognizing the name. "What's he talking about?" The beggar told him. *This guy's some kind of spiritual nut,* the young man thought. "Uh, no, thanks," he said.

He reached into his wallet to pull out the two dollars so he could be on his way. As he handed the beggar the money, the beggar said to him, "The blessings of God, the Sugmad, are with you." Then

As he handed the beggar the money, the beggar said to him, "The blessings of God, the Sugmad, are with you."

the beggar turned and disappeared into the crowd.

The third time the young man met an ECK Master was in the dream state when he was a soldier in Vietnam. Gopal Das, an ECK Master who served years ago in Egypt during his term as the Mahanta, the Living ECK Master, took the soldier out of the body into the high planes of God every night.

They attended a spiritual study class at one of the Temples of Golden Wisdom on the inner planes, but after a time the young man got tired of these journeys. School was not his idea of spiritual adventures. Gopal Das said to him, "If you leave the class we won't meet again." But the young man decided to explore elsewhere.

Years later the young man discovered the path of ECK. He realized then how precious the gift of meeting these ECK Masters was. As the spiritual travelers worked with him, he had expanded his awareness of the inner worlds and developed the self-discipline that's needed to learn spiritually.

As the spiritual travelers worked with him, he had expanded his awareness of the inner worlds and developed the self-discipline that's needed to learn spiritually.

THE MOTORCYCLE MAN

An ECKist told me about her experiences with "the motorcycle man." She was only three or four years of age when they began.

Every night, just before she went to sleep, she would hear a motorcycle coming down the street. The driver would rev the motor as he brought the motorcycle in through the front door and down to the basement. She could hear the motor humming very quietly as the driver came up the stairs. But as soon as he walked into her room, she would quickly close her eyes.

She was always afraid when the man on the

motorcycle came while she was physically awake. But when she shut her eyes, the fear would dissolve. She could then see things as Soul.

And when the man said, "Want to go for a ride on the motorcycle?" she would immediately say, "Sure!"

Together they would walk down to the basement, ride out of the house on the motorcycle, and go on all kinds of adventures. The next morning she would wake up and run to tell her parents, "The motorcycle man gave me a ride again last night!" "You were only dreaming," they would say each time. But she knew it was more than a dream. The experiences with this kindly man, who was an ECK Master, went on for a couple of years.

LIGHT AND SOUND

When she was twelve or thirteen, she had another type of experience. It gave her the feeling of vibration.

This was the ECK, the Holy Spirit—the Sound Itself. She also began to see a Light. It came down the hall while she was in her bedroom at night. The Light always frightened her, so she would shut her eyes and eliminate the scene from her mind.

She was now having experiences with the two aspects of the Holy Spirit, the Light and Sound of God. They manifest in many different ways, and she was experiencing them in her own way. Although they were very real, no one could explain them to her.

She was unable to sleep because of the Light coming down the hallway.

She was unable to sleep because of the Light coming down the hallway. When she told her parents about it, they decided to take her to a doctor. He gave her sleeping pills so that she could get her rest, and eventually the Light went away.

This was the Inner Master coming in his Light body, which also is a manifestation of the Light of God. It's made out of the same spiritual fabric, you might say, as the cloth of God.

At the age of sixteen, the girl had a serious allergic reaction to a prescription medication. Too ill to get out of bed, she called out to her father. But it was late and he didn't hear her. Finally she began to pray, "Dear God, please come and stay by me. I need your love."

Once again, she saw this Light coming down the hall, but this time she wasn't afraid. The Light filled her room, and then It filled her heart with the most joyful love she had ever known.

Suddenly she felt herself being pulled out of the human shell. She found herself in the Soul body, in a world of beautiful Light and the sound of orchestral music more uplifting than she could have imagined. With the experience came healing, and when she awoke in bed, her fever was gone.

Long after the experience was over, she often wondered how she could find that joy and happiness again.

LOOKING FOR HAPPINESS

Long after the experience was over, she often wondered how she could find that joy and happiness again. As she got older, she became interested in psychic phenomena, and once again she began to have inner experiences.

She told her mother about some of them, and also about the Light and Sound and the feelings of love she had experienced when she was sixteen. This time her mother did not suggest that she go to the doctor for sleeping pills. Instead, she handed her a copy of *The Tiger's Fang* by Paul Twitchell, saying, "I think you'll find your answers here." Her mother also told her about *ECKANKAR—The Key to Secret Worlds.* "That book will explain where you go during your inner experiences," she said.

The ECKist has since come to realize that the Light, the Sound, and the love are one and the same. They all go together.

FIRST CONNECTION

A woman from Australia, whose first connection with ECK was through the dream state, recently wrote to request information about the ECK teachings. In her letter she explained how her introduction to the teachings came about.

She had shared a large home with her fiancé for four years, and when the relationship broke up, she moved to a dingy little apartment. Emotionally, it was a very difficult time for her.

"Can I do something to brighten up the place?" she asked her new landlord.

"Sure, go ahead," he said. She then proceeded to clean and paint until she had turned the apartment into a warm haven from the stress of the working world.

Several months later, many of the belongings that she had brought with her from the big house were still in boxes. Now that the apartment was fixed up, she decided to begin the tedious task of unpacking.

In a box of books she came across *The Flute of God* by Paul Twitchell.

That's strange, she thought. She hadn't bought it, didn't remember ever seeing it before, and had never heard of Eckankar.

The ECKist has since come to realize that the Light, the Sound, and the love are one and the same. They all go together.

It was an earlier printing of *The Flute of God*. The cover was a pretty, pale yellow, the same color she had just painted her apartment. Turning the book over, she saw on the back cover a picture of the ECK Master Paul Twitchell.

The woman immediately recognized him. He was the man who had come to her in her dreams for the past nine months.

ACCEPTING THE LOVE

The first night it happened, she was asleep when suddenly she got the feeling that someone else was in the room. Opening her eyes, she saw a light that grew brighter and brighter until it filled the entire room. In the center of this light stood a being, the man she later learned was Paul Twitchell.

He came to the side of the bed and, without touching her, held his hands above her. The power of the love of God she felt in him took away all her fear.

"Be quiet," he answered. "Just accept the love." And then he was gone.

"Who are you?" she asked. "What are you doing here?"

"Be quiet," he answered. "Just accept the love." And then he was gone.

He came back several more times during those months she was going through that rough emotional time in her life. When she came across the book and saw his face on the cover, she was struck by the fact that the book said he had died in 1971. Yet she knew he was alive; he had come and talked with her.

That's when she decided to write me to learn more about Eckankar.

Her letter had one date at the top. Ten days

later she had added a note at the bottom: "You'll notice that I didn't mail this letter after I finished writing the first part."

She explained that a few days after she wrote the letter to me, Paul Twitchell came to her again, surrounded by light.

He said, "You now have the Light and Sound of God," and he left. After meeting Paul and experiencing the Light of God, she knew that the power of love had more meaning in her life than she had ever realized.

A Dream with Rebazar Tarzs

In the early 1930s, a girl in the first grade had a series of very vivid dreams on a similar theme. She was in a candle-lit cavern full of buried bodies. Wolves were growling in the distance, and she could hear them running after her. The dream repeated itself for several nights.

One night the wolves caught up with her, and she called out for help. Instantly two men appeared, one dressed in a maroon robe. The man said, "Turn around, and face them." But the girl was too afraid.

The next night, as she ran through the cavern, the girl noticed that the candles were flickering. They were almost used up. "I'd rather die in the light than in the dark," she said and turned to face the wolves. To her surprise, they vanished. The two men were standing next to her, smiling.

Through the years, the girl continued to have dream experiences with the man in the maroon robe. He emanated such love and kindness that she grew to trust him. As she grew older, he began appearing in her outer life in dramatic ways. Once

After meeting Paul and experiencing the Light of God, she knew that the power of love had more meaning in her life than she had ever realized.

she saw him save her parents from two men who were trying to kill them. Another time his whispered instructions helped her rescue a cousin who was drowning.

It wasn't until 1940, in her sophomore year of high school, that the woman was able to learn the man's name. It was Rebazar Tarzs.

Still following Catholicism, the woman began meeting with both Jesus and Rebazar in her dreams. One night, Jesus told her that she would begin studying exclusively with Rebazar. When she met Rebazar the next night, she asked him why.

"It's time to move on to higher planes. Jesus teaches up to this region, but it is time to go on." The next night the woman sought out Jesus and asked about what Rebazar had said. He repeated the same thing, saying, "Now return to your Master."

In 1970, when the woman read Paul Twitchell's *ECKANKAR—The Key to Secret Worlds,* she was very surprised to learn that Paul had known Rebazar Tarzs too.

The ECK Masters taught this woman how to face her own fears. As long as you have fear, you will never have true freedom of Soul.

The ECK Masters taught this woman how to face her own fears. As long as you have fear, you will never have true freedom of Soul. This is the whole point of Eckankar: to teach the individual how to reach spiritual freedom and go back to God in this lifetime.

Spiritual Exercise:
Beach Walk with Rebazar Tarzs

If you would like to try a Soul Travel exercise, here is an easy one that should let you meet the ECK Master Rebazar Tarzs or enjoy a short journey into the heavens of God.

Picture yourself on a beach, walking in the sand at the edge of the water. The warm waves wash about your feet, and a light spray from the ocean leaves a refreshing mist on your face. Overhead, white gulls sail silently on the wind.

Now breathe in as the incoming waves wash toward you on the beach. Then on the outgoing breath, sing *Rebazar* (REE-bah-zahr) softly in rhythm with the waves returning to the sea. Do this exercise for twenty to thirty minutes every day. After you are skilled at this exercise, Rebazar will come and give you the wisdom of God.

If you live near the seashore, walk along the beach to get a feeling of the sounds of the ocean. Or imagine the feeling of sand under your feet, the ocean spray, and the many blue-green waters that reach the horizon. Use your impressions from the seashore in your daily Soul Travel exercise.

You may not ever see Rebazar or another ECK Master on your short Soul Travel journey, but someone is always near at hand to lend a hand, should you need it.

At first, you may feel that you have only met Rebazar in your imagination, but in time and with practice, you will find that he is every bit a flesh-and-blood individual, even as you are.

Picture yourself on a beach, walking in the sand at the edge of the water.

A DREAM WITH GOPAL DAS

A Japanese woman who recently became an ECKist had a dream. She was riding on a bus with a few other passengers. She mentioned to the bus driver that she wanted to be let off at a certain stop.

"That's a very dangerous place at night," he cautioned her. "You don't want to get off there by yourself."

"I'll go with you," a man on the bus offered.

The ECKist and the other passenger got off the bus. They were met by a woman, a child, and one or two other people. The ECKist could see the moon in the darkening sky as they walked down the road.

Soon they came to a path that took them to a house high up in the mountains. The man from the bus opened the glass door, and they went inside.

On one wall in this house was a picture of a man with long golden hair. "Who's he?" the woman asked.

"You remember, don't you?" the man from the bus said.

All of a sudden she did remember: She had come to this mountain home many times before, on that very same bus, accompanied by the man in the picture. The dream ended at that point, but she retained a vivid memory of it.

Shortly after that she attended an ECK Satsang (spiritual study) class. Sketches of four ECK Masters were displayed on a table as part of the class discussion. As she glanced at each one, suddenly her eyes widened in surprise. "That's the man I saw in the picture in my dream!" she said, pointing to one of the sketches. It was the ECK Master Gopal Das.

"That's the man I saw in the picture in my dream!" she said, pointing to one of the sketches. It was the ECK Master Gopal Das.

 Spiritual Exercise: Meeting Gopal Das

Sit in an easy chair with your eyes closed, and chant the word *Gopal*. Gopal Das is one of the guardians of the Temples of Golden Wisdom. He guards the fourth section of the Shariyat-Ki-Sugmad. This is the holy book for those who follow Eckankar.

The word is chanted in two syllables. It is a

sacred name and must be sung as *GOH*, then *pahl*.

Keep this up with a clear mind, and you will suddenly find yourself out of the body. You will be accompanied to the Temple of Golden Wisdom where you can listen to Gopal Das speak on the Shariyat-Ki-Sugmad.

You will be accompanied to the Temple of Golden Wisdom where you can listen to Gopal Das speak on the Shariyat-Ki-Sugmad.

When the Seeker Is Ready

About ten years ago, a soldier stationed at a military base in the Midwest had a persistent urge to keep a dream journal.

He wasn't quite sure why, since he didn't remember any of his dreams. But as soon as he took the step of keeping a notebook and pen by his bed, he began to remember dreams, and he faithfully wrote each one down.

Pretty soon the experiences changed. They were no longer dreams; he was going into the other worlds in full consciousness.

One day, while reviewing the notes of his travels out of the physical body, he realized there was a pattern. Although he was in a state of awareness greater than the dream state, he was not in control of this travel; something else was directing his experiences.

While the soldier was out of the body one night, a spiritual traveler came to him in the Light body. Also called the Nuri Sarup, the Light body is a glittering form that appears to be made of a million little stars. The traveler took him by the hand, and together they soared high above a city. This being then directed his attention to a Temple of Golden

Wisdom of such awesome beauty that the neophyte traveler was moved to tears.

GOLDEN WISDOM TEMPLES

There are many Temples of Golden Wisdom. Each houses a portion of the Shariyat-Ki-Sugmad, the sacred scriptures of Eckankar, which contains the secret knowledge and wisdom of the Light and Sound. These works are under the guardianship of one of the ECK Masters.

There he saw a picture of Paul Twitchell, whom he instantly recognized as the being who had taken him out of the body to the Temple of Golden Wisdom eight years earlier.

This individual was eventually discharged from the service and returned to civilian life. Eight years later, while browsing in a bookstore, his friend pulled a book off the shelf and handed it to him. "I think you'll like this one," he said. It was *ECKANKAR— The Key to Secret Worlds,* by Paul Twitchell. He took the book from his friend and turned it over to read the back cover.

There he saw a picture of Paul Twitchell, whom he instantly recognized as the being who had taken him out of the body to the Temple of Golden Wisdom eight years earlier. The memory of that beautiful temple came rushing back, and he finally understood the purpose of the experience.

Eight years earlier he had not yet been ready to come into ECK. He needed more experience, he had to overcome his fear, and certain other preparations had to be made before he could take this step to meet the Master. When the chela is ready, the Master appears.

The Mahanta comes in the radiant body that sparkles and shines with a million lights, like twinkling stars. The inner experiences occur more often and with more vividness in ECK than in possibly any other spiritual path on earth, because this teaching has the Light and Sound as its living elements.

The Light and Sound are the heart of ECK; they are the ECK. This is why Eckankar is the most direct path to God.

HOW TO VISIT TEMPLES IN YOUR DREAMS

There are several Temples of Golden Wisdom in the lower worlds, including the Katsupari Monastery and the temple at Agam Des here on the Physical Plane, as well as those on the Astral, Causal, Mental, and Etheric Planes. The ECK writings generally mention the main Temple of Golden Wisdom on each plane, but there are numerous minor temples too.

In the dream state or during Soul Travel, the seeker is accompanied to one of the temples by an ECK Master, such as Rebazar Tarzs, Peddar Zaskq (Paul Twitchell's spiritual name), or Wah Z (my spiritual name).

There the seeker can read from one of the books of the Shariyat-Ki-Sugmad. This is part of the ECK path. There are two volumes of the Shariyat in print here on earth, but many more are kept in the other temples on the inner planes. Sometimes the human mind cannot contain what the individual takes in while traveling in the Soul body. But even if he doesn't remember what he has read, the golden truth is within him.

There the seeker can read from one of the books of the Shariyat-Ki-Sugmad. This is part of the ECK path.

Though the temples on the lower planes are usually located in a building of some kind, on the Soul Plane and higher there is no such structure. Here you find the action of the Sound and Light working directly with you as Soul, coming into you to uplift and give the knowledge and wisdom to which your state of consciousness entitles you. Here it is impossible to speak of what you take in, because there simply are no words for it.

 Spiritual Exercise: Temple Technique

One of the Temples of Golden Wisdom here on the physical plane is the Temple of ECK in Chanhassen, Minnesota. Any of you who visit will find that it has a special character, a presence of its own. That presence is the love of God.

Go there with an open mind, without any ideas or notions about what this presence should be. Look around, listen to the tour guide, and just be there.

Later, if you are ever in need of spiritual help, imagine yourself back at the Temple.

Do this at some quiet time—in your private moments of contemplation or at bedtime. Ask the question that is on your mind, that you need help with, and then just go to sleep. Often you'll wake up in the morning with an entirely different view of the situation.

The Temple of ECK in Chanhassen, Minnesota, is here for a spiritual purpose, and it's not just for ECKists. It's for people of all religions.

The Temple of ECK in Chanhassen, Minnesota, is here for a spiritual purpose, and it's not just for ECKists. It's for people of all religions. You don't have to leave your religion and become a member of ECK to enjoy the benefits of the ECK Temple; just come.

No one there will be pushy; it's not our way. The missionary effort in ECK is unlike that of most religious groups in that we don't feel the need to push the blessings of God, as we imagine them to be, upon other people. To do that is to take on the burdens of these Souls, and the burdens are especially heavy when you push somebody who is not ready into your religion. You become responsible for that person.

An ECKist with any degree of awareness at all will not push others to come to ECK. If they come before they're ready, you'll have to help carry them along. And believe me, no matter how strong you think you are, you are not strong enough for that.

An ECKist with any degree of awareness at all will not push others to come to ECK.

Seeing Loved Ones in Dreams

An ECKist had a friend who had just lost a son to a drug overdose. The friend came to work that day very distraught, so the ECKist began telling her about HU and teaching her a technique to travel in the dream state to see her son.

"How do you do it?" the mother asked. The ECKist said, "Well, you say to your master or whoever you're comfortable with, 'I want to have a dream with my son.' And then you chant HU. It's an ancient name for God. It lifts you in your state of consciousness so that you should be able to meet your son."

The mother said she would try it, but she asked if the ECKist would do the technique at the same time and be with her in the dream. And the ECKist said, "Sure, I'll try."

So the mother went home, and the ECKist went to her home. That night the ECKist woke up on the inner planes in a hospital. She walked through the corridors until she came to a room, and there she found the son recuperating from his drug overdose.

The ECKist went to him and said, "Your mother is very concerned about you."

"I'm OK now," he said. "Just tell her I'm fine." Then they talked a little bit, laughed and joked, and the ECKist said to him, "I'm going to try to find your mother and tell her that you're OK."

She left the room, met the mother, and told her that her son was fine. In the dream state the mother said, "I want to see him too." And then the ECKist woke up.

The next morning at work the mother was very happy. "I had the dream," she said. "And in the dream, I remember you telling me that my son was OK." The mother hadn't remembered the full details of the ECKist's visit with her son, or the fact that the mother had then gone to visit her son herself—just the assurance that they had shared the same dream somewhere in the other worlds, the assurance that her son was truly alive. This gave the mother great comfort.

FINDING THE MASTER IN DREAMS

Some ECK initiates have experiences on the inner planes where they are helping a person find someone else.

Some ECK initiates have experiences on the inner planes where they are helping a person find someone else. They are able to do this in full consciousness. In the past, the dreamer had had the opportunity to travel through the mazes of a particular region—on the Astral or Causal Plane, sometimes on the Mental Plane—and he or she knows the territory.

A person who lives in Orlando or who has traveled to Disney World several times can tell you, from firsthand experience, the best time to avoid the crowds. But if your guide has never been to Orlando before, you're probably going to have a disillusioning experience at Disney World. You'll probably spend a lot of time in long lines. It's the same way in the other worlds.

An initiate woke up in a dream and saw a maze of streets. Three children were coming down one of the streets toward her. "Do you know where our father is?" they asked.

The dreamer had been this route before. "Sure," she said and gave the three children directions. Looking at it with spiritual symbology, the children were Souls, and they were saying, "Do you know where the Mahanta, the Dream Master, is?"

The children were Souls, and they were saying, "Do you know where the Mahanta, the Dream Master, is?"

Two of them ran off immediately because that was all the direction they needed. Soon they were out of sight. But the third child seemed to be having difficulties; he was a little slower in walking. The dreamer felt that the child had karmic problems which made it difficult for him to progress on the spiritual path.

The dreamer guided the child through the streets. They kept up a pleasant conversation about one thing or another, until finally they came to a wall that had a window in it, decorated with lights and little teddy bears.

She could act as a guide on the inner planes, working with the Dream Master to show people how to make the spiritual connection with the Mahanta.

"Here's the window," the dreamer said to the little boy. "I don't know how you're going to get through it."

"Oh, I know how," the boy said. "And I know what to do when I get through it. I get in the boat and row to the island, and there's my father."

When the dreamer awoke, she knew that no matter how inadequate she sometimes felt about her knowledge of ECK, she had something to give to others. She could act as a guide on the inner planes, working with the Dream Master to show people how to make the spiritual connection with the Mahanta.

This is one example of how an ECK initiate works with other Souls in the dream state. In this case, the little boy trying to find the island was a symbol of Soul looking for the Isle of Bliss, or Paradise.

A DREAM CLASS WITH FUBBI QUANTZ

At first, she couldn't remember the dream, but then it slowly came back. While traveling in the other worlds, she had met the ECK Master Fubbi Quantz.

Another ECKist, whom we'll call Nancy, awoke from a dream, giddy with excitement. At first, she couldn't remember the dream, but then it slowly came back. While traveling in the other worlds, she had met the ECK Master Fubbi Quantz.

"I haven't seen you at Katsupari in such a long time," he said. "Will you come to visit me?" She promised she would, and they parted.

Next, Nancy found herself in a garden at the Katsupari Monastery. On a whim, she decided to attend a Satsang class led by Fubbi Quantz. She slipped into his classroom and took a seat against the back wall, liking the feel of being a student. Fubbi had just told the class about a visitor from the Soul Plane. When he finished his introduction for the guest speaker, he called Nancy to the front of the room. The topic he gave her was, "Why God's Love Is Worth Anything and Everything to Attain."

Her situation struck her as humorous. She realized how quickly ECK Masters set to work any chela who accepts their invitation to visit.

Looking at the sea of expectant faces in class, she began to talk. She spoke of all the suffering that a person may endure, but how trivial it is in comparison to the happiness, majesty, and splendor of God's love. This is everywhere: in a child's hug, in a puppy's eagerness to play, and in the blooming of wildflowers on the lawn. The more we can accept divine love, the more we can receive. Yet accepting God's love is only half of it. The other part is giving it back through service.

Then she asked the class, "What can you do to serve?" This led to a spiritual discussion. Afterward, she asked them to pick a day, and at its onset to dedicate it to ECK. "See what happens."

This meeting with Fubbi Quantz was why she awoke so happy.

Secret Teachings

An ECKist from Africa, an electrical engineer, went to the home of a retired school principal to do some electrical work. Although the retired principal was up in years, he told the ECKist he shared his house with his father.

As they worked on the wiring together, the ECKist was telling him about ECK when a very old man came into the room.

"Hey, what are you doing there, telling the secrets of ECK to this child?" said the old man. The child, of course, was the old man's son, the retired principal.

"Hey, what are you doing there, telling the secrets of ECK to this child?" said the old man.

"They are not secret anymore," the ECKist said. "A man named Paul Twitchell brought them out to the public in 1965."

The old man thought about this for a while. Then he said, "I first heard about Eckankar in 1914." He described the ECK Master who had taken him to a Temple of Golden Wisdom in the inner worlds, the inner heavens. "He spoke to me about Eckankar. I see this teaching has finally made it out to the earth plane."

"What did this Master look like?" the ECKist asked.

How can you find the elusive love of God? Follow the example of the stories in this chapter.

"He had long blond hair," the old man said.

"I think I know who you met. I'll bring you a picture." The ECKist went home and found a picture of Gopal Das, an ECK Master who once served as the Mahanta, the Living ECK Master—the position I fulfill today as the spiritual leader of Eckankar. He brought the picture to the old gentleman, who recognized the face immediately.

"Yes," the old man said, "that is the man who first told me about the teachings of ECK in 1914."

How can you find the elusive love of God? Follow the example of the stories in this chapter. Divine love comes through giving, and in no other way.

About this time he had a vivid dream in which Simha, the Lady of ECK, appeared to him.

11

Active Dreaming

The dreamer's inner life begins to straighten out once he takes up the study of ECK. The arena of the dreamer's subtle worlds is graced by the entrance of the Mahanta, who erases karmic burdens through the creative use of dreams.

A common reason for failure in this study is that one accepts inferior spiritual goals. These ambitions include begging the Deity for better health, more wealth, or a loving mate, which are merely desires of the human consciousness. The only profitable object for any Soul is Its return to God.

The Living ECK Master introduces the most direct path back to the Ocean of Love and Mercy. He consistently points to the inner temple, where the Mahanta meets the dreamer.

The dreamer's inner life begins to straighten out once he takes up the study of ECK.

DREAM LETTER

The connection between the Inner and Outer Master was indicated by a woman from the Philippines who expressed thanks for a recent response from the Living ECK Master. "Around the time postmarked on your letter," she writes, "I received a similar letter from you in the dream state. I can recall only a few phrases now, but it has given me so much reassurance."

The dream experience affords a compatible teaching tool to the ECK discourses. It lets the dreamer sidestep the fear and doubt that often paralyze him during contemplation. With confidence he now greets the Inner Master, who lifts him into higher planes of heaven. Upon invitation, the Mahanta establishes an esoteric link between himself and the ECKist. Gently he removes obstructions of fear, depression, and loneliness. Thus the dreamer's consciousness opens to receive a measure of Light and Sound.

DREAM SOFTENS FEAR OF DEATH

The fear of death is softened through dreams.

An ECKist from the Great Lakes region in the U.S. says: "A couple of nights ago I had a dream . . . dealing with the fear of death. I was sitting by a campfire with the Inner Master and asked if Soul survives the body after death. The campfire started to move until it was under me and my body was consumed by the fire. When my body had burned up entirely, I could see that I was still there!"

He learned through his own experience that Soul is eternal and that It has no beginning nor ending.

Fear is confronted numerous times within the dreamer's kingdom.

Fear is confronted numerous times within the dreamer's kingdom. Another individual found herself lost in the basement of a museum. This image represented the imprisonment of Soul in the material worlds. Finally chancing upon the exit, she emerged from the basement into the outdoors. Instantly a tornado loomed on the horizon, but she choked down her terror by singing her secret word. A white light, like a ball of lightning, then swept toward her, causing even more fright than the tornado. As she continued singing her word, she lost her fear of the white ball of light that now blended smoothly with her aura. The tornado was forgotten.

Surrender to Divine Spirit conquers fear. An inner experience of the sort that she reported builds stamina to meet other trials in day-to-day living.

The fear motif emerges repeatedly in dreams. A chela from the West Coast of the United States dreamed of an attack by a pack of wolves. She called for help, and in response she heard a "pop." The wolves howled and ran away. Next, the face of Wah Z, the Inner Master, appeared on the screen of her mind, and this touched upon an important realization: Remember to call on the ECK.

And what is the Inner Master? Only the ECK! The Divine Power forms the matrix of a spiritual traveler with whom the dreamer has developed a close rapport.

INNER COMMUNICATION LINE

Eckankar seminars help set the inner communication line between Master and chela.

At an Eckankar regional seminar in Greensboro, North Carolina, someone told of having arrived there several hours earlier—but in the dream state. Word had reached him that the Living ECK Master wished to see him. A million and one details cropped up before he could get there. Personal burdens had to be resolved before the meeting. Perplexed, he wondered if the myriad details signified his unworthiness to answer the Master's call. The Mahanta soothed his concern: "Take your time!"

Eckankar seminars help set the inner communication line between Master and chela.

After cleaning up the odds and ends, he was ready to meet the Light Giver—first in his dream, and shortly thereafter in the physical.

GOING BEYOND PASSIVITY

People who look at everything in a practical, down-to-earth way often find it difficult to get into a higher state of consciousness. The higher mind is so powerful that when it sees the creative process begin—when Soul moves into a higher state of consciousness—it says, "That doesn't work."

"It doesn't?" says the lower part of the mind.

"Of course it doesn't," the higher mind says. "You can't do that. It just doesn't happen like that."

"Right," says the lower mind, "it just doesn't happen like that."

An ECKist wrote to me about this very problem. She couldn't get out of the body into the higher states of consciousness; she couldn't hear the Sound or see the Light of God; she couldn't have any of these life-giving experiences which are the food of Soul. "Please help me," she wrote.

She described a dream she'd had where she saw herself as a stone statue.

A group of ECK Masters were gathered around her trying to lift the statue, but she was too heavy. She was convinced the dream meant she was hopelessly fixed in the human state of consciousness and could never rise into the spiritual states.

"What should I do?" she asked.

Taking the material at hand to help the dreamer construct something out of that very dream, I wrote back to her to suggest she try a spiritual exercise I call "The Big Stone Statue."

Spiritual Exercise: The Big Stone Statue

Before you go to sleep, imagine seeing yourself as a big stone statue. Visualize the ECK Masters Peddar Zaskq, Rebazar Tarzs, Fubbi Quantz, and Wah Z gathered around the statue with moving equipment. Wah Z and Peddar Zaskq each have a crowbar, while Fubbi Quantz and Rebazar Tarzs are operating a tow truck.

Visualize Peddar and Wah Z prying up the edge of the statue and the hoist from the tow truck being slipped under it. The tow truck groans under the dead weight of the statue, but it lifts it. How high it lifts it doesn't matter.

The Masters now move the statue from one place to another—from the Physical to the Astral to the Causal Plane. Fubbi Quantz then drives the tow truck up a ramp into a Temple of Golden Wisdom where they have a restoration room. In this big, empty room the ECK Masters turn statues back into living spiritual beings.

The ECK Masters are all very happy that they have gotten the statue this far. It's a lateral move but better than no move at all. Fubbi Quantz carefully lowers the statue and sets it down in the center of the room. He brings in a few plants, including large ferns, and places them around the statue to make it pretty.

Now watch carefully to see what the ECK Masters are doing.

Each Master has a little can, which he pries open with a screwdriver. Inside is a very special oil designed to dissolve crust, the crust of ages that gets on Soul after being hardened by the problems of daily living.

The ECK Masters very carefully put this dissolving oil all over the statue. Remember, this statue is you. Shift your viewpoint from watching what is happening, to being the statue itself. Feel the dissolving oil being smeared all over you. After a moment, the crust of ages begins to crumble, and underneath it is healthy skin.

The ECK Masters stand back and look. "There's somebody in there," they cry jokingly.

They watch as Soul breaks free of the human consciousness. When this happens, the ceiling opens up and the sun, or Light of God, touches the real being that was trapped inside the statue of human consciousness.

As you progress in the Light and Sound, the ECK will begin to enliven your spiritual pulse.

Repeat the Big Stone Statue exercise for one month. As you progress in the Light and Sound, the ECK will begin to enliven your spiritual pulse. You will begin to listen, and you will hear the Sound of the spheres, which may sound like the wind in the trees.

Tip: See Yourself Alive in Spirit

Try the Big Stone Statue exercise tonight to see how it works for you, but don't expect too much at first; it may take a month or so.

The first step is the imaginative technique, which then takes you directly into the dream state, where there will be some kind of an experience. It may be totally different from the one you set up in the imaginative state, but you've got to start there.

It might help if you can see yourself with humor in a totally different environment, under totally different circumstances, being alive in Spirit for the first time. Once this happens, the ECK begins to enliven your spiritual life, which begins to affect your daily life a little bit at a time. You become able to work more fully in your true spiritual presence and to act more and more as a Co-worker with God.

SOUL TRAVEL IN DREAMS

An ECKist lived in an apartment. She had learned to Soul Travel in her dreams but often wondered why she never seemed to travel any farther than her apartment building.

Each time she fell asleep and woke up in the Soul body, she was able to see her Physical body lying on the bed. She would generally walk through her front door and out into the hallway of her building. And then she'd wait awhile.

Pretty soon, the Inner Master would come around the corner. "Where do you want to go?" he'd ask the woman. And she'd answer, "I want to go to a Golden Wisdom Temple." But the only place she went was her apartment building.

One night she asked the Inner Master why she never seemed to go anywhere else in her dreams. "Please show me what I need to do," she said.

"How did you learn to Soul Travel?" he asked. So she began thinking about the first time she had found herself out of the body.

She had walked into the kitchen, into the bedroom, and looked around a little. "Hey, this is great," she had said. Each step of the way she'd thought of what to do next. It took her awhile in the dream state to think of chanting Wah Z, the spiritual name of the Inner Master, but she finally did. This took her to another level. Then she felt she ought to be doing something else, but it took another bit of time for her to think of sitting on the couch and doing a spiritual exercise.

The spiritual exercise took her out of her apartment into the hallway where she met the Inner Master. This had been the last experiment she tried.

She had learned to Soul Travel in her dreams but often wondered why she never seemed to travel any farther than her apartment building.

Finally she understood why the Master didn't come up to her and just say, "OK, we'll go off to a Wisdom Temple. I'll do everything for you; you don't have to do anything." The Dream Master was letting her use her own creativity.

The Dream Master was letting her use her own creativity.

Most often a person fails at Soul Travel or dream travel because inside the individual is the fear of death. As this ECKist began to experiment and have the experience of Soul Travel under her own terms, it began to diminish this fear.

OPENING THE HEART CENTER

Many people want to know how to get rid of fear. Fear isn't something you can be talked out of. The secret to getting rid of fear is to open the heart center.

Spiritual Exercise: How to Open Your Heart

In contemplation or before sleep, imagine yourself sitting in the audience at a gathering with the Living ECK Master speaking from the stage.

Visualize the golden Light of God coming into your heart center, coming in so quietly and gently that you may not realize It's there. Imagine your heart center reacting like the pupil of an eye, opening gently to allow more Light to come in.

There is a way for each person to control the opening of the heart center and the flow of Light within. Ask the Inner Master how to maintain the inner connection with the ECK, the Holy Spirit, to find a balance that is right for you.

LEVELS OF HEAVEN

A spiritual exercise that will be of help in the dream state and also with Soul Travel is called the Formula technique. It was given to me by Peddar Zaskq (Paul Twitchell). It can help you reach any level from the Second to Fifth Planes.

You may want to go to the second level, the Astral Plane, which corresponds to the emotional body, to find out why there is an emotional bond with another person. The third level, the Causal Plane, is where you find the seed of all karma created in the past and learn about the past lives that influence you today. The Mental Plane is the level where mental processes originate, where inspiration and ideas may be found in whatever field you are interested in. At the top of this fourth level is the Etheric Plane, which corresponds to the subconscious or unconscious attitudes that motivate you. Then comes the Soul Plane, the level of Self-Realization, the first of the true spiritual worlds.

Like so many other ECKists, I used to go into contemplation and then drop off to sleep. I just assumed that my contemplation would carry over into the dream state, like a natural bridge. But so often when I had an experience on the inner planes, I would wonder whether it happened on the Astral, Causal, or Mental Plane.

I couldn't always distinguish the difference. Many of the experiences on the Mental Plane and the Astral Plane, for instance, are similar enough that sometimes you can't tell on which plane they occurred. It would be nice if someone held up a brightly painted sign in the dream state: "You have arrived on the Astral Plane!" But you can't count on it.

The Formula technique is like a visitor's pass

A spiritual exercise that will be of help in the dream state and also with Soul Travel is called the Formula technique.

The Formula technique is like a visitor's pass to the other planes.

to the other planes. It can even be used by a First or Second Initiate to visit the Soul Plane.

This spiritual exercise, which takes about fifteen to twenty minutes, is done at bedtime. It's very simple, and it goes with the sound of HU, a holy name for God. This is how it was given to me.

Spiritual Exercise: The Formula Technique

To reach the Second, or Astral, Plane, use Formula Two. First chant HU two times, then breathe deeply two times. Repeat it again—chant HU twice and breathe deeply twice. Then do it again—HU two times, breathe two times.

You don't have to set your timer, because all of a sudden you will know that it's time to stop chanting. Then go to sleep. If you do the spiritual exercise lying on your back, just roll over, make yourself comfortable, and very gently hold the thought "Formula Two" in mind as you go to sleep.

You needn't worry about it or perform some special ritual, such as lying straight in bed with your toes pointing up to the ceiling and your hands folded on your chest, or anything like that. Just keep "Formula Two" lightly in mind, and drift off to sleep.

If you wake up and remember something that happened on the inner planes, try to write it down right then, because you'll probably forget most of it by morning.

If you wake up and remember something that happened on the inner planes, try to write it down right then, because you'll probably forget most of it by morning. Writing these experiences down as soon as they come is a most difficult discipline. But if you can get in the habit, you will find the full spectrum of your life slowly opening to you, like the petals of a flower.

Going to the Third, or Causal, Plane, the plane of seed karma and past lives, is equally simple with Formula Three: Chant HU three times and breathe deeply three times. Repeat it again—three HUs, three breaths. Keep doing this until you know within that it's time to quit. As you go to sleep, very gently, without becoming locked on it, try to hold the thought, "Formula Three."

You can aim for the Mental Plane by chanting four HUs, taking four deep breaths, and falling asleep with "Formula Four" lightly in mind.

To visit the Soul Plane, chant HU five times, breathe five times, and gently think "Formula Five."

And that's all there is to the Formula technique.

Once you have any degree of success with this Formula technique, you will start to see a different texture to the experiences on each plane.

Once you have any degree of success with this Formula technique, you will start to see a different texture to the experiences on each plane. Try to see if there is a thread that runs through them. In one way or another, Soul will try to come through to give you what you need to know for your spiritual unfoldment.

Tip: Recording the Experiences

When writing the experiences in your dream journal, you will find it helpful to write at the top of the page which formula you used, to help you remember what you were trying to achieve that night. Then add the date and write down the experience. Eventually you will develop a feel for which plane you should be working on that particular evening.

WORKING CONSCIOUSLY
WITH SOUND AND LIGHT

The Sound and Light of God are very real in ECK.

The Light we speak of is the manifestation of the Holy Spirit at a certain rate of vibration.

The Light we speak of is the manifestation of the Holy Spirit at a certain rate of vibration. It's a rate of vibration in which the atoms of God can be seen. As these atoms move faster at a higher level of vibration, they can be heard as the Sound Current of ECK.

The Light is seen in many different ways, depending upon the individual's state of consciousness. It may come as a blue flash, like flashbulbs going off, or as a blue globe which looks like a very steady small blue light. This is known as the Blue Light of the Mahanta.

Another form is the white light or a yellowish-white light. Sometimes it looks like the sun but much more brilliant and pure. It can be seen as a green, lavender, or pink light. Jakob Böhme, the mystic cobbler, saw everything with an aura of pinkness about it, which is one of the preliminary stages of the Light of God. Any of these manifestations simply means that the Light of God is coming to show Soul the way home to the heavenly kingdom, to the Godhead.

The Sound does not come as the voice of an awesome deity speaking to you. Instead, depending upon your level of consciousness during contemplation or in the dream state, It can come in the form of music, the different sounds of nature, or any number of ways.

For instance, you might hear It as the buzzing of insects, the twittering of birds, the tinkling of bells, or musical instruments. What it means is that, at this particular time, the Sound of God is entering into you to bring about the purification of Soul.

In your dream state, return your attention to the Living ECK Master, who will appear as the Dream Master.

Spiritual Exercise: Dreaming Consciously

To learn to move consciously into a new or higher plane in the dream state, try this technique.

Before sleep gently place the attention on the Living ECK Master. In your dream state, return your attention to the Living ECK Master, who will appear as the Dream Master.

In your dream, anchor your attention on some solid object in the room. While you are focused, give yourself this thought command: *I am awakening in my dream.* As you anchor your attention on the object as a point of concentration, you will find yourself rising as if through veils of consciousness. You will move into a new plane just as solid as the physical.

If you fail to maintain your concentration on the object in the dream, you will sink into the dream state and awaken in a natural way.

The Light and Sound are actual, definite aspects of the Holy Spirit, understood and achieved through the Spiritual Exercises of ECK.

Sometimes people have experiences with the Light and Sound before coming to ECK, but they don't know what it all means.

The Light and Sound are actual, definite aspects of the Holy Spirit, understood and achieved through the Spiritual Exercises of ECK. Many of these are given in books such as *The Spiritual Exercises of ECK.* The ECK teachings are built specifically upon these two pillars of God in a direct, knowable way.

Tip: How Do I Get Back?

The question always arises: What should I do if I am consciously dreaming or on a different plane and I want to get back into the awareness of the physical body?

There is one basic rule: Assume with the sense of feeling that you are in your physical body. This will happen immediately.

SOUND EXPERIENCES

The Mahanta may sometimes contact a person years before he comes across Eckankar.

The Mahanta may sometimes contact a person years before he comes across Eckankar.

The person may have no conscious recall of the Mahanta, Soul Travel, or the Sound and Light of ECK. This contact, however, is made in response to his disillusionment with old religious beliefs.

For ten years a certain woman belonged to a metaphysical religion. During all that time she felt as if she had come to a dead end. It seemed that she had gone as far as possible with reality, at least in this plane of existence. What would happen to her after death remained to be seen. Perhaps nothing lay beyond death. Perhaps religion really was the great opiate of the masses. But in her heart, she did not fully believe that.

She finally took steps to remove her name from the files of the metaphysical church. All this took place before she heard of Eckankar.

Then she found ECK. But it was still several years before she actually heard the Sound Current for the first time. It happened at an Eckankar seminar in Chicago.

Until then she had counted herself outside the

group that would ever hear It. When she heard the Sound of God within her, she felt joy. During the intervals when It was silent, she felt empty.

This brief description of her experience gives only the barest indication of the grandeur and majesty of the Sound Current, which has the power to transform the life of an individual. It is a wave of indescribable proportions that flows from the Sugmad (God) to all creation. It is the purifier of Soul.

NIGHT SOUNDS

This next example is of a woman who heard the Sound years before she came across the teachings of ECK. One night, as she lay awake in bed, she became aware of a sound inside her that was difficult to describe. It was like a multitude of crickets, but also like many ticking clocks. The more she listened, the louder it became. The intensity increased until it changed into a whistle, or better, into the single note of a flute. The musical sound had the peculiar ability to be inside her, yet it was also outside her.

Now the Sound began to prepare her for Soul Travel, but fear prevented her from going on with the experience. She felt herself floating outward in the Soul body.

At the same time she was floating inward toward the Sound. Timidity got the best of her, and she resisted the Mahanta, who was trying to lift her into a higher state of consciousness via Soul Travel.

Today she wishes she had followed the experience to its end. After her reluctance in regard to

At the same time she was floating inward toward the Sound.

Soul Travel, the Mahanta simply continued by other means to insure her spiritual purification.

The Shariyat-Ki-Sugmad, Book One, of the holy scriptures of ECK, says that "the ECK descends and ascends in vibratory currents, producing life in all forms; producing music inherent and inborn that gives joy to the heart of those who have the power to hear Its melody." And "With this comes freedom, the liberation that brings to Soul the very essence of happiness."

CELESTIAL LIGHT

The other aspect of the ECK is the Light. Some people have experiences with It rather than with the Sound. It all depends upon the line of spiritual unfoldment they have chosen to follow in their past lives upon earth.

A boy of thirteen experienced the Light of God in an unusual way. One particular night a lightning bolt shot past his left shoulder.

The sky was absolutely clear, so he could not understand what might have happened to him. This incident took place about the time that he began searching through books for a truth greater than that of his own religion.

The Mahanta was responsible for this experience to further awaken the Spiritual Eye of Soul.

Years passed. One night he and a childhood friend were sitting outside on a car. Suddenly the whole southern horizon lit up as if it were daylight. They both sat stunned for a second, then asked each other, "Did you see that?" The Mahanta was responsible for this experience to further awaken the Spiritual Eye of Soul. No one else in the area reported the unusual phenomenon of celestial light.

By and by the young man moved to another

state and joined the Mormon Church. During his youth he had seen occasional flashes of light, and now they began to return. He was coming closer to the day that he would find Eckankar.

At a church meeting he tried to describe to others the Blue Light he often saw: it was about the size of a quarter and appeared at unexpected intervals. Nobody knew what he was talking about, since the Light of God was not a part of their experience.

About this time he had a vivid dream in which Simha, the Lady of ECK, appeared to him.

About this time he had a vivid dream in which Simha, the Lady of ECK, appeared to him. He had just fallen asleep when he found himself standing before a blond woman. She wore a blue robe and called him her son. She assured him that he was progressing well in his spiritual unfoldment, but he was to continue his search for truth.

What astounded him was the tremendous love he felt in her presence. It was like a wave rolling across the ocean. The wave of love was the Sound Current, which was pouring out to him through the Lady of ECK. That was years ago. Since then, Divine Spirit has brought a change to his life: mainly, fear is fading away. In its stead he is developing a compassionate, yet detached, love for all living things.

Divine Spirit has brought a change to his life: mainly, fear is fading away.

SERIES DREAMS

A certain woman had many important spiritual dreams since she began to study ECK.

In one series of dreams, she found herself exploring the rooms of sometimes a one-storied, sometimes a two-storied apartment. She awoke with the feeling that someone had been with her, but mainly, she just wanted to know the meaning of these recurring dreams.

*The spiritual
traveler who
had gone
with her
to this place
was telling
her that she
was now
beginning her
journey to God.*

The spiritual traveler who had gone with her to this place was telling her that she was now beginning her journey to God. The dream image of the one-storied apartment meant that in Soul awareness she was dwelling on the first plane, the Physical Plane. The two-storied apartment indicated that her dream travels were now taking her to a higher level—one step closer to God—to the Astral Plane, which is immediately above the Physical Plane.

In another dream, an ECK Master came in the Soul body to give her a blessing. He came again later, but this time in his physical body: to consolidate her inner and outer awareness of the ECK teachings.

She had quite forgotten the dream meeting with this ECK Master, the day she rode a subway in a city on the East Coast of the United States. The car was nearly empty except for a man sitting across from her and four people on the far end. She decided to use the time to contemplate upon God and shut her eyes to silently sing HU, the sacred name of God. The word raises Soul to an awareness of the Sound and Light of the Holy Spirit, the ECK. Once an individual contacts these two qualities of God, he will never rest until entering fully into God Consciousness.

When the train pulled out from the stop before hers, the man was still in the seat opposite her. She again shut her eyes to sing HU, but when she opened them an instant later, he was gone, nowhere in sight.

His strange disappearance haunted her the rest of the day. Late in the afternoon, she suddenly realized he was the same man who had appeared to her in a recent dream. In the dream he had greeted her with the ancient blessing of the ECK Masters. "May the blessings be," he had said simply, handing her a ring with many keys on it.

These were her keys to heaven, given to her because she loved God with all her heart; the holy name of HU was always on her lips.

Even today she continues to hear the divine Sound of God. She knows that God communicates to mankind through this Sound and Light. The sounds of ECK are many, but the one she heard recently was a clicking sound, which then became a medium-pitched tone that rose to an ever-higher pitch. The Sound of ECK, however It is heard, spiritually elevates anyone who is so fortunate as to hear this celestial melody. But one is twice-blessed who both hears the Sound and sees the Light.

Even today she continues to hear the divine Sound of God. She knows that God communicates to mankind through this Sound and Light.

OPENING THE INNER VISION

Another time she was in contemplation, and the Light came to accompany the Sound. Her Spiritual Eye opened to a soft white light.

At first she moved toward the light, but then the white light began to pour into her in huge waves. The Sound and Light were purifying her of karma, so that she would never need to return to earth in the seemingly endless cycles of death and rebirth.

Purification by Sound and Light is the only way for Soul to enter the higher kingdoms of God. Therefore, the ECK Masters endorse these two aspects of the Holy Spirit. Neither baptism nor confirmation give Soul the passkeys to the true heaven, which begins at the Soul Plane.

Purification by Sound and Light is the only way for Soul to enter the higher kingdoms of God.

WAH Z

If someone who loves God wants the divine melody and celestial light, he may chant HU. This is a spiritually charged word. Together, the Sound and Light provide Soul with the surest known way home to the Kingdom of God.

But if one is unsuccessful with HU, he may use another term in its place: Wah Z.

The woman in the following story was new to ECK. She attended lectures and discussions on the spiritual teachings, chanted HU as directed, but this produced no conscious experiences of either Sound or Light. A friend suggested she try chanting Wah Z.

One night, just before going to sleep, she felt a strong need to chant Wah Z, which she did not then know was the spiritual name of the Mahanta, the Living ECK Master. And when she sang it, a wondrous feeling of peace came upon her; moreover, a heavenly sound drifted down over her. This startled her, but she sensed there was nothing to fear. So she relaxed to enjoy the music from heaven.

It seemed "as though a chorus of angels and every beautiful sound in the universe had combined" to reassure her that she was not alone. The music soon reached a crescendo, was in her and of her, indicating that she was in and with the Holy Spirit. This kind of spiritual experience is highly uncommon in most religions, except for secondhand reports from the lives of saints. But ECKists are quite familiar with such experiences with the Holy Spirit because Eckankar is certainly the most dynamic and direct path to God on earth today.

The Sound gradually faded to where she had to strain to hear It, before It vanished completely. Yet the very essence of her room had changed, and so had she; tears of bliss and joy streamed down her face. Ever after she would hunger for that Sound, because It was the Voice of God calling her to come home.

DREAM MUSIC

A man wrote me of the following experience he had in a dream.

He said that whenever he was waking up from sleep, he would feel as though he were falling from a great height and as if he were out of the body. He said that he never felt afraid because he felt familiar with the vibrations of those heights. What was most interesting, he said, "was the beautiful music I always heard. Often I heard madrigals, with mostly female voices."

When he was waking up, Soul was coming back to the body from the higher planes. This gives the feeling of falling from a great height and is a Soul Travel experience.

Hearing the madrigal indicates Soul Travel on the Mental Plane, since this form of song particularly develops the Mental body. The madrigal is another expression of the Sound Current there in addition to the sound of running water.

Ever after she would hunger for that Sound, because It was the Voice of God calling her to come home.

Hearing the madrigal indicates Soul Travel on the Mental Plane, since this form of song particularly develops the Mental body.

Spiritual Exercise:
Golden Musical Notes

Here is a simple exercise to help you experience the Sound of ECK.

Sit or lie down, close your eyes, and place your attention on the Spiritual Eye. Chant HU. As you chant, listen carefully in a gentle way. Use the creative imagination. Try to visualize the Sound as golden musical notes flowing down from a place above you.

As you see them, know that each golden note has an accompanying sound. Listen for the melodies as they pass into and through you in a continuous stream.

Visualize something connected with the music that strikes a definite image on your mind, perhaps a stringed instrument, a flute, or woodwinds. First try to see, then try to hear the golden notes flowing down from this musical instrument. Know that you are listening to the melody of God.

Try to visualize the Sound as golden musical notes flowing down from a place above you. As you see them, know that each golden note has an accompanying sound.

DREAMS OF TEACHING

An ECKist often dreamed of carrying a small boy in her arms down a long white hall. She recognized the boy as a person she knew who had muscular dystrophy. He had no control over his muscles, and he was deaf.

She wondered why she dreamed about him so often. Sometimes in her dreams she carried him out of the hallway to a swimming pool. He had spent his whole life in a wheelchair, so on the inner planes she was helping him get used to a new environment. She helped him swim as much as he could, but in each dream the boy became sicker and sicker.

One day there was an ECK event on the West Coast. She saw the young boy in his wheelchair by a window. He motioned her over and signed to his mother, "I swim, I swim." He remembered what the ECKist was teaching him on the inner planes, something he could never do in his physical body.

A short time later the boy got very sick. Just before he translated (died), he signed to his mother, "I'm finished." The doctors were astounded because they had never met anyone who made the transition into death so easily with this kind of illness.

The ECKist was grateful that she had been allowed to be an inner teacher, to teach the boy in the other worlds and allow him to understand that life continues. Life always continues in a way that is greater and more beautiful than before.

Spiritual Exercise: Getting Answers in Dreams

At some level Soul knows everything. If there is something that you would like to bring into consciousness, here is a way to get help.

Before you go to sleep, relax and decide that upon awakening you will have an answer to whatever it is that you desire.

When you awaken, it will be in the forefront of your thoughts. At the moment of slipping from or into sleep, you are opened to truth and in direct contact with it. It is at this point that you will perceive your answer.

Immediately make note of it in your dream journal.

At some level Soul knows everything.

Learn the value of doing a spiritual exercise just before retiring or upon awakening.

We know that there is an answer for every situation that comes up in our life. There is always a way, somehow. What holds us back is our attitudes. Learn the value of doing a spiritual exercise just before retiring or upon awakening. It works to your advantage during these times of change in conscious awareness.

Dream travel is your ticket to a world of wonder.

12

Dream Travel to Soul Travel

*D*ream travel is your ticket to a world of wonder.

The ECK-Vidya, ancient science of prophecy, deals with the causes and effects that play in the lives of people, places, and things. One of its tools is the dream state. A person may use the Spiritual Exercises of ECK to visit some unusual and very interesting locales. The purpose is to learn more about oneself as a spiritual being.

Why go to the world of dreams?

Dream travel adds another side to human experience, giving an insight into life that would take lifetimes of ordinary living. The basis for the ECK-Vidya is that the dream worlds are as real as this physical world. So the people we meet there are also real—real people in real places. Each holds beliefs that reflect a sliver of divine truth. We can learn much about ourselves and the structure of the divine order by meeting people from these dream worlds.

To me, the dream worlds are actual places. Continuity of events is the same as here. Since most people there are not yet God-Realized beings, they

Dream travel adds another side to human experience, giving an insight into life that would take lifetimes of ordinary living.

267

also like to practice as many deceptions and abuses of power as they can get away with. For our part, we advance our own education by having to deal with them. Those experiences lend us wisdom and strength.

SELF-REALIZATION

In the inner worlds, I met two college students after class. They were going to the philosophy room, so I went along to pass the hour. The subject for the day was Self-Realization. The teacher felt it necessary to give a broader view about the many kinds of thought her students would meet in life. It was a study of different frames of mind.

The main problem I saw with her instruction was that it all came from a book. So I asked one of my young friends, "How does she know whether a certain set of behavior shows a person with Self-Realization, cosmic consciousness, an emotional breakdown, or some other state? How could she know the God-Realized state?"

"Oh, she'd know," my young friend assured me. "In fact, a student from this very class had Self-Realization last semester."

"How do you know he wasn't on drugs?" I asked.

"Oh, you can tell the real thing," she said. And of course, that opinion came from a person who had not had Self-Realization herself. But in her ignorance, she didn't know that.

People who like people are more likely to find success with dream travel than the vain or arrogant.

From my observations, people who like people are more likely to find success with dream travel than the vain or arrogant. The desire to learn requires a genuine love for something. Few realize that a deep love for God also implies a love for learning. How can one separate the Creator from Its creation?

So a dream traveler is merely acting out divine

love in making the effort to explore the inner worlds, while many so-called experts study the human mind and debate its experiences in the life of an individual.

Dream travel will round out your spiritual life. It is one of the most fascinating classes in life's schoolhouse. And the Spiritual Exercises of ECK are your passport to travel there.

Dream travel will round out your spiritual life.

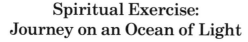

Spiritual Exercise:
Journey on an Ocean of Light

Tonight when you go to bed, close your eyes and locate the Spiritual Eye. It is at a point right above and between the eyebrows. Now very gently look for the Light, which can come in a number of different ways.

At first you may see just a general glow of light that you think is merely your imagination. It might appear as little blue spots of light or as a ray of light. Or it could look like a beam of light coming through an open window from the sunshine outside. The white light may also show up in any number of ways.

As you look for the Light, chant your secret word or HU, a name for God which has a power greater than the word *God* for many people. Watch as this Light turns into an ocean of light. Then, as you see It turn into an ocean, look for a little boat that's coming to shore very near where you are standing. At the helm is the Mahanta or one of the ECK Masters, who will invite you into the boat. Don't be afraid; just get in.

When you get to this point, allow any experience to follow that may. Set no limitations on it. You may end up in a video arcade, or you may end up near or inside a Temple of Golden Wisdom. Or you may have an experience of the Light and Sound of God coming directly into Soul.

SOUL TRAVEL AND
SPIRITUAL UNFOLDMENT

Soul Travel is one of several ways for us to experience the Light and Sound of the Holy Spirit. To draw a fine line, Soul Travel is different from the expansion of consciousness.

Life carries all people and beings onward to the expansion of consciousness.

Soul Travel is part of the whole, while the expansion of consciousness is the whole. Soul Travel is one way the Mahanta, the Living ECK Master may speed up the unfoldment of an individual. Other ways include dreams, the Golden-tongued Wisdom, events in family or business life, or a spiritual realization. Yet each of these is only a part of the expansion of consciousness.

Life carries all people and beings onward to the expansion of consciousness. For those outside of ECK, life is usually a winding road lined with blind alleys. This route to God, the Wheel of the Eighty-four—the cycles of karma and reincarnation—is a slow journey due to Soul's many lives in the lower universes. The Physical, Astral, Causal, and Mental Planes are the rooms where Soul toils in God's school.

As you study and check your dream journal, you're going to find that you remember your dreams better and better.

Experiences in the Sound and Light of God, however, accelerate Soul's unfoldment. The HU Song, singing a holy name for God, sets these spiritual experiences into motion. Some people then find a better recall of their dreams, while the Mahanta lifts others directly into the heavens by Soul Travel. Each experience expands their consciousness.

DREAMS TO SOUL TRAVEL

As you study and check your dream journal, you're going to find that you remember your dreams better and better. Soon after that, you'll move on to the next step, which is Soul Travel. This is a level of consciousness above the dream state.

The difference between a dream and Soul Travel is as great as the difference between imagination and a dream. Once you begin to Soul Travel, you'll continue to do it until about the time you become a Fifth Initiate, established on the Fifth Plane. At that point, you generally don't Soul Travel anymore. Instead, when you do the spiritual exercises, you move directly into the Soul Plane; or if you're going to work in one of the lower worlds, even someplace here on earth, you are there instantly.

There are different levels of learning that you are going to undergo on this spiritual path, and the first step is to use the creative imagination.

There are different levels of learning that you are going to undergo on this spiritual path, and the first step is to use the creative imagination.

Spiritual Exercise: Using the Imaginative Body

The imaginative faculty within yourself is like a muscle. You're going to have to train it day after day. What you are actually doing is learning how to become aware and observant of yourself in a different state of consciousness.

One way is to go to different places in your imagination. Maybe you'll want to re-create a plane ride: I'm sitting in the airplane seat. What do I see? What do the people look like? What happens when I walk down the aisle? What is on the food tray?

As you go through the day, you'll find yourself looking at objects and making mental notes, because that physical information about the dresser or the clothes in your closet will be helpful when you sit down in your chair and try to visualize it for Soul Travel.

WHAT IS SOUL TRAVEL?

In the 1960s, Paul Twitchell, the modern-day founder of Eckankar, referred to out-of-body travel as bilocation, but that term was misleading. He found that people had it mixed up with astral projection, which is a limited form of travel that requires separating the Astral body from the physical body. In astral projection you have to drag the connecting silver cord with you, and you end up no higher than the Astral Plane.

But Paul's teachings went beyond the Astral Plane, and eventually he came up with the term *Soul Travel.*

He explained that Soul Travel took place in two ways: (1) by projection (a term which he later put on the shelf along with bilocation), and (2) by the movement of consciousness.

Soul Travel enables Soul to go into a higher state of consciousness where It takes on one of the bodies already operating on the other planes.

Soul Travel enables Soul to go into a higher state of consciousness where It takes on one of the bodies already operating on the other planes. Soul inhabits the physical body but is not imprisoned in it; therefore, It can also move to the Astral Plane and take on the Astral body which is already residing there with some fragment of the consciousness of Soul.

The Astral Plane is the area where many of our dream experiences occur. There is also a delicate interplay—a tuning in to the unconscious mind, on the Etheric Plane—that deals with remembrances and the source of the impulses for the experiences which take place on the Astral Plane.

Soul then can move on to the Causal Plane, and then to the Mental Plane. It picks up one of the bodies stationed on each plane. There is always one body in each of these universes, and sometimes there are several, depending upon the individual's state of consciousness.

The Mental Plane is generally the level that one can reach if he sees the Blue Light of the Mahanta. A person can usually get to this plane before he translates or dies. The Blue Light comes from the Mental Plane. This Light of the Mahanta appears blue because It is shining through the Mental Plane from the highest of the God Worlds. But if you see It just as you are getting into ECK, it means you are between the First and Second Planes.

Some of this gets very esoteric. The deeper instruction comes through the inspiration you get from reading the ECK discourses. But the real teachings come on the inner planes as you, Soul, move into the invisible worlds with the Mahanta.

The term *Mahanta* refers to the Inner Master. His appearance on the inner is often the same as he appears on the outer as the Living ECK Master. The Mahanta is the Inner Master, and the Living ECK Master is the Outer Master.

The term Mahanta *refers to the Inner Master. His appearance on the inner is often the same as he appears on the outer as the Living ECK Master.*

NATURAL MOVEMENT OUT OF THE BODY

The spiritual exercises generally take you into the higher worlds without a lot of fanfare.

Sometimes you find yourself in the presence of a rushing wind, which is one of the sounds of the Holy Spirit. The Sound is the force, or power, which raises the vibrations of Soul. Soul is then lifted from the human body, either through the heart center or the skull area.

ECKists often leave the body smoothly and naturally without feeling any effect on the physical body. We simply find ourselves on another plane,

The spiritual exercises generally take you into the higher worlds without a lot of fanfare.

where the surroundings and architecture are of a higher, finer nature. We are usually working and being among other people the same way as here.

Through these travels out of the body, we are preparing for the time when we must leave the physical body permanently. There is no fear at the time of death because we have already visited the inner planes many times in the Soul body in a very natural way.

We have more than one home on these inner planes. Soul visits many different places during the dream state.

That's why the individual sometimes brings back a distorted memory of the experience. What actually happens is that the Inner Master has taken Soul out of the body during sleep to a higher plane of consciousness. Sometimes he may be taken to see a loved one who has passed on or to meet with other people from earth who are also on a Soul Travel journey.

STEPS TO HIGHER CONSCIOUSNESS

The purpose is to lead you to a fuller awareness of yourself as a being who operates and meets people on all planes of existence.

As we go farther in ECK, we make steps from the human state of awareness to the higher levels of consciousness through dreams, Soul Travel, and experiences with the Light and Sound.

For those of you who are new to the teachings of ECK, I put more attention on the first step, the dream state. This will help you learn the validity of the inner planes in which you, as Soul, live, move, and have your being. The purpose is to lead you to a fuller awareness of yourself as a being who operates and meets people on all planes of existence. You then learn to work more fully as a Co-worker with the Mahanta, so that you too can earn your mastership.

As you work and travel on the inner planes, whether in the dream state or through Soul Travel, you are opening yourself for experiences in the Light and Sound of ECK, the Holy Spirit. These two elements of ECK are the purifiers of Soul. They uplift you into the higher states of being, where you begin to act and think in ways which will eventually create a better life for you. What we do in the present makes our future.

Begin with a Dream

The ECK dream discourses can help many of you learn to make the bridge from your present daily consciousness to the inner teachings, to the area where the highest truths can be gleaned.

Here you can receive the information and knowledge to begin restructuring your life in ways that will be beneficial for you and others. This is meant quite literally, because the path of ECK recognizes that as one person unfolds, everyone is uplifted.

I recall my experiences with Paul Twitchell, who was the Living ECK Master when I was learning dream travel and Soul Travel. This particular Soul Travel experience began as a dream. Our destination was a sub-Astral Plane, a parallel world to earth that is just beyond its physical boundaries.

The humming sound had taken me out of the body in full awareness. Then I entered into a dream of home; the sound drew me to the lawn outside our farmhouse.

To the north of the barn, a gigantic orange planet hung in the sky over the woods. It seemed so close I thought my outstretched hand could touch it. Below it, off to the side, a smaller planet was also

As you work and travel on the inner planes, whether in the dream state or through Soul Travel, you are opening yourself for experiences in the Light and Sound of ECK, the Holy Spirit.

in orbit around the earth.

This smaller planet was brownish-grey, but orange light reflected on it from the larger one. The color of the orange planet was so pure that I caught my breath in wonder. Suddenly Paul appeared beside me and said, "They are of the Sun and Moon Worlds!" In this experience, a dream had turned into the full consciousness of Soul Travel.

REMEMBERING YOUR INNER EXPERIENCES

Everyone who goes to sleep is out of the body.

Everyone who goes to sleep is out of the body. A dream is nothing more than one's experience beyond the physical plane, and even those who claim not to dream are really out of the body when asleep.

Soul Travel, then, is the conscious movement of Soul between the outer and inner selves, and gives one the ability to remember what the average person does not. Stop and think about it: In sleep, you are naturally out of the body.

Soul Travel is the conscious movement of Soul between the outer and inner selves.

The Spiritual Exercises of ECK help us have spiritual experiences in the sleeping hours. Many Higher Initiates in Eckankar have learned the art of being aware during most of a twenty-four-hour day, because they know how to use the periods of normal sleep for unfoldment.

While the body sleeps, Soul makes journeys of seeing, knowing, and being. At bedtime, we simply place our thoughts upon some ideal, such as the Sound or Light of God. This image is gently held in mind for about twenty minutes. When sleep comes, an ECK Master is always nearby for protection, should we need it.

Contemplation helps us to sharpen our spiritual ideal. Daily practice manifests a worthy goal, such as having the Light and Sound in our life, meeting with an absent loved one, or gaining love, wisdom, freedom, or understanding. All of these are uplifting ideals for one's contemplative sessions.

HERE'S A SOUL TRAVEL EXPERIENCE

One always goes out of the body when he falls asleep, but it is an unconscious act. In Soul Travel, the only difference is that we are trying to get out of the body in full awareness.

The moment Soul leaves the body, It finds Itself in a blue-grey zone near the Physical Plane.

The moment Soul leaves the body, It finds Itself in a blue-grey zone near the Physical Plane. This zone is an approach to the Astral Plane. The sensation of moving from the Physical to the Astral body is like slipping through a large iris of mild wind currents; this iris is the Spiritual Eye. Soul enters this neutral zone of blue-grey tones in Its Astral form, a sheath which looks like a thousand sparkling stars.

This buffer zone, or corridor, between the Physical and lower Astral Planes, resembles the underground silo of an enormous rocket that is perhaps two hundred feet in diameter and more than two thousand feet deep. The ceiling of this circular pocket is open and may display a brilliant canopy of white light, or you may see a night sky sprinkled with specks of twinkling stars. There may even be a pastoral scene by a river, whose waters murmur their pleasure at life.

Whatever scene is displayed in the opening of that vast ceiling, Soul is drawn toward it at a mighty speed. Most people begin to recall their dreams only after their departure from this launching zone between the two worlds, and after their arrival at a faraway destination on the Astral Plane.

SOUL TRAVEL TODAY

Soul Travel is a modern way to speak of Soul on Its journey home to God.

The old misunderstanding about Soul Travel still remains: that it is an occult projection out of the body, into the Astral Plane. Soul Travel is all-inclusive, however. It is a modern way to speak of Soul on Its journey home to God.

Several phases one may experience while in ECK are these: vision, dream, Soul Travel, ECKshar consciousness, and God Consciousness. Each of these facets is distinguished by an increase in Light and Sound for the individual.

THE VISION EXPERIENCE

Each stage has a unique order of experience, and each leads to a higher phase. The vision is a pre-Soul Travel experience. The individual is still bound to the physical body and is unwilling to admit to a new search for God, especially if it means venturing outside the security of his narrow human consciousness. But a vision is a good beginning toward reaching the Kingdom of God, or God-Realization, in this lifetime.

An example of a vision is this report from a doctor in California.

In contemplation, he relaxed and declared himself a channel for the Mahanta *(pause);* the Sugmad, or God *(pause);* and Sat Nam, who is the manifestation of God on the Soul Plane *(pause).* After a short wait, he was about to give up, as nothing seemed to happen. Then, via his Spiritual Eye, he saw different colored rays coming down from heaven into him. The different colors were for the Mahanta, the Sugmad, and for Sat Nam, the ruler of the Soul Plane.

Then a voice said to him, "That's not all there is."

He got the impression that the rest was the ECK, the Holy Spirit of God. Now he declared himself a vehicle for the ECK, and the whole heavens filled with the ECK, as Light and Sound. "A wonderful experience," in his words.

If one has a vision like this, he is on the brink of seeing the deeper things of ECK.

THE DREAM EXPERIENCE

The dream is commonly the next phase that the Mahanta, the Living ECK Master uses to instruct a new chela, the spiritual student. The individual will find his dreams beginning to change texture from his pre-ECK days. The vague cloudiness, the pointlessness, of dreams begins to melt away. One finds a new direction taking place in his inner worlds; it is first noticed as dreams of increasing clarity and meaning.

The illuminated dream is thus the second part of the Mahanta's teaching. Understand, there are no fixed borders between the various phases of experience.

Even an advanced ECK initiate may have ordinary dreams and visions, although this is rare. Usually, the higher one goes toward God, the more he actually lives and moves in full consciousness in all the worlds he enters. Dreams and visions are a heightened level of consciousness in comparison to what most people outside of ECK know, but in ECK, our goal is total awareness.

Now he declared himself a vehicle for the ECK, and the whole heavens filled with the ECK, as Light and Sound.

Usually, the higher one goes toward God, the more he actually lives and moves in full consciousness in all the worlds he enters.

GIVING AND RECEIVING

This example of a dream shows the two-part play of ECK: giving and receiving. In a dream, the Mahanta handed the ECK dreamer a photograph of the dreamer and two young men. They were standing next to a lamppost, and the dreamer was giving them something. When the ECKist awoke, the meaning of the dream was clear: He was giving light to these two individuals.

But this dream led to another experience. In an effort to understand the dream further, he went into contemplation and again fell asleep.

Now he awoke to find himself in Sat Lok, the Soul Plane. This was no dream, but an actual visit to this first of the true spiritual worlds. Here he met ECK Master Rebazar Tarzs, who taught him the way of spiritual maturity. The individual had enough understanding of ECK to teach others. The message was for him to get involved in life.

This was a dream experience that ended in a visit to the Soul Plane, which is the dividing line between the material and spiritual worlds. Notice how there is no hard line of demarcation here between the dream phase and a higher one.

After the vision and dream comes Soul Travel.

THE SOUL TRAVEL EXPERIENCE

After the vision and dream comes Soul Travel. This is all-important in one's spiritual unfoldment. It means he is making the effort to consciously go into the invisible worlds of God. This is in keeping with the aim of Soul, which is to work for the Sugmad, for God, in ever-greater awareness.

Although Soul Travel belongs to the lower worlds

of space and time, it is often how one passes through the material worlds to the spiritual ones in the most direct way. Therefore, it is a valuable skill that can be learned by almost anyone who is willing to invest the time and patience. Soul Travel is a bridge over the gulf that divides the human from the spiritual consciousness.

Soul Travel is a natural progression that is reached through the Spiritual Exercises of ECK.

A ECKist in Africa lay down in bed, covered his ears with pillows, and listened to the ECK Sound, which was like a sibilant, rushing wind in the distance—but still very close and within him. Soon, he felt a sucking motion at the top of his head, but he was not afraid.

He then felt himself totally withdraw from his physical body and hover in space over the bed.

"The whole of this space was lighted with shimmering atoms and bright giant and small stars," he said. He looked at himself and discovered he was in the radiant Soul body, very youthful and full of energy and power.

Then he sang "Sugmad" in a gentle lullaby. In that moment he realized that all the atoms and all the stars were part of him. As he sang quietly to himself, an energy vibrated continuously and flowed out from him to sustain all things and beings in this unending universe of stars. He felt mercy and love for all beings in this universe of light. He experienced a great Sound flowing from his center, touching and giving joyful bliss, life, and power to all in his universe. This left him in spiritual ecstasy, because of the act of giving.

The ecstasy returns to him even now in his physical state. This was an experience of brief

Soul Travel is a bridge over the gulf that divides the human from the spiritual consciousness.

He felt mercy and love for all beings in this universe of light.

homage paid to the Sugmad (God), and it has enhanced his life in every way.

*This experience
began as Soul
Travel, but it
went beyond
that and ended
as a spiritual
journey to God.*

This experience began as Soul Travel, but it went beyond that and ended as a spiritual journey to God. A touch of God is not the Sugmad in Its fullness, because the God experience, all at once, would devastate the individual, causing a setback for many ages.

THE ECKSHAR EXPERIENCE

The classic Soul Travel experience is leaving the human body in full awareness and having the Light and Sound of God flow directly into the Soul body. But some people have done that in earlier incarnations and have no desire to go through the ABCs of spiritual school again.

The Mahanta may give them a few brief refresher Soul Travel experiences, and from then on they go on to seeing, knowing, and being. This phase of experience in ECK is the ECKshar consciousness. To see, know, and be are the qualities of Soul that are at the forefront of attention in the Soul Plane and above.

Beginners in Soul Travel usually stay close to the body. The Mahanta or his designee will help the individual get above the human state of consciousness and take a short journey in the near Astral Plane. These experiences may include the awareness of moving out of the body, going through ceilings or walls, and flying into a blackness. A patch of light glimmers at the edge of the blackness, and the novice Soul Traveler emerges into the light, which is a world of light.

Here he may walk city streets that closely resemble those on earth. The people, however, are busy with duties that are unknown on earth: welcoming new arrivals who have died on the Physical Plane and are ready to resume their lives on the Astral, guiding people who have come to the Astral Plane by chance during a dream, and serving the spiritual hierarchy in many other things that are routinely done to make life go on in the worlds of God.

HEARING AND SEEING GOD

Soul Travel is a means of hearing the Sound and seeing the Light of God, in a way which cannot be done in the human body.

The Sound and Light are the wave upon which Soul rides back into the kingdom of heaven; they are the twin aspects of ECK. When an individual has gone through the phases of visions, dreams, Soul Travel, and the ECKshar consciousness, and is an experienced traveler in all the regions of God, then he receives the enlightenment of God. This is God Consciousness, and nothing more can be said about it here because words fail.

Experience is everything in ECK. An individual can read all the books on faith and spirituality in the library, but reading will net him nothing in the worlds of God.

Only experience can take us through the detours and dead ends of life and bring us to the realm of the All. A milestone in Soul's supreme journey to God is the art and science of Soul Travel.

Soul Travel is a means of hearing the Sound and seeing the Light of God, in a way which cannot be done in the human body.

PROMISE OF THE ECK MASTERS

If the dream teachings of ECK achieve anything, may it be to show people how the Holy Spirit teaches through both Its inner and outer guidance. This lifetime is our spiritual laboratory.

We lay out our spiritual chemistry kit on a table and make experiments in our lives regarding the far-reaching, but often unseen and unknown, laws of life. Experience alone lets us determine what is good for us or not.

Experience alone lets us determine what is good for us or not.

Whoever seeks God with a pure heart shall find Him. This promise of the ancient ECK Masters is renewed today.

We learn first by dreams. Then, by one of the many aspects of Soul Travel, whether it includes the fantastic out-of-the-body experience or something more subtle. After that comes our first important spiritual realization, which is from the Soul Plane.

And finally, if Soul desires God badly enough, It enters God Consciousness.

The most direct, yet most fulfilling, path to the Kingdom of God is still love. It is the beginning and ending of all things. The path of ECK, then, provides the way for us to receive the joy of God into our hearts and lives. Even so, we must *return* this holy love to all life. No matter how far we venture into the uncharted reaches of God, we find it to be the endless journey.

Rebazar Tarzs once summed up this matter of love in the ECK book *Stranger by the River.* "The way of love is better than wisdom and understanding," he said, "for with love you can have all."

And that is exactly what the dream teachings of Eckankar and the ECK Masters, Travelers of the Far Country, offer you.

Soul's Dream of God

Why do we dream? Why is it important to dream? Because dreaming comes from the creative imagination, which is God's gift to you and me. It is the nature of immortal Soul to dream. This is why your dreams, both in everyday life and while asleep, are so important.

Through your ability to dream, you often have experiences in the other worlds where you act as an observer. But as you move farther along in ECK, you become the participant in your dreams. You become the actor.

You begin to see goals, spiritual goals which may be as valid as finding a home for your family. You want a place where they can be happy, a haven away from the fast pace of today's society. You create a warm place where friends are welcome.

It's a place where you can go, a home, a spiritual dream. Because as we plan our homes, whether it's a rented home or one we buy, we're just thinking of a higher home. It's the home of Soul. The place where Soul has come from, from the heart of God in the Ocean of Love and Mercy.

Dream. Dream your way home. Dream your way back to God. Use your creative imagination, because that's the only way you can return to the source of all life.

I would like to give you my blessings on your journey home, today and forever. May the blessings be.

Why do we dream? Why is it important to dream? Because dreaming comes from the creative imagination, which is God's gift to you and me.

Dream your way back to God.

Glossary

Words set in SMALL CAPS are defined elsewhere in this glossary.

ARAHATA. *ah-rah-HAH-tah* An experienced and qualified teacher of ECKANKAR classes.

CHELA. *CHEE-lah* A spiritual student.

ECK. *EHK* The Life Force, the Holy Spirit, or Audible Life Current which sustains all life.

ECKANKAR. *EHK-ahn-kahr* Religion of the Light and Sound of God. Also known as the Ancient Science of SOUL TRAVEL. A truly spiritual religion for the individual in modern times. The teachings provide a framework for anyone to explore their own spiritual experiences. Established by Paul Twitchell, the modern-day founder, in 1965. The word means "Co-worker with God."

ECK MASTERS. Spiritual Masters who can assist and protect people in their spiritual studies and travels. The ECK Masters are from a long line of God-Realized SOULS who know the responsibility that goes with spiritual freedom.

GOD-REALIZATION. The state of God Consciousness. Complete and conscious awareness of God.

HU. *HYOO* The most ancient, secret name for God. The singing of the word HU is considered a love song to God. It can be sung aloud or silently to oneself.

INITIATION. Earned by a member of ECKANKAR through spiritual unfoldment and service to God. The initiation is a private ceremony in which the individual is linked to the Sound and Light of God.

LIVING ECK MASTER. The title of the spiritual leader of ECKANKAR. His duty is to lead SOULS back to God. The Living ECK Master can assist spiritual students physically as the Outer Master, in the dream state as the Dream Master, and in the spiritual worlds as the Inner Master. Sri Harold Klemp became the MAHANTA, the Living ECK Master in 1981.

287

MAHANTA. *mah-HAHN-tah*   A title to describe the highest state of God Consciousness on earth, often embodied in the LIVING ECK MASTER. He is the Living Word. An expression of the Spirit of God that is always with you.

PLANES. The levels of existence, such as the Physical, Astral, Causal, Mental, Etheric, and Soul Planes.

SATSANG. *SAHT-sahng* A class in which students of ECK study a monthly lesson from ECKANKAR.

SELF-REALIZATION. SOUL recognition. The entering of Soul into the Soul Plane and there beholding Itself as pure Spirit. A state of seeing, knowing, and being.

THE SHARIYAT-KI-SUGMAD. *SHAH-ree-aht-kee-SOOG-mahd* The sacred scriptures of ECKANKAR. The scriptures are comprised of twelve volumes in the spiritual worlds. The first two were transcribed from the inner PLANES by Paul Twitchell, modern-day founder of ECKANKAR.

SOUL. The True Self. The inner, most sacred part of each person. Soul exists before birth and lives on after the death of the physical body. As a spark of God, Soul can see, know, and perceive all things. It is the creative center of Its own world.

SOUL TRAVEL. The expansion of consciousness. The ability of SOUL to transcend the physical body and travel into the spiritual worlds of God. Soul Travel is taught only by the LIVING ECK MASTER. It helps people unfold spiritually and can provide proof of the existence of God and life after death.

SOUND AND LIGHT OF ECK. The Holy Spirit. The two aspects through which God appears in the lower worlds. People can experience them by looking and listening within themselves and through SOUL TRAVEL.

SPIRITUAL EXERCISES OF ECK. The daily practice of certain techniques to get us in touch with the Light and Sound of God.

SRI. *SREE* A title of spiritual respect, similar to reverend or pastor, used for those who have attained the Kingdom of God.

SUGMAD. *SOOG-mahd* A sacred name for God. Sugmad is neither masculine nor feminine; It is the source of all life.

WAH Z. *WAH zee* The spiritual name of Sri Harold Klemp. It means the Secret Doctrine. It is his name in the spiritual worlds.

Index

Aberration, 126
Abuse, 89–91
Acceptance, 121
  social, 218
Accounting, 200
Advice, 218
  Africa, 8, 112, 201, 239, 281.
    See also Ghana
Afterlife, 79
Agam Des, 233
Aggressor, 202
Aging, 121
Agnostic, 136
Air force, 3, 28
Airplane dream, 69
Alaska, 106, 107
Alien, 74
Ambitions, 243
Anger (angry), 79, 83, 86, 156,
  169, 219
Animals, 12. *See also* Bear;
  Camels; Crickets; Dog;
  Duck-in-the-furnace story;
  Eagle; Falcon; Gulls; Oxen;
  Puppy; Robins; Sid the
  Horse; Turkey-headed snake;
  Vulture; Whale(s); Worms
Answer(s), 19, 91, 165, 265
Answering machine, 213
Anxiety, 156, 199
Apartment, 249, 259–60
Appreciation, 6
Astral projection, 272, 278
Atheist, 136

Atoms, 254, 281
Attachment(s), 11, 148
Attention, 41, 217
Attitude(s), 27, 128, 251, 266
  harmful, 169
  unconscious, 87
Attributes, 3, 198
Audible Life Stream, 16, 130,
  132. *See also* Light and
  Sound; Sound Current
Auditorium, 116
Auditors, 201
Aura, 245, 255
Australia, 116, 117, 225
Authority, 156
Auto accident, 204, 208–9
Aware(ness), 16, 61, 102, 105,
  235, 271, 275, 280
  conscious, 210, 266
  dreams as a tool of, 16
  of ECK teachings, 260
  experience brings, 76
  HU lifts into a higher state of,
    95
  human, 274
  of inner worlds, 222
  leaving body in full, 276–77,
    282
  of physical body, 256
  Soul, 260
  spiritual, 111, 152
  state of, 49, 231
  total, 279

Balance, 61, 130, 155, 192, 219
    karmic, 76
    social, 91
Ballast, 159
Baptism, 261
Baseball diamond, 166–67
Basement, 38–40, 116, 222–23,
    244
Beach, 229
Bear, 167
Beggar (begging), 221–22, 243
Behavior, 268
Being. *See* Seeing, knowing, and
    being
Belief(s) (believing), 41, 75, 210,
    267
    old religious, 256
Belong(ing), 46
Bilocation, 274
Black magic (magician), 8, 130–
    31
Blame (blaming), 16, 70. *See also*
    Responsibility: self-
Blessing(s), 45, 235, 260, 286
Bliss, 263, 281. *See also* Isle of
    Bliss
Block(s), spiritual, 35, 63, 81,
    156
Blue, 116, 138
    Curtain of God exercise, 20
    Light, 254, 259, 269, 273
Boat, 237, 269
Body (bodies)
    Astral, 54, 130, 272, 277
    emotional, 251. *See also* Body
        (bodies): Astral
    Mental, 35
    out of the, 214, 222, 231, 263,
        274, 276, 277, 282–83
    physical, 41, 53, 61, 78, 114,
        124, 231, 249, 256, 274, 278
    running several, 52, 272–73
    Soul, 118, 169, 217, 224, 233,
        249, 257, 260, 274, 281, 282
    Soul and the, 37, 244
Böhme, Jakob, 254
Book(s), 29, 94, 254, 268, 283.
    See also Eckankar: books

of dream symbols, 35, 163, 168
Bookstore, 232
Breathe, 229, 252–53
Bridge, 251, 275, 281
Broken necklace, 190
Buddha consciousness, 25
Budget, 201
Buffer zone, 277
Burdens, 234, 245
Bus, 108, 143–44
Bus dream, 229–30
Business, 10, 106, 145, 200
Businessman, 16
Busybody, 171. *See also* Eaves-
    dropping

Camels, 83
Campfire, 244
Canada, 76, 143–44
Car(s), 98, 106, 165–66
    buying, 59
    white used, 11
    won't start, 79
Career, 97, 113, 123
Catholic(ism), 138–39, 228
Cause and effect, 267
Cavern(s), 74, 227
Celestial beings, 133
Censor. *See* Dream censor
Challenge, 129
Change(s), 34, 44, 56, 70, 198, 259
    in conscious awareness, 265
    resistance to, 5, 148
Channel, 44, 278
Chanhassen, Minnesota, 234
Chant(s) (chanting), 158, 229,
    230, 252–53. *See also* HU:
    chanting; HU Chant
Chaos, 157
Chela(s), 238, 245, 279
    and Master, 232
Chicago, 107–9, 257
Child(ren), 101–2, 116–17, 124,
    192, 201–2; 207, 220–21,
    237, 239, 264–65
Chore(s), 13, 38

Christ, 42, 76, 228
  consciousness, 25
Christian(s)(ity), 75, 76, 82, 113,
    218. *See also* Catholic(ism);
    Christ
  concept of heaven, 206
  fears about, 137
  fundamentalist, 136
Church(es). See also
    Catholic(ism);
    Christian(s)(ity); Mormon
    Church; Seventh-day
    Adventists
  doctrines, 137
  dream, 136–37
  leaving, 137
  the pull of our former, 136–37
  unable to find comfort in, 18
Circumstance(s), 70, 118
Civil War, 74
Class, spiritual, 222. *See also*
    Satsang
Clemens, Samuel. *See* Twain,
    Mark
Clubs, 10
Code Blue. *See* Near-death
    experience
Coincidence, 146
Color(s), 20, 105, 111, 276–79.
    See also Blue; Green;
    Lavender; Orange; Pink;
    White
Comfort, 95, 236
Commitment, 160
Communication
  between higher worlds and
    physical, 65
  inner, 29
  between Master and chela, 245
  modes of, 169
Complaining, 190
Composure, 198
Computer-room dream, 115
Computer(s), 112
  games, 80, 81
Concentration, 255
Concern, 168
Conestoga wagons, 73

Confidence, 42, 70, 113, 244
  self-, 127–28
Confirmation, 108, 261
Connection(s)
  inner, 62, 250
  between inner and outer life,
    15, 168
  between Inner and Outer
    Master, 243
Conscious(ness), 33, 34, 35, 105,
    147, 168, 266. *See also*
    Buddha consciousness;
    Christ: consciousness
  bridge between spiritual and
    human, 281
  cosmic, 268
  expansion of, 136, 244, 270
  full, 18, 37, 163, 204, 231,
    236, 279
  higher, 43, 274
  human, 6, 15, 37, 55, 58, 152,
    207, 243, 248, 278, 282
  level(s) of, 10, 61, 255, 271, 274
  movement of, 272
  Soul, 69
  state(s) of, 10, 15, 25, 27, 29,
    40–41, 54, 71, 88, 118, 233,
    235, 246, 254, 257, 271,
    272, 273
  victim, 91
Contact lenses, 147
Contemplation, 8, 9, 84,142,
    254, 276–77
Control, 71, 79, 231
  losing, 95
  of the mind, 130
Copper coin, 146
Counselor(s)) (counseling), 130,
    207–10
Courage, 56
Co-worker
  with God, 71, 75, 248
  with the Mahanta, 274
Creation, 44, 268
Creative (creativity), 127, 134
  abilities, 71
  dreamer, 70–71
  power, 128

Creative (creativity) *(continued)*
  process, 246
  use of dreams, 243
  using, 73, 250
Creator, 270
Crickets, 257
Criticism, 154
Crisis, 89
Crossroad(s), 106, 165
Crust of ages, 247–48
Crutch, 62
Curtain(s), 42–43, 60, 70, 152
  blue, 20
  invisible, 72
  of memory, 61
Cycle(s), 39–40, 111
  of death and rebirth, 261
  of karma, 270. *See also* Karma
    (karmic); Reincarnation

Darkness, 130, 152
  lord of, 131. *See also* Kal
Daydream(s)(ing), 8, 122–23,
  125, 197
Dead battery, 145
Dead end, 256
Death, 1–2, 18–19, 70, 75, 113–
  14, 204–5, 208–10, 256, 261,
  264–65
  dreams about, 9, 100–101, 113
  helping others in, 283
  overcoming fear of, 38, 69,
    204, 214, 244, 250, 274
  Soul can conquer, 124
Debt(s), 60, 75–76, 156. *See also*
  Karma (karmic)
Deity, 133, 243, 254
Depression, 244
Desert, 83, 154
Desire(s), 59, 65, 78, 243
  to give up smoking, 62
  to learn, 268
Destiny, 14
Destruction, 130
Detachment, 192. *See also*
  Attachment(s)
Details, 50, 200, 245

Deus ex machina, 133–34
Dhyana technique. *See*
  Technique(s): Dhyana
Diet, 194
Difficulties, 148
Discipline, 5, 252
  of remembering dreams, 141–
    42
  self-, 62, 79, 89, 222
Disillusionment, 256
Disney World, 236–37
Distortions, 204
Distress signal, 135
Distributor(ship), 145–46
Divine intervention, 134
Divine love, 3, 102, 268–69
  accept, 239
  chanting, 45
  giving and, 240
  protection of, 78
Divine order, 267
Divine Spirit, 5, 17, 35, 97, 156,
  259. *See also* ECK; Holy
  Spirit
  commitment with, 30
  ECK Masters and, 25
  and healing, 89, 130
  power of, 217
  spiritual exercises and, 19
  surrender to, 245
Divorce, 4
Doctor(s), 223
Dog, 12–13
Do-gooders, 27
"Don't Pass the Buck," 70. *See
  also* Blame (blaming);
  Responsibility: self-
Doomsday. *See* World(s): end of
Door(s)
  glass, 152
  of protection, 131–32
  white, 115
Doorbell. *See* Wake-up call(s)
Dorms, 10
Doubt(s), 128, 244. *See also*
  Fear(s); Intrusion
Drapery, 152. *See also*
  Curtain(s)

Dream(s)(ing), 1–4, 5–8, 9, 18, 45, 51, 58, 66, 70, 87, 93–94, 96–98, 106, 127, 144, 145, 155, 158, 164, 270, 276, 279–80, 283, 285. *See also* Dream state; Initiation: dreams of; Intrusion: dream(s) of; School: dreams of. For dreams on specific subjects, look under those subjects, also, e.g., for dreams of elevators, see Elevator dreams.
  are a divine gift, 164
  of aspiration, 98–99
  of catastrophe, 99–101
  changing, 197
  confused, 2, 54, 64, 71, 141
  detail, 189
  eight categories of, 122, 161
  about fear, 219, 244–45
  have meaning, 64, 104, 163, 199, 279. *See also* Dream interpretation
  help you in life, 2, 6, 54, 118, 203
  of home, 285
  illuminated, 279
  importance of, 285
  levels of, 164
  monsters in 130
  not going anywhere in, 249
  not merely symbolic, 35
  occur on Astral Plane, 272
  recurring, 4, 93, 114–16, 117, 259
  the secret knowledge of, 8
  seeing loved ones in, 208, 235–36
  spiritual, 10–11, 141, 154–55, 259, 285
  structure of, 168
  study of, 6–7, 10, 12, 82, 94, 96, 118
  symbol(s)(ism), 12, 35, 61, 82, 163, 165, 168, 199, 219, 238
  telescope of, 3
  of understanding, 122, 152–53, 155
  universal nature of, 3, 12–13, 14
  universe of, 20
  value of, 94, 164
  vivid, 227, 259
  writing down. *See* Dream journal
Dream censor, 55, 56, 57, 58, 65, 90, 168–69, 171
Dream dictionary, 166–67
Dreamer(s), 10, 11–12, 16, 28, 43, 61, 93, 124, 164, 192, 243, 245, 280
  becomes the knower, 41
  in ECK, 70, 150, 157
  Inner Master talking to, 170
  universal, 13
  viewpoint of, 125
  worlds of, 6
Dream exercise, 95–96, 196
Dream experience(s), 89, 141, 199
Dream Initiation. *See* Initiation: First
Dream interpretation, 97, 100, 163–64, 168
Dream journal, 31, 50–51, 53, 54, 56, 65–66, 96, 142, 167, 195, 196, 231, 253, 265, 270
Dream Master, 8, 10, 17, 55, 58–60, 71–72, 77, 88, 105, 106, 108, 124–25, 137, 170, 171, 191, 192, 197, 237, 250, 255. *See also* Inner Master; Mahanta; Spiritual traveler(s)
  attention on, 53
  does not work with smokers, 62
  and dream state, 33
  gives wake-up calls. *See* Wake-up call
  learning to recognize, 24
  message from, 55
  mocks up situation, 31, 167
  must be invited, 23, 24, 28, 63

Dream Master *(continued)*
and nightmares, 60. *See also*
Nightmare(s)
and Outer Master, 45
teaches, 44, 197
works with chela, 24, 27, 61,
168–69, 238
Dream Master, The (Klemp), 63
Dream state, 23, 24, 25, 26, 27,
30, 33, 37, 54, 56, 69, 75, 77,
101, 121, 122, 127, 141, 142,
150, 157, 159, 160, 168, 192,
194, 201, 203, 209, 231, 238,
248, 251, 255, 267, 271, 275
attending seminar in, 245
attention on, 53
awake in, 40, 256
ECK Masters work in, 217
first connection with ECK
through, 225
guidance in. *See* Guidance: in
dream state
karma in, 35, 60, 78
learning in, 141, 284
meeting others in, 32, 205, 210
meeting the Master in, 197,
217, 218
reality of, 2, 66, 204, 268
remembering, 7, 21, 27, 29,
30–31, 50–53, 60–61, 64–65,
75, 95, 141, 231, 270–71,
273. *See also* Dream censor;
Dream journal
Dream teachers. *See* Dream
Master; ECK Master(s);
Inner Master; Mahanta;
Master(s)
Dream teachings
contemporary, 27, 82
of ECK, 4, 31, 46, 56, 70, 71,
76, 81–82, 86, 95, 121, 136,
283–84
inner, 7
truth of, 112, 114
Dream travel, 8, 36, 43, 214,
235, 260, 269, 274, 278. *See
also* Soul Travel
success with, 269

technique for, 235
Dream world(s). *See* Dream
state; World(s): dream
Drug(s), 270
overdose, 235
Duck-in-the-furnace story, 38–
40
Dungeon, 88

Eagle, 167
Earrings, 146
Earth, 8, 19, 74, 276
life on, 4
purpose for being on, 134
social balance on, 91
Earth plane, 26, 239. *See also*
Earth
Earthquake dream(s), 34–35, 56,
93
Eavesdropping, 170–71
ECK, 5, 10, 16, 24, 33, 34–35,
51–52, 75, 95, 97, 129, 132,
145, 156, 157, 171, 254, 255,
256, 259, 261, 274, 275, 278,
279, 285. *See also* Divine
Spirit; Eckankar; ECK
teachings; Holy Spirit; Light
and Sound; Path of ECK;
Voice of God
arranges the waking dream, 149
belief in, 16
connection with. *See* ECK:
linkup with
declaring oneself a vehicle for,
279
dedicating a day to, 239
dream discourses. *See ECK
Dream Discourses*
enlivens your spiritual life,
248
event, 264. *See also* ECK
seminar(s)
experiences with, 26
finding, 19
flow of, 154
holy scriptures of. See

Shariyat-Ki-Sugmad, the;
Shariyat-Ki-Sugmad, The
knowledge of, 160, 237
linkup with, 125, 225, 250
missionary, 106, 234
new to, 37, 262
not ready for, 232, 235
people outside of, 27, 270, 279
principles, 218
remember to call on, 245
speaks, 84, 151. *See also*
Golden-tongued Wisdom;
Sound
spiritual standard of, 17
student (study) of, 9, 57, 243,
259
telling the secrets of, 239
traveling for, 105
trust in, 76, 154
twin aspects of, 275, 283. *See
also* Light and Sound
understanding, 282
as vibration, 223, 258
wisdom of, 83
working of the, 29, 31
Eckankar, 8, 26, 46, 78, 106, 136,
166, 205, 209, 210, 214, 215,
226, 239, 256
advantages of being in, 78
books, 19, 45, 63, 94, 97, 105,
218, 220, 225, 232, 284. *See
also Dream Master, The;
ECKANKAR—The Key to
Secret Worlds; Eternal
Dreamer, The; Flute of God,
The; Shariyat-Ki-Sugmad,
The; Spiritual Exercises of
ECK, The; Spiritual Note-
book, The; Stranger by the
River; Tiger's Fang, The*
as direct path, 81, 233, 263
discourse(s), 19, 84, 86, 94, 101,
124, 160, 168, 244, 275
emphasis on dreams in, 118
finding, 18–19, 40, 204, 220,
225, 259
member(s) of, 10, 31, 84, 93,
101, 104, 117, 207, 210, 234.

See also ECKist(s); Higher
Initiate(s); Initiate(s)
modern-day founder of. *See*
Twitchell, Paul
newsletter, 213
not ready for, 217, 221
people not in, 24, 39, 86, 165
point of, 228
primitive form of, 88
sacred scriptures of. *See*
Shariyat-Ki-Sugmad, the;
Shariyat-Ki-Sugmad, The
spiritual leader of, 8, 29, 37,
218, 240. *See also* Harji;
Living ECK Master;
Mahanta; Wah Z
study of, 7, 17, 24, 196
telling about, 206
*ECKANKAR—The Key to Secret
Worlds* (Twitchell), 225,
228, 232
ECK center(s), 218
ECK Dream Discourses, The,
84. *See also* Eckankar:
discourse(s)
ECK Initiator, 125. *See also*
Initiation
ECK insignia ring, 209
ECKist(s), 57, 75, 151, 168, 246,
249
African, 112, 201, 239, 283
dreams of, 31–32, 85, 88, 113,
124, 135, 154, 159–60, 165,
189–91, 222–23, 229–30,
238–39, 244–45
leave the body smoothly, 276
and Master, 24
and non-ECKists, 76, 138–39,
205–6, 213–15, 220, 235
and Temple of ECK, 234
and waking dreams, 108,
146–47
ECK Master(s), 11, 25, 40, 42,
83, 220, 221, 223, 228, 229,
233, 238, 239, 246–48, 260–
61, 269, 284. *See also*
Dream Master; Fubbi
Quantz; Gopal Das; Harji;

ECK Master(s) *(continued)*
    Inner Master; Lai Tsi;
    Living ECK Master;
    Mahanta; Peddar Zaskq;
    Rebazar Tarzs; Twitchell,
    Paul; Wah Z; Yaubl Sacabi
  chanting HU, 159
  guard the Shariyat-Ki-
    Sugmad, 232
  help from, 217–18
  as manifestations of Divine
    Spirit, 25
  meeting, 218, 221–22, 232,
    260
  never interfere, 27
  pictures of, 218, 230
  the promise of, 284
  protection of, 217, 276
ECK path. *See* Path of ECK
ECK seminar(s), 23, 29, 117,
    143, 152, 245, 256
ECKshar consciousness, 278,
    282, 283
ECK teachings, 7, 19, 45, 46, 76,
    82, 83, 164, 209, 218, 255,
    260. *See also* Dream
    teachings: of ECK;
    Eckankar
  the essence of, 122. *See also*
    Light and Sound
  finding, 105, 225
  gaining understanding
    through, 87
  inner, 23, 29
  not familiar with, 99
  outer, 23
  secret. *See* ECK teachings:
    inner
ECK-Vidya, 104, 122, 267
ECK works. *See* ECK teachings
ECK writings, 233. *See also*
    Eckankar: books; Eckankar:
    discourse(s)
Ecstasy, 281
Education, 268
Effort, 17, 75, 280
Egypt, 1, 222
1880, 75

Einstein, Albert, 57
Electrical engineer, 239
Elevator dreams, 10
Emotion(s), 131, 163, 164, 196.
    See also Body (bodies):
    Astral; Body (bodies):
    emotional; Plane(s): Astral
Employment agency, 191
Energy, 78, 281
  field, 72
  invisible, 130
Enlightened (enlightenment),
    203, 283
Esoteric, 273
Eternal dreamer, 121, 127, 160
Eternal Dreamer, The (Klemp),
    63
Exercise(s). *See* Spiritual
    exercise(s); Spiritual
    Exercises of ECK
Expectation(s), 60, 136
Experience(s), 16, 24, 26, 29, 69,
    83, 87, 121
  dream, 54, 71, 161, 274. *See
    also* Dream state;
    Dream(s)(ing); Plane(s):
    Astral
  drinking in, 51
  with ECK Masters, 24–25. *See
    also* ECK Master(s)
  of the future, 72
  is everything in ECK, 283–84
  gaining, 44
  God, 284
  higher, 41, 159
  human, 269
  humbling, 11
  inner. *See* Inner experience(s)
  learning through, 43, 76, 81
  with the Light and Sound of
    God. *See* Light; Light and
    Sound (of God); Sound
  from the Mahanta, 15
  mean little by themselves, 17
  negative, 60
  outer, 15, 150, 199
  out-of-body, 214, 282. *See also*
    Travel(s): out-of-body

painful, 155
past-life, 75, 87–88. *See also*
    Past life (lives)
phases of, 278
remembering, 37, 49–50
spiritual, 262, 270, 276
study the details of, 50
thread of common, 160
writing, 253. *See also* Dream
    journal
Experiments, 284
Exploration(s), 44
Eye doctor, 204
Eyes, 63, 216
    Master's, 158
Eyesight, 147

Failure dreams, 97–98
Faith, 75–76
Falcon, 94–95
Falling, 263
Family, 10
Far Country, 9. *See also*
    Heaven(s); Plane(s)
Farmer(s), 38–40, 213
Farmhouse, 275
Fast(ing), 63–64
Fatigue, 207
Fear(s), 3, 25, 79, 87, 105, 130,
    141, 155, 157, 216, 219–20,
    223, 226, 244, 257, 259, 262
    of animals, 101
    of being an outsider, 219
    about church and Christianity,
        138
    of death, 38, 204, 210, 244, 250
    dream about, 219
    facing, 228
    of going outside, 89
    of heights, 87, 89
    of living, 210. *See also* Fear(s):
        of death
    of looking at inner experiences,
        49
    of opposite sex, 89

overcoming, 37, 70, 100, 122,
    136, 191, 232, 250
    and past-life experience, 88
    subconscious, 60
    of talking about Eckankar,
        88, 165
    at time of death, 276
    of unworthiness, 158
Ferris-wheel dream, 49
Fever, 224
Finances, 134
"Finders keepers," 6
Flat tire, 98
Flooding-river dream, 93
Flute, 84. *See also* Sound: of
    flute
Flute of God, The (Twitchell),
    225
Fly(ing), 15, 69
    into a blackness, 285
Flying saucers, 87
Food(s), 203, 219. *See also* Ice
    cream; Milk; Sugar-water
    story
    eating the wrong, 144
    sensitivity to, 194
Football-coach story, 96–99
Force(s), 130, 273
    conflict of opposing, 58
    evil, 24
    field of love, 128
    negative, 60
    spiritual, 59
    universal, 16
Formula technique, 251–53
Fortune-cookie story, 151
Foster home, 209
Freedom, 71, 156, 258, 279. *See
    also* Spiritual freedom
    in the physical body, 215
    of religion, 210
    of Soul, 28, 130, 228
French Revolution dream, 76–77
Freshness date, 102–3
Friendship, 205–6
Fubbi Quantz, 238–39, 247
Future, 65
    contained in the present, 73

Future *(continued)*
  dreams let us see, 2, 7, 93, 117
  made by what we do in
    present, 275
  not every dream will predict,
    66

Geraniums, 12, 13–14
Germany, 189
Ghana, 93
Ghosts, 87
Gift(s), 11, 164, 285
Giving, 240, 281, 282
Glass, 150
  decanter. *See* Sugar-water
    story
Glasses, 147
Goal(s), 59, 243, 276, 279, 285
God, 4, 18, 136, 198, 261, 279,
    280, 285. *See also* Sugmad
  becoming instruments for, 44
  blessings of, 221
  the Blue Curtain of, 20
  chanting, 42
  the cloth of, 224
  communicates through Sound
    and Light, 261. See also
    Light; Light and Sound;
    Sound
  creative power of, 71
  grace of, 75
  heart of, 288
  heavens of. *See* God: worlds of
  jewel of, 29
  journey to, 8, 144, 260, 282,
    283
  joy of, 284
  Kingdom of. *See* Kingdom of
    God
  Light of, 20. *See also* Light;
    Light and Sound
  love for, 19, 240, 268
  love of, 156, 226, 234, 239, 240
  love song to, 19, 157, 215. *See
    also* HU; HU Chant
  name for. *See* HU; Sugmad
  nature of, 8

opening the heart to, 5
  path to, 2, 26, 76, 81, 217, 220,
    233, 270
  planes of *See* Plane(s): of God
  qualities of, 260
  relationship with, 164
  return to, 228, 243, 285
  search for, 6, 9–10, 44, 278,
    284
  Soul is a child of, 3
  Sound(s) of. *See* Audible Life
    Stream; Light and Sound;
    Sound: of God
  spark of. *See* Soul(s): is a
    spark of God
  touch of, 282
  trust in, 107
  truth of, 76
  two pillars of, 255. *See also*
    Light and Sound
  wisdom of, 229
  worlds of, 7, 8, 19, 36, 41, 227,
    273, 280, 283, 284. *See also*
    Heaven(s); Inner planes;
    Plane(s)
God Consciousness, 260, 278,
    283, 284
Godhead, 254
Godlike, 3
God-Realization, 43, 268
  in this lifetime, 278
God Worlds. *See* God: worlds of
Golden-cup exercise, 51–52
Golden-musical-notes exercise,
    263–64
Golden seeds, 154
Golden-tongued Wisdom, 15, 29,
    102–4, 151, 272
  as category of dreams, 122,
    150
Gondola dream, 157
Goodwill, 65
Good works, 8
Gopal Das, 222, 230, 240
Go-slower exercise, 198
Gossip, 10, 219
Grace, 3, 5, 6, 21, 121. *See also*
    God: grace of

Grass, 12
Grateful, 190, 265
Great Lakes, 244
Greek playwrights, 132
Green, 111, 254
Grief, 18–19
Group meetings, 10
Growth, 14, 28, 70
Guidance, 10, 21, 106
  asking for, 219
  in dream state, 7, 31, 167
  from ECK, 93
  of Holy Spirit, 93, 283–84
  inner, 108
Guillotine, 77
Gulls, 229

Habit(s), 16, 136, 170
  breaking, 98
  harmful, 62, 169
  of writing down experiences, 253
Happiness, 41, 224, 258
Harji, 217. *See also* Living ECK
    Master; Mahanta; Wah Z
Harm, protection from, 129
Harmony, 16, 17, 21
Harvey, Paul, 57
Hate, 86, 87, 89
Hawaii, 124
Heal(ing), 2, 89, 91, 189, 194–95,
    196, 224
  asking for, 171
  from Divine Spirit, 130
  through Light and Sound, 5
Health, 10, 18, 27, 114, 134, 192,
    203
  begging God for, 243
  problem(s), 194, 196
Hearing, spiritual, 20
Heart, 9, 132, 258
  center, 64, 250, 273
  opening to God, 5
  welcoming Master into, 63
Heaven(s), 8, 25, 41, 44, 60, 124,
    239, 244, 270. *See also*
    Dream(s)(ing); Dream State;

God: worlds of; Plane(s);
    World(s)
  Christian concept of, 75, 206
  colored rays from, 278–79
  of dreams, 163
  dreams are road to, 7, 9, 10, 12
  expectations about, 60
  journey into, 228–29
  keys to, 261
  kingdom of, 254, 283
  level(s) of, 52. *See also*
    Plane(s)
  study of, 9
Help, 6, 154, 160, 264
  accepting, 62, 216
  asking for, 65, 134, 159, 245
  from ECK Masters, 217
  not conscious of, 24
Hero, 133
Hesitation, 132
Higher Initiates, 276
Higher self. *See* Soul
Holy Spirit, 16, 21, 44, 51, 61,
    76, 95, 125, 157, 158, 223,
    250, 254, 261, 262, 270,
    275, 279. *See also* ECK
  becoming a vehicle for, 44, 52
  and dreams, 6, 96
  gifts of the, 147
  guidance from. *See* Guidance:
    of Holy Spirit
  linkup with. *See* Initiation:
    inner
  sounds of, 276. *See also*
    Audible Life Stream; Light
    and Sound; Sound Current
  speaks to us, 15, 29, 84
  teachings of, 165, 283–84
  two aspects of, 14, 223, 256,
    261. *See also* Light and Sound
  warnings from, 146
  works through medical
    profession, 130
  works through other people,
    196. *See also* Golden-
    tongued Wisdom
Horse. *See* Sid the horse
Households, 10

Howe, Elias, 1
HU, 95, 138, 214, 252
  chanting, 20, 30, 36, 42, 58,
    64, 79, 95, 102, 131, 139,
    147, 196, 252–53, 260–61,
    262, 263, 270. *See also* HU
    Chant
  name for God, 9, 20, 95–96
  for protection, 78
  singing. *See* HU: chanting
  sound of, 158–59
  tape, 215
  telling about, 235
HU Chant, 157–58, 270
Human
  body, 2
  nature, 46
  race, 61
  self, 4, 61
  spirit, 98
Humor, 248
HU Song. *See* HU Chant
Hypnotism, 89

Ice cream, 194
Ideal, spiritual, 79, 276–77
Ideas, 251
Illness, 76
Illusion, 121
Image(s), 150, 171, 264, 276
  dream, 260
  Master's, 217
  personal, 121
Imagination, 38, 102, 197, 229,
    269
  creative, 263, 271, 285
  different from dreams, 271
  going to different places in,
    271
Imbalance, 60
Impatient, 38
Initiate(s), 41, 167, 236, 279. *See
    also* ECKist(s); Higher
    Initiates
  work with other Souls, 238

Initiation(s), 85, 124, 125
  dreams of, 122, 123–24
Inner experience(s), 2, 15, 26,
    36, 70, 171, 224, 245
  establishing time frame of, 73
  hidden meanings behind, 56,
    199
  with Light or Sound, 157
  not having, 62
  occur more often in ECK, 232
  as part of everyday life, 66
  reason we forget, 142
  recording, 65–66. *See also*
    Dream journal
  remembering, 52, 56
  upset by, 40, 46, 60
Inner Master, 8, 9, 15, 23, 25,
    33, 54, 71, 99, 107, 109, 113,
    141, 142, 145, 148, 150, 157,
    158, 170, 190, 192, 198, 199,
    202, 213, 216, 220, 224, 244–
    45, 249–50. *See also* Dream
    Master, Mahanta; Wah Z
  appearance, 273
  going into other worlds with,
    89
  help from, 65
  is ECK, 245
  is Mahanta, 25
  mental conversation with, 100
  messages from, 148
  takes Soul out of body during
    sleep, 274
  trusting, 105
  voice of. *See* Golden-tongued
    Wisdom
Inner planes, 73, 148, 150, 157,
    158, 159, 192, 197, 220, 222,
    235, 264, 274. *See also*
    Dream(s); Dream state;
    Plane(s)
  acting as guide on, 237
  attending seminar on, 153
  experience(s) on, 165, 171,
    236, 251
  fight on, 131
  guidance given on, 220
  learning on, 113

meeting with loved ones on, 277
phone call on, 124
purpose of experiences on, 171
real teachings come on, 273
temples on, 233. *See also* Temple(s) of Golden Wisdom
validity of, 274
we have more than one home on, 274
write down experiences about, 253. *See also* Dream journal
Inner security, 220
Inner tangles, 65
Inner teacher, 265. *See also* Inner Master; Living ECK Master; Mahanta; Master(s)
Inner teachings, 144, 275
Inner vision, 148. *See also* Spiritual Eye
Inner world(s), 128, 160, 222, 239, 268–69. *See also* Heaven(s); Inner planes; Plane(s)
ability to go into, 203
Inquisition dream, 88
Insight, 21, 27, 66, 104, 147, 149, 163, 166, 199, 205, 267
from dreams, 10
into how life works, 81
needed to overcome weak points, 171
from past lives, 71–72
into past lives, 82–83
into relationships, 2
spiritual, 15, 150
for spiritual benefit, 60
into spiritual nature, 164
Inspiration, 251, 273
Interference, 169–71
Intrusion, 101, 129, 171
dream(s) of, 122, 125–26, 127–29, 132
Intuition, 106, 108
Investment(s), 145, 203
Iris, 277
Isle of Bliss, 238

Jealousy, 126
Jesus. *See* Christ
Job(s), 107, 112, 134, 189
changing, 205
Joke, 151
Joseph, 1
Journey to God, 8, 160
dreams as starting point of, 7
Joy, 3, 21, 257

Kal, 90
Karma (karmic), 5, 25, 35, 71, 87, 237. *See also* Past life (lives); Reincarnation
to avoid making, 79
conditions, 28, 196
creating, 76, 78
facing, 60
patterns, 136. *See also* Habit(s)
purification of, 261
seed, 252
underlies all relationships, 155
worked out in dreams, 78, 243
Katsupari Monastery, 233, 238
Key(s), 109–10, 145
to heaven, 261
to spiritual understanding, 95
Kingdom of God, 262, 278, 284
Klemp, Harold. *See also* Mahanta; Mahanta, the Living ECK Master; Wah Z
Dream Master, The, 63
Eternal Dreamer, The, 63
Spiritual Exercises of ECK, The, 256
Knowing(ness) (knower), 41, 45. *See also* Seeing, knowing, and being
Knowledge, 8, 36, 76, 233
secret, 232

Lady of ECK. *See* Simha
Lai Tsi, 219–20
Lamppost dream, 280
Lavender. *See* Light: lavender
Law(s)
    of Divine Spirit, 5, 114
    of life, 43, 284
    of Love, 207
    of Noninterference, 207
    of protection, 131
    of Silence, 10
    social, 91
    spiritual, 4, 25, 91
Lesson(s). *See also* Eckankar:
        discourses; *ECK Dream
        Discourses, The*
    from dream state, 194
    from previous lifetimes, 80–81
    spiritual, 15, 79, 142, 148
Letter(s),
    from Living ECK Master, 243
    to Master, 11, 37, 215–17,
        226–27
Letting go. *See* Attachment(s)
Level(s), 163–64. *See also*
        Conscious(ness); Plane(s)
    of dreams, 164
    of obstacles, 129
    at which Dream Master
        works, 169
Library, 94, 106, 221
License plate, 106
Life,15, 17, 18, 27, 45, 75, 86,
        134, 142, 198, 199, 265, 270.
        See also Past life (lives)
    accepting, 154
    daily, 66, 94, 164, 168
    detours of, 283
    fulfillment of, 154
    inner, 66, 243
    restructuring, 275
    taking a chance on, 105
Light, 19, 55, 152–53, 223, 226,
        254, 269, 283. *See also* Light
        and Sound
    blue, 111, 254, 269. *See also*
        Blue: Light
    celestial, 258, 262

    controlling flow of, 250
    of ECK, 152
    giving, 280
    of God, 111, 224, 227, 246,
        248, 250, 254, 259, 283
    Golden, 52
    green, 111, 254
    lavender, 254
    as lightbulb, 111
    mountain of. *See* Mountain-of-
        Light exercise
    orange, 276
    pink, 111, 254
    seen as fire, 111
    seen as sunlight, 248, 269
    universe of, 281
    white, 111, 129, 244–45, 255,
        261, 269, 277, 280
Light and Sound, 18, 75, 153,
        157, 224, 244, 248, 279. *See
        also* Audible Life Stream;
        Light; Sound
    chanting HU opens one to, 102
    of ECK, 26, 107
    of God, 14, 16, 25, 51, 110,
        214, 220, 227, 270, 282
    experiences with, 26, 122, 255,
        270, 274
    having in our life, 277
    healing through. *See*
        Heal(ing): through Light
        and Sound
    as heart of ECK, 233
    increase in, 278
    knowledge and wisdom of, 232
    Lord of, 131
    manifest in different ways, 223
    telling others about, 105
    twin pillars of God's love, 111
    worlds of, 132
Light body, 224, 231
Light Giver, 246. *See also* Living
        ECK Master; Mahanta
Lightning-bolt story, 259
Limitations, 269
Link. *See also* Zelda II: Legend
        of Link
    between Mahanta and ECKist,

29, 244
Listen, 98
Living ECK Master, 11, 36, 245,
    250, 255, 275. *See also*
    Dream Master; Eckankar:
    spiritual leader of; Inner
    Master; Mahanta; Outer
    Master
  gazing at face of, 217
  introduces path back to God,
    243
  is Outer Master. *See* Outer
    Master
  in role of Scotty, 135
Loan, 145
Locked out, 145
Logic, 34
Loneliness, 244
Love, 6, 65, 87, 105, 110, 114,
    202, 205, 218, 219, 221, 224,
    277
  accepting, 45, 226
  for all beings, 259, 281
  bond, 209
  capacity for, 5
  fill yourself with, 42
  force field of, 128
  God's, 110–11
  human, 10, 45
  is better than wisdom and
    understanding, 284
  is path to God, 284
  for learning, 268
  learning how to, 75
  of Master, 111
  opens heart, 5
  power of, 227
  same as Light and Sound, 110–
    11, 225
  search for, 19
Luck, 94
Lying, 210

Madrigal(s), 263
Magazine-writer story, 122–23
Mahanta, 11, 15, 21, 28, 52, 75,
    109, 135, 154, 170, 209, 232,
    240, 245, 258, 270, 273,
    280, 282. *See also* Dream
    Master; Inner Master;
    Living ECK Master;
    Mahanta, the Living ECK
    Master
  asking for help, 70, 134, 202,
    206
  Blue Light of. *See* Blue: Light
  contact with, 256
  Co-worker with, 274
  as Dream Master, 17, 53, 61,
    124, 137, 155, 198, 218, 237
  dreams with, 122, 156–59,
    201
  entrance into dreamer's life,
    243
  Initiator as channel for, 125
  inner guidance from, 108
  as Inner Master, 89, 142, 148,
    158, 200, 273
  is state of consciousness, 25
  making connection with, 237,
    244
  meeting, 157
  messages from, 103, 151, 197
  presence of, 157
  protection of, 8–9
  put your attention on, 53
  recognizing, 158
  resisting, 257
  teaching on inner planes, 113
  voice of, 150, 194
  works through Golden-
    tongued Wisdom, 102–3
Mahanta, the Living ECK
    Master, 10, 19, 135, 262,
    272, 281. *See also* Gopal
    Das
  contemplation upon, 63
  as Dream Master, 27, 29, 106
  love of, 156
  may speed up unfoldment,
    270
Malignancy, 69
Maroon robe, 227. *See also*
    Rebazar Tarzs
Marriage, 158

Martial arts, 131
Master(s). *See also* ECK
　　Master(s)
　true test of, 24
Mastership, 274
Matrix, 25, 157, 245
Maturity, spiritual, 280
Meddle, 170. *See also* Interfer-
　ence; Intrusion
Melody (melodies). *See* Audible
　Life Stream; Light and
　Sound; Music, Sound
Memory (memories), 26, 29, 36,
　42, 54, 199. *See also* Past
　life (lives): memory (memo-
　ries) of
　Causal, 73
　distorted, 274
　dream, 4, 51, 64, 115, 124
　as subjective side of Causal
　Plane, 87
Mental. *See also* Mind
　distortions, 36
　plane. See Plane(s): Mental
　screen, 50
Message(s), 205. See also Dream
　Master: message from;
　Inner Master: messages
　from; Mahanta: messages
　from
　dreams, 54, 56, 61, 201
　recognizing, 104
Milk, 102–3, 194
Mind, 28, 55, 60, 78, 87, 118,
　233. *See also* Plane(s):
　Mental
　Etheric, 58, 168–69, 171. *See
　also* Dream censor
　higher, 246
　lower, 90, 246
　obstacle of, 10
　passions of, 135
　peace of, 94, 96
　physical, 52, 141, 169
　power of, 146
　putting Soul in control of, 198
　screen of the, 90, 217, 245
　study of, 268

subconscious, 55, 87, 90, 251
unconscious, 54, 272
Minnesota. *See* Chanhassen,
　Minnesota
Miracle(s), 98, 147
Mirror, 121, 129
Missionary for ECK, 106
Mississippi River. *See* Twain,
　Mark
Mistake, 16, 76
Mock up (mock-up), 31, 167
Moloch, 131
Money, 93, 106, 108, 201
　hidden in a paper bag, 5
　security in, 35
Mormon Church, 259
Motive(s) (motivation), 11, 191
Motorcycle
　accident, 18
　man, 222–23
Mountain-of-Light exercise, 132
Mount Saint Helens, 93
Movie, 77, 116
Moving, 5, 205, 225
Muscular dystrophy, 264
Museum dream, 244
Music, 224, 263–64. *See also*
　Flute; Madrigal(s)
　heavenly, 97, 262
　Sound comes as, 254
　synthesized, 84
Musical instruments, 196, 264.
　See also Flute; Sound: as
　musical instruments

Nap, 53. *See also* Sleep(ing)
Near-death experience, 214
Negativity, 127, 219
Nest, 13–15, 39
New York City, 74, 123, 218
Nightmare(s), 1, 7, 58, 60, 101–
　2, 130, 138, 219. *See also*
　Dream(s)(ing)
Noise, 38, 41, 144
Nourishment, spiritual, 15
Nudge(s), 107, 194

from Mahanta, 106
Nuri Sarup. *See* Light body

Observer, 285
Obstacle(s), 58, 129
Occult, 278
Ocean, 11, 52, 153
    of Light exercise, 269
    sounds of. *See* Sound: of ocean
Ocean of Love and Mercy, 97,
    243, 285
Offend(ed)(er), 170
Old American West, 72–74
Old Testament, 1
Opinion(s), 61
    imposing on others, 171
    negative, 128
Opposition, 59, 80, 86
Options, 97
Optometrist, 147–48. *See also*
    Eye doctor; Eyes; Eyesight
Oregon Trail, 73
Orlando, 236
Ornade dream, 195
Outer Master, 8, 23, 25, 273. *See*
    also Living ECK Master
Oxen, 73

Pain, 5, 147
Panic, 198, 219. *See also* Anxiety
Paradise. *See* Isle of Bliss
Past, 93. *See also* Karma
    (karmic); Past life (lives)
    events of, 87
    feelings and impulses created
        in, 82
    follower of ECK in, 218
    and present or future, 118
Past life (lives), 82–83, 87–88,
    89–91, 156, 196, 251, 258.
    See also Karma (karmic);
    Plane(s): Causal
    dreams of, 10, 71–72
    memory (memories) of, 85, 101

regression, 89–90, 91
    subconscious fears from, 60.
        See also Fear(s)
Path of ECK, 233, 275, 284. *See*
    also Eckankar
    commitment to, 160
Patience, 198, 281
Peace, 19, 219, 262
Peddar Zaskq, 233, 247, 251
Perception, direct, 43
Permission
    giving to Master, 28, 42, 65, 142
Perspective(s), 71–72
    spiritual, 220
Personality worship, 131
Pharaoh, 1
Philippines, 243
Phobia. *See* Fear(s)
Photograph(er), 121, 280
Picture frame, 190–91
Pilot, 69
Pink. *See* Light: pink
Plane(s), 49, 256, 274–75. *See*
    also World(s)
    Astral, 52, 54, 72, 87, 141,
        164, 214, 247, 270, 272,
        277–78, 283
    and dreams, 40, 54, 101, 233,
        236, 251–52, 260, 272
    Causal, 46, 52, 73, 87, 164,
        233, 236, 247, 251–52, 270,
        272
    difference between, 251
    different languages on, 169
    of emotions. *See* Plane(s):
        Astral
    Etheric, 54, 87, 164, 233, 251,
        272
    of existence, 164, 256, 274
    experiences on each, 253
    Fifth, 251, 273. *See also*
        Plane: Soul
    of God, 43, 222. *See also*
        Plane(s): high(er)
    high(er), 41, 72, 87, 228–29,
        264
    inner, 3, 8, 25, 26, 37, 44, 46,
        96, 102, 124, 157

Plane(s) *(continued)*
  Mental, 46, 54, 72, 87, 164,
    169, 233, 236, 251, 253, 263,
    272–73. *See also* Mind
  physical, 43, 52, 87, 164, 233,
    247, 260, 270, 277, 283
  Second, 251
  Soul, 43, 164, 233, 238, 251–
    52, 253, 261, 271, 279, 280,
    282
  spiritual, 52, 61
  sub-, 52, 275
  temples on the lower, 233. *See
    also* Temple of ECK;
    Temple(s) of Golden Wisdom
  transportation in inner, 169
  visitor's pass to. *See* Formula
    technique
Plateau, spiritual, 63
Position, misuse of, 156
Potential, spiritual, 164
Power, 1, 25, 78, 273, 281
  abuses of, 268
  of black magic, 8, 130
  Divine, 245
  of HU, 30
  of love of God, 226
  negative. *See* Kal
  to work inwardly and out-
    wardly, 24
Practice, 44, 276
Prayer, 8, 18–19, 139, 224
Prescription(s), 194, 224
Present, 87, 93, 277
  past and future contained in,
    73, 118
Principle(s), 17
  creative, 70
  divine, 158
  of ECK, 39
  spiritual, 62, 81, 150
Priorities, 17
Prison-inmate dream, 219
Problem(s), 138, 196
  with alcohol, 89
  and dream teachings of ECK,
    71
  karmic, 237. *See also* Karma

  (karmic)
    solving, 81, 98, 134–35, 199,
      203
Prophecy. *See* ECK-Vidya
Protection. *See also* ECK
    Master(s): protection of;
    Mahanta: protection of
  screen of, 127
  self-, 129–30
  spiritual. *See* Mountain-of-
    Light exercise
Psychic
  attacks, 126, 130–31
  criminal(s), 9
Psychotherapy (psychothera-
    pist), 89–91
Purification, 255, 258, 262

Question(s), 74, 95
Quitter's dreams, 4

Radiant body, 217, 232. *See also*
    Light body; Mahanta
Raft dream, 159–60
Rays, 278–79
Reader's Digest, 66
Realization, 4–5. *See also* God-
    Realization; Self-Realization
  degrees of, 43
  dream of, 153
  spiritual, 284
Rebazar Tarzs, 214, 218, 228,
    233, 247, 282, 284
Rebirth. *See* Reincarnation
Receiving, 280
Reincarnation, 75, 80–81, 102,
    218, 262, 272
Relationship(s), 86, 155, 204
  dreams give insight into, 2
  with Inner Master, 134
Relaxation, spiritual. *See*
    Contemplation
Religion(s), 41, 220, 262. *See also*
    Catholic(ism); Chris-

tian(s)(ity); Church(es);
    Mormon Church; Seventh-
    Day Adventists
  followed in the past, 136
  HU available to all, 139
  metaphysical, 256
  Temple of ECK for all. *See*
    Temple of ECK
Remembrances. *See* Memory
    (memories); Plane(s): Etheric
Resistance. *See* Change: resis-
    tance to
Responsibility, 71, 88, 235
  for our inner worlds, 126
  not facing, 191
  self-, 70, 76, 91
Rest, 131
Restaurant, 114–16
Resurrection, 69
Retirement, 146
River. *See* Flooding-river dream;
    Raft dream; Twain, Mark
Riverboats. *See* Twain, Mark
Robins, 13–15
Roman-galley dream, 85–86

Saints, 262
Sat Lok, 280. *See also* Plane(s):
    Soul
Sat Nam, 278–79
Satsang class, 86, 230, 238
Scales of justice, 155
School
  counselor, 207–10
  dreams of, 4, 10, 16–17
  God's, 270
  principal, 208, 210, 239
  suspension from, 208
Seattle, 105, 107
Secret word, 244–45
Security, 35, 128
Seed karma. *See* Karma (karmic):
    seed
Seeing, knowing, and being, 276,
    282
Self-discipline. *See* Discipline:
    self-
Self-Realization, 43, 251, 268
Self-righteous(ness), 90, 91
Service, 239
Sewing machine. *See* Howe,
    Elias
Shariyat-Ki-Sugmad, the, 230,
    232, 233
Shariyat-Ki-Sugmad, The, 63,
    83, 258
Sid the horse, 31, 32–33
Sign(s), 18, 70, 107
  asking for, 146
Silence. *See* Law(s): of Silence
Silver cord, 272
Simha, 259
Sin, 76
Sisyphus, 79
Sleep(ing), 122, 266
  dreamless, 7
  drop off to in contemplation,
    252
  dying in, 9
  hard time, 138, 223
  pursuing spiritual activity
    during, 63
Smoker, 62
Soldier, 231
Solomon, 23
Soul(s), 12, 35, 52–53, 61, 69,
    144, 198, 272–73, 274, 275,
    277–78, 284, 285. *See also*
    Body (bodies): Soul
  aim of, 280
  always works in present
    moment, 73
  awareness. *See* Awareness:
    Soul
  birthright of, 25, 136
  creative principle of, 70
  in dream state, 210
  enters many bodies, 75
  eye of, 63. *See also* Spiritual
    Eye
  food of, 246
  freedom of. *See* Freedom: of
    Soul
  home of, 97, 285

Soul(s) *(continued)*
  imprisonment of, 90, 244, 248,
    272
  Inner Master works with, 141
  is a spark of God, 70, 199
  is eternal, 41, 70, 124, 205,
    244
  knows everything, 265
  linkup with ECK, 158
  polishing of. *See* Soul: purifica-
    tion of
  purification of, 91, 255, 257,
    275
  qualities of. *See* Seeing,
    knowing, and being
  seeing as, 20, 197, 223
  testing ground of. *See* Experi-
    ences: negative
  working on different planes,
    52, 141
  you are, 3, 61, 64, 124
Soul Plane. *See* Plane(s): Soul
Soul Travel, 7, 8, 18–19, 32, 40–
    42, 45, 87, 214–15, 249–53,
    263, 271–79, 280–84
  definition of, 36, 276
  difference between dream and,
    36, 271
  dream state is preparation for,
    54
  exercise, 228–29
  and expansion of conscious-
    ness. *See* Conscious(ness):
    expansion of
  failing at, 250
  meeting loved ones during, 274
  misunderstanding about, 278.
    See also Astral projection
  technique(s), 42, 81
  visualizing for, 271
Sound, 30, 58, 223, 262–63, 281.
    See also Audible Life
    Stream; Light and Sound;
    Madrigals; Music; Sound
    Current
  as buzzing of insects, 254
  clicking, 261
  as crickets, 257

  of drumbeat, 84–85
  of flute, 111, 257, 264. *See also*
    Flute
  of God, 84, 86, 153, 255, 261,
    285
  hearing, 19, 246, 258
  humming, 115, 275
  knocking, 31. *See also* Wake-
    up call(s)
  of machinery, 115
  as musical instruments, 254
  of nature, 254
  of ocean, 84, 229
  peeping, 13
  raises vibrations of Soul, 273
  of running water, 263
  of spheres, 248
  as ticking clocks, 257
  of tinkling bells, 254
  of twittering birds, 254
  as vibration. *See* Vibration(s)
  of whistle, 257
  as wind. *See* Wind
Sound and Light, 283. *See also*
    Light; Light and Sound;
    Sound
  action of, 233
  and consciousness, 33
  of ECK, 61, 256
  of God, 255, 270
  of Holy Spirit, 260. *See also*
    Holy Spirit
  purification by. *See* Purifica-
    tion
Sound Current, 16, 254, 257, 259
Space, 84
  spiritual, 127, 170
Spain, 88
Spirit, 25, 34, 154. *See also* Holy
    Spirit; Divine Spirit
  being alive in, 249
  reliance on, 35
Spiritual exercise(s), 37, 41, 44,
    84, 206, 273. *See also*
    Formula technique; Spiri-
    tual Exercises of ECK;
    Technique(s)
  Big Stone Statue, 246–48

Blue Curtain of God, 20–21
for direct knowingness, 45
Game of Chess, 197–98
Golden Cup, 51–52
How to Heal Yourself, 196
How to Open Your Heart, 250
Inviting the Dream Master, 28
to remember dreams, 30, 51
The Rest of the Story, 57–58
to Soul Travel, 36, 42
using the imaginative body,
    271
value of, 266
Spiritual Exercises of ECK, 19,
    34, 89, 111, 192, 255, 269,
    281
help us have spiritual experi-
    ences, 276
open the consciousness, 147
purpose of, 269
Spiritual Exercises of ECK, The
    (Klemp), 255
Spiritual existence, 66
Spiritual Eye, 36, 148, 259, 269,
    277, 278
Spiritual freedom, 3, 25, 28, 136,
    218, 228. *See also* Freedom:
    of Soul
Spiritual geography, 46
Spiritual hierarchy, 283
Spiritual laboratory, 284
Spiritual life, 4, 18, 40, 94, 122,
    192
dream travel rounds out, 269
ECK enlivens, 248
initiation in, 124
insight, harmony, and joy in,
    21
step backward in, 11
Spiritual message, 58
Spiritual needs, 136
Spiritual Notebook, The
    (Twitchell), 19, 63
Spiritual path, 26, 81, 233, 271.
    See also Eckankar; Path of
    ECK
advancement on, 192
difficulty progressing on, 237

Spiritual principle(s), 170, 199
Spiritual traveler(s), 8, 221,
    231, 245, 260. *See also* ECK
    Master(s)
Stability, 33. *See also* Security
Stamina, 128, 245
Star(s), 220–21, 277, 281
blue and white, 221
Star Trek, 133–34
Star Trek dream, 135
Stone statue. *See* Spiritual
    exercise(s): Big Stone
    Statue
Story (stories), 12, 19, 40, 111
using images in telling, 150
Stranger by the River
    (Twitchell), 63, 284
Strength, 15, 129, 268
Stress, 3, 196
haven from, 225
Stroke, 206
Student, 238
Study
of dreams. *See* Dream(s)(ing):
    study of
spiritual, 17
Subconscious. *See* Mind:
    subconscious
Subway, 260
Success, 71, 99
Sugar-water story, 192–93
Sugmad, 221, 257, 279, 281. *See
    also* God
homage paid to, 282
the way home to, 97
Sun and Moon Worlds, 276
Sundial, 84
Surrender, 158, 198, 245
Survival, 62
Suspicions, 219
Sweden. *See* Teacher(s): in
    Sweden
Swimming pool, 264
Swing, 10
Symbol(s)(ism)(ogy), 27, 237.
    See also Dream(s)(ing):
    symbols; Dream dictionary

Tacks, 149
Taking chances, 105
Talent(s), 75, 81, 87
Talk(s), 62, 117, 152
    audiotape of, 29
    about ECK, 37
    introductory, 106
Teacher(s), 17, 196
    inner, 108. *See also* Dream
        Master, Inner Master;
        Mahanta
    Living ECK Master as outer,
        25
    in Sweden, 201
Teaching(s). *See also* Teachings
        of ECK
    the Mahanta's, 279
    of Paul Twitchell. *See*
        Twitchell, Paul: teachings of
Teachings of ECK, 18, 25, 75,
        111, 134, 205, 257
    Divine Spirit working
        through, 217
    new to, 124, 274
Tears, 263
Technique(s), 43, 132, 142, 255.
        See also Spiritual
        exercise(s); Spiritual
        Exercises of ECK
    Dhyana, 217
    in discourses, 168
    dream, 81
    imaginative, 248
    inner, 130
    Soul Travel. *See* Soul Travel:
        technique(s)
    Temple, 234
    to travel in dream state. *See*
        Dream travel: technique for
    visualization. *See* Visualize
        (visualization): technique
    writing, 122
Teddy bears, 237
Teenager, 59
Temper tantrum, 116
Temple, 215. *See also*
        Technique(s): Temple;
        Temple of ECK; Temple(s)

of Golden Wisdom
    inner, 243
Temple of ECK, 234
Temple(s) of Golden Wisdom, 65,
        142, 158, 222, 232–34, 239,
        247, 269. *See also* Agam
        Des; Katsupari Monastery;
        Temple of ECK
    guardians of, 230
Tension, 65, 86
Test(s), 5, 16–17, 112
Theology, 76
Thought(s), 164
    breaking up patterns of, 168
    creates karma, 78
    disturbing, 128
Tiger's Fang, The (Twitchell),
        224
Time, 85, 114. *See also* Old
        American West
    and space, 121
    track, 88, 118, 156
Timidity. *See* Fear(s)
Tool(s), 80–81
Tornado, 244–45
Tragedy, 18
Translate (translation). *See*
        Death
Translator function, 169, 171.
        See also Dream censor
Travel(s), 49
    on inner planes, 277. *See also*
        Soul Travel
    out-of-body, 274, 276
Treasure, 5
Trials, 245. *See also* Problem(s)
Truck(s), 247
    dream about, 199–200
Trust, 105, 108, 227
Truth(s), 60, 104, 233, 275
    censor blocks, 58
    direct contact with, 265
    duty to speak, 97
    and inner teachings, 29
    mind and accepting, 2
    reveals itself constantly, 102
    search for, 19, 42, 258–59
Turkey-headed snake, 138–39

TV, 107, 206
Twain, Mark, 1–2
Twelve-step program, 138
Twitchell, Paul, 26, 218, 221,
    227, 239, 272, 275–76. *See
    also* Peddar Zaskq
  book(s) by, 19, 94, 224, 225–26,
    228, 232. *See also* Eckankar:
    books
  *ECKANKAR—The Key to
    Secret Worlds,* 225, 228, 232
  Flute of God, The, 225
  Spiritual Notebook, The, 19, 63
  Stranger by the River, 63, 284
  teachings of, 272
  Tiger's Fang, The, 224

Unconscious, 87, 127, 251. *See
    also* Mind: subconscious;
    Mind: unconscious
Underground city, 74
Understand(ing)
  dream(s) of.
    See Dream(s)(ing): of
    understanding
  how life really works, 76
  inner experiences, 52
  from inner experiences, 36
  love is better than, 284
  not, 29
  spiritual, 61, 95, 122, 144
  why things happen, 76, 83
Unfoldment, 16, 158, 272
  spiritual, 14–15, 42, 75, 87,
    104, 124, 253, 258, 259, 280
  using sleep for, 276
Universe, 85
Unpacking, 225
Unworthiness, 158, 245

Veil(s), 152–53, 255. *See also*
    Curtain(s)
Vibration(s), 110, 157, 223, 254,
    263, 273

Victim(s), 90, 91, 202
Video arcade(s), 80, 269
Vietnam, 222
Viewpoint, 123
  as Soul, 197
Vision(s), 17, 66, 75, 278, 279,
    280, 283. *See also* Eyesight
Visualize (visualization), 58,
    216, 264
  technique, 51
Voice of God, 97, 263. *See also*
    Golden-tongued Wisdom
  agreement with, 18
  two aspects of, 16. *See also*
    Light and Sound
Voyage to forever. *See* Raft
    dream
Vulture, 168

Wah Z, 233, 245, 247
  chanting, 217, 249, 262
Wake-up call, 24, 30–31
Waking dream(s), 13, 15, 106,
    108, 122, 144, 148, 149
  happen constantly, 147
  meaning of, 104
  purpose of, 142
Waking state, 122
Wall(s), 129, 142
  going through, 282
Wall-hanging story, 148–49
Warn(ing)(s), 100, 102, 145
  in dreams, 17, 93
  how we miss, 146
Wastebasket, 197
Waters, 277. *See also* Sound: of
    running water; Sugar-
    water story
  spiritual, 154
Wave(s), 229, 283. *See also*
    Light and Sound
  of light, 261
  of love, 259
  from the Sugmad, 257
Weakest points, 171
Wealth, 93, 243

West Coast, 245, 264
Western culture, 82
Whale(s), 153–54
Wheel of the Eighty-four, 270
Wheelchair, 264
Wheels, 111
    of life, 88
Whisper. *See* Fortune-cookie
    story
Whistle. *See* Sound: of whistle
White. *See* Light: white
Wildflowers, 238
Will. *See* Desire(s): to give up
    smoking
Wind, 248, 273, 277, 281
Window, 150, 237
Winning, 99
Wisdom, 3, 8, 25, 36, 62, 163,
    218, 232, 233, 268, 277
    of dreams, 95
    of ECK, 83
    love is better than. *See* Love:
        is better than wisdom and
        understanding
    source within, 203
Witchcraft, 95
Wolves, 227, 245
Wonder, 5
Wood duck. *See* Duck-in-the-
    furnace story
Woodwinds. *See* Sound: as
    musical instruments
Word(s), 15. *See also* Golden-
    tongued Wisdom
    holy, 42
    initiate's personal, 131. *See
        also* Secret word
Work
    on the inner planes, 273, 277
World(s), 15, 80. *See also*
    Plane(s)
    dream, 2, 3, 60, 204. *See also*
        Dream state
    end of, 99–100
    of God. *See* God Worlds
    inner, 18, 29, 42, 44, 49, 50,
        52, 58, 121
    invisible, 7, 46, 116, 273

launching zone between, 277
of Light and Sound. *See* Light
    and Sound: worlds of
lower, 75, 87, 90, 166, 271
material, 244, 281
Mental, 55. *See also* Mind;
    Plane(s): Mental
other, 37, 60–61, 74, 89, 210,
    236
physical, 40, 58, 59, 61, 102,
    108, 121, 126, 267
problems of the, 56
secret, 19
of space and time, 280–81
spiritual, 16, 91, 251, 281
traveling in higher, 217, 238
you create your, 197
Worry (worries), 28, 148, 197
Wounds, 5
Writer's Digest, 122
Writing. *See also* Dream Journal
    for magazines, 123
    inner experiences, 56

Yaubl Sacabi, 83, 84, 86
YWCA, 109

Z, 217. *See also* Wah Z
Zelda II: The Legend of Link, 80

313

314

For Further Reading and Study

A Modern Prophet Answers Your Key Questions about Life
Harold Klemp

A pioneer of today's focus on "everyday spirituality" shows you how to experience and understand God's love in your life—anytime, anyplace. His answers to hundreds of questions help guide you to your own source of wisdom, peace, and deep inner joy.

Our Spiritual Wake-Up Calls
Mahanta Transcripts, Book 15
Harold Klemp

When God calls, are you listening? Discover how God communicates through dreams, the people you meet, or even a newspaper comic strip. Learn how you are in the grasp of divine love every moment of every day. The Mahanta Transcripts are highlights from Harold Klemp's worldwide speaking tours.

The Spiritual Exercises of ECK
Harold Klemp

This book is a staircase with 131 steps. It's a special staircase, because you don't have to climb all the steps to get to the top. Each step is a spiritual exercise, a way to help you explore your inner worlds. And what awaits you at the top? The doorway to spiritual freedom, self-mastery, wisdom, and love.

35 Golden Keys to Who You Are & Why You're Here
Linda C. Anderson

Discover thirty-five golden keys to mastering your spiritual destiny through the ancient teachings of Eckankar, Religion of the Light and Sound of God. The dramatic, true stories in this book equal anything found in the spiritual literature of today. Learn ways to immediately bring more love, peace, and purpose to your life

Available at your local bookstore. If unavailable, call (612) 544-0066. Or write: ECKANKAR, Dept. BK16A, P.O. Box 27300, Minneapolis, MN 55427 U.S.A.

There May Be an
Eckankar Study Group near You

Eckankar offers a variety of local and international activities for the spiritual seeker. With hundreds of study groups worldwide, Eckankar is near you! Many areas have Eckankar centers where you can browse through the books in a quiet, unpressured environment, talk with others who share an interest in this ancient teaching, and attend beginning discussion classes on how to gain the attributes of Soul: wisdom, power, love, and freedom.

Around the world, Eckankar study groups offer special one-day or weekend seminars on the basic teachings of Eckankar. For membership information, visit the Eckankar Web site (www.eckankar.org/membership.html). For the location of the Eckankar center or study group nearest you, click on "Other Eckankar Web sites" (www.eckankar.org/ekcenters.html) for a listing of those areas with Web sites. You're also welcome to check your phone book under **ECKANKAR**; call (612) 544-0066, Ext. BK16B; or write **ECKANKAR, Att: Information, BK16B, P.O. Box 27300, Minneapolis, MN 55427 U.S.A.**

☐ Please send me information on the nearest Eckankar center or study group in my area.

☐ Please send me more information about membership in Eckankar, which includes a twelve-month spiritual study.

Please type or print clearly

Name _____
　　　　　first (given)　　　　　　　　　　last (family)

Street _____ Apt. # _____

City _____ State/Prov. _____

ZIP/Postal Code _____ Country _____

About the Author

Sri Harold Klemp was born in Wisconsin and grew up on a small farm. He attended a two-room country schoolhouse before going to high school at a religious boarding school in Milwaukee, Wisconsin.

After preministerial college in Milwaukee and Fort Wayne, Indiana, he enlisted in the U.S. Air Force. There he trained as a language specialist at Indiana University and a radio intercept operator at Goodfellow AFB, Texas. Then followed a two-year stint in Japan where he first encountered Eckankar.

In October 1981, he became the spiritual leader of Eckankar, Religion of the Light and Sound of God. His full title is Sri Harold Klemp, the Mahanta, the Living ECK Master. As the Living ECK Master, Harold Klemp is responsible for the continued evolution of the Eckankar teachings.

His mission is to help people find their way back to God in this life. Harold Klemp travels to ECK seminars in North America, Europe, and the South Pacific. He has also visited Africa and many countries throughout the world, meeting with spiritual seekers and giving inspirational talks. There are many videocassettes and audiocassettes of his public talks available.

In his talks and writings, Harold Klemp's sense of humor and practical approach to spirituality have helped many people around the world find truth in their lives and greater inner freedom, wisdom, and love.

International Who's Who of Intellectuals
Ninth Edition

Reprinted with permission of Melrose Press Ltd., Cambridge, England, excerpted from *International Who's Who of Intellectuals, Ninth Edition,* Copyright 1992 by Melrose Press Ltd.